mathematics

mathematics

VOLUME **2**
Da-Lo

Barry Max Brandenberger, Jr., Editor in Chief

MACMILLAN REFERENCE USA

GALE GROUP
™
THOMSON LEARNING

New York • Detroit • San Diego • San Francisco
Boston • New Haven, Conn. • Waterville, Maine
London • Munich

Macmillan Reference USA   Macmillan Reference USA
300 Park Avenue South   27500 Drake Rd.
New York, NY 10010   Farmington Hills, MI 48331-3535

Library of Congress Cataloging-in-Publication Data
Mathematics / Barry Max Brandenberger, Jr., editor in chief.
   p. cm.
Includes bibliographical references and index.
ISBN 0-02-865561-3 (set : hardcover : alk. paper) - ISBN 0-02-865562-1 (v. 1 : alk. paper)
ISBN 0-02-865563-X (v. 2 : alk. paper) - ISBN 0-02-865564-8 (v. 3 : alk. paper) -
ISBN 0-02-865565-6 (v. 4 : alk. paper)
   1. Mathematics-Juvenile literature. [1. Mathematics.] I. Brandenberger, Barry Max, 1971-
QA40.5 .M38 2002
510-dc21   00-045593

Printed in the United States of America
1 2 3 4 5 6 7 8 9 10

Table of Contents

Dance, Folk

Both mathematics and dance are languages that use symbols to convey ideas and expressions. Mathematics uses written symbols to represent abstractions so that users can arrive at a greater understanding of a problem without **ambiguity**. Dancers use **abstract** symbols to represent thoughts, feelings, emotions, and ideas, and these symbols may be interpreted in multiple ways. Both disciplines rely to a large extent on pattern recognition.

Many forms of dance, such as classical ballet, involve complex patterns and take years of practice to master. Yet other forms of dance use everyday movements with more simplistic patterns. For example, folk dances have evolved from common movements of work and play.

Although folk dances require concentration and focus, their use of everyday movement invites observers to participate. Similarly, mathematics can be studied at the basic level of arithmetic, which is used to make simple transactions and to understand how things work. More advanced mathematics, such as **calculus**, **chaos theory**, or **abstract algebra** require years to master.

Discreteness in Mathematics and Dance

Many dances are based on a simple method of counting and **discrete** sequences, which enables participants to recognize and learn a variety of dances. The word "discrete" also has a common, similar usage in mathematics. Discrete mathematics involves counting separate elements, such as the number of arrangements of letters on a license place, or the number of ways that a presidential candidate can visit all fifty states. Solutions in discrete mathematics can be only whole units. Discrete math is therefore one of the most accessible areas of modern mathematics since many of the questions are easy for anyone to understand.

Contradancing. Contradancing is a popular form of folk dance in the United States that illustrates the mathematics of dance. Its origins go back to colonial days, and its roots can be traced to English country dances.

Contradancing, which shares elements of traditional square dancing, is a form of **set dancing** in which a dancer's position relative to another dancer traces patterns on the dance floor. As in most dancing, timing is crucial, as is the ability to rapidly carry out called instructions.

ambiguity the quality of doubtfulness or uncertainty

abstract having only intrinsic form

calculus a method of dealing mathematically with variables that may be changing continuously with respect to each other

chaos theory the qualitative study of unstable aperiodic behavior in deterministic nonlinear dynamical systems

abstract algebra the branch of algebra dealing with groups, rings, fields, Galois sets, and number theory

discrete composed of distinct elements

set dancing a form of dance in which dancers are guided through a series of moves by a caller

Counting is crucial to timing in dance, which can be very structured. Traditional folk dancers—like this troupe from Morocco—often form lines, circles, squares, and other geometric figures while keeping rhythm.

matrix a rectangular array of data in rows and columns

permutation any arrangement of ordering, of items in a set

Music for contradancing is highly structured. Everything occurs in multiples of four. In one common format, the band plays a tune for sixteen beats, repeats the tune, then plays a new tune for sixteen beats and repeats. An eight-beat section is known as a call, during which each block of four dancers executes a called-out instruction.

When contradancers line up in their groups of four to produce a long column "down" the dance floor (extending away from the band), each square block of two couples can be thought of as a mathematical **matrix** with the dimension 2×2. Each dancer, or element of the matrix, is in a specific position within the array. The called instructions correspond to re-arrangements of the elements (dancers). After sixty-four beats, for example, the first and second rows of the matrix may be interchanged. Of course, this could be done in one step, but the fun of dancing comes from performing the various **permutations** by which groups of four can reach the end result.

There are many called instructions in contradancing, ranging in complexity from simply circling once around to the left or right within each group of four to sequences of moves that involve exchanging partners or stepping one-quarter, one-half, or three-quarters of the way around the ring. With each call, the matrix representing four dancers changes. In the final configuration, the two rows of the original 2×2 matrix may be interchanged, or they may be the same as when the dance started.

Chaos Theory and Dance

Computer scientists have applied the basics of chaos theory to generate variations on dance movement sequences. Special symbols represent human body postures, and positions for each of the body's main joints are encoded by defining an **axis** and **angle of rotation** given in the form of a mathematical expression called a **quaternion**. A motion sequence is then mapped onto a **chaotic attractor**. Following a new **trajectory** around the attractor produces a variation of the original motion sequence. To smooth out abrupt transitions introduced by the chaotic mapping, the researchers have developed schemes that capture and enforce particular dance styles. SEE ALSO CHAOS, MATHEMATICS OF.

Marilyn K. Simon

Bibliography

Devlin, Keith. *The Language of Mathematics: Making the Invisible Visible.* Chicago: W. H. Freeman, 2000.

———. Using Chaos to Generate Variations on Movement Sequences." *Chaos* 8, no. 4 (1998).

Internet Resources

Bradley, Elizabeth. "Chaographer and MotionMind: Using Mathematics to Generate Choreographic Variations." *Chaography Software.* <http://www.cs.colorado.edu/~lizb/chaotic-dance.html>.

Contradancing. <http://www.io.com/~entropy/contradance/dance-home.html>.

Country Dance and Song. <http://www.cdss.org/>.

What Is Contra Dance? <http://www.sbcds.org/contradance/whatis/>.

Data Analyst

A data analyst does more than simply analyze information. Data are collected for a variety of reasons—to learn about something new, to find relationships and generate statistics, or to create **information databases**. Likewise, there are numerous fields of study that collect data, such as finance, medicine, sales and marketing, and engineering, to name a few. All this data needs to be correlated into useful and relevant information.

When a data analyst faces a printout of numbers or facts, he or she must make sense of it all. First, a data analyst will determine where the data came from, if anything has corrupted the collection, and if more data is needed. As data is sorted, the analyst needs to find relationships among the data, select samples that are indicative of the whole, convert data from one form to another, and even predict results. In short, the analyst helps make the data useful.

Data analysts may also summarize the data in a report and communicate this information to colleagues or the public. Sometimes data analysts maintain routine records in a database or archive data for future use and analysis. Those data analysts with more advanced computer and engineering training may be called upon to design programs or models that collect data, calibrate instruments that run tests, or troubleshoot systems that are not functioning properly.

THE COMMUNICATION OF MATHEMATICS AND DANCE

According to Keith Devlin in *The Language of Mathematics*, mathematics seeks to communicate a sense of what humans experience. The simplicity, precision, purity, and elegance of mathematical expressions and patterns give mathematics an aesthetic value. The mathematical connections to dance similarly give dancers a creative, aesthetic, and interpretive means of expressing the human experience.

---

axis an imaginary line about which an object rotates

angle of rotation the angle, measured from an initial position to a final position, that a rotating object has moved through

quaternion a form of complex number consisting of a real scalar and an imaginary vector component with three dimensions

chaotic attractor a set of points such that all nearby trajectories converge to it

trajectory the path followed by a projectile; in chaotic systems, the trajectory is ordered and unpredictable

information database an array of information related to a specific subject or groups of subjects and arranged so that any individual bit of information can be easily found and recovered

Mathematics and computer programming are essential skills for data analysts. The most important math skills are strong knowledge of **statistics** and statistical analysis, since a data analyst will often be asked whether a set of data is statistically significant. Data analysts must also have the computer skills necessary to operate a wide variety of databases. SEE ALSO DATA COLLECTION AND INTERPRETATION.

Lorraine Savage

Bibliography

Career Information Center, 8th ed. New York: Macmillan Reference USA, 2002.

Data Collection and Interpretation

Data interpretation is part of daily life for most people. Interpretation is the process of making sense of numerical data that has been collected, analyzed, and presented. People interpret data when they turn on the television and hear the news anchor reporting on a poll, when they read advertisements claiming that one product is better than another, or when they choose grocery store items that claim they are more effective than other leading brands.

A common method of assessing numerical data is known as **statistical analysis**, and the activity of analyzing and interpreting data in order to make predictions is known as **inferential statistics**. Informed consumers recognize the importance of judging the reasonableness of data interpretations and predictions by considering sources of bias such as sampling procedures or misleading questions, **margins of error**, **confidence intervals**, and incomplete interpretations.

Why Is Accurate Data Collection Important?

The repercussions of inaccurate or improperly interpreted data are wide-ranging. For example, every 10 years a major census is done in the United States. The results are used to help determine the number of congressional seats that are assigned to each district; where new roads will be built; where new schools and libraries are needed; where new nursing homes, hospitals, and day care centers will be located; where new parks and recreational centers will be built; and the sizes of police and fire departments.

In the past 30 years there has been a major shift in the U.S. population. People have migrated from the northern states toward the southern states, and the result has been a major shift in congressional representation. With a net change of nearly 30 percent (a 17 percent drop in the Northeast and Midwest coupled with a 12 percent gain in the South), the South has gone from a position of less influence to one of greater influence in Congress as a result of population-based **reapportionment**. This is just one of many possible examples that reveal how data gathering and interpretation related to population can have a marked affect on the whole country.

Gathering Reliable Data

The process of data interpretation begins by gathering data. Because it is often difficult, or even impossible, to look at all the data (for example, to

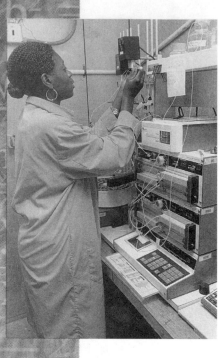

Some data analysts with engineering expertise may work with electronic instrumentation that measures and processes data.

statistics the branch of mathematics that analyzes and interprets sets of numerical data

statistical analysis a set of methods for analyzing numerical data

inferential statistics analysis and interpretation of data in order to make predictions

margin of error the difference between estimated maximum and minimum values a given measurement could have

confidence interval a range of values having a predetermined probability that the value of some measurement of a population lies within it

reapportionment the process of redistributing the seats of the U.S. House of Representatives, based on each state's proportion of the national population

In data presentations, the audience must think critically about both the data collection methods and the interpretation being offered by the presenter.

poll every high school student in the United States), data are generally obtained from a smaller unit, a subset of the population known as a **sample**. Then data from the sample are used to predict (or infer) what the characteristics of the population as a whole may be. For example, a telephone survey of one thousand car owners in the United States might be conducted to predict the popularity of various cars among all U.S. car owners. The one thousand U.S. car owners who are surveyed are the sample and all car owners in the United States are the population.

But there both an art and science to collecting high-quality data. Several key elements must be considered: bias, sample size, question design, margin of error, and interpretation.

Avoiding Bias. In order for data interpretation to be reliable, a number of factors must be in place. First and perhaps foremost, an **unbiased sample** must be used. In other words, every person (or item) in the population should have an equal chance of being in the sample.

For example, what if only Ford owners were surveyed in the telephone survey? The survey would be quite likely to show that Fords were more popular. A biased sample is likely to **skew** the data, thus making data interpretation unreliable. If we want to know what sorts of cars are preferred by U.S. car owners, we need to be sure that our sample of car owners is representative of the entire car owner population.

One way of ensuring an unbiased sample is to choose randomly from the population. However, it is often difficult to design a study that will produce a truly unbiased sample. For example, suppose a surveyor decides to choose car owners at **random** to participate in a phone interview about car preferences. This may sound like a good plan, but car owners who do not have telephones or whose telephone numbers are unavailable will not have a chance to participate in the survey. Maybe car owners with unlisted telephone numbers have

sample a randomly selected subset of a larger population used to represent the larger population in statistical analysis

unbiased sample a random sample selected from a larger population in such a way that each member of the larger population has an equal chance of being in the sample

skew to cause lack of symmetry in the shape of a frequency distribution

random without order

BIAS IN NEWS CALL-IN POLLS

Many news programs have call-in polls. The results of the poll are usually shown later in the program. This type of data collection is very unreliable because the information is coming from a biased sample.

People who watch or listen to the news make up only a small percentage of the population. Of that group, only an even smaller percentage will call to offer their opinion. And of those who call, more are likely to disagree with the question because people with strong feelings against an issue are more likely to respond.

biased sampling
process of obtaining a nonrandom sample; choosing a sample to represent a particular viewpoint instead of the whole population

very different car preferences than the broader population, but we will never know if they are not included in the sample.

Biased sampling continues to challenge census takers. In 1990, nearly 35 percent of the households that were mailed census forms did not mail them back. If a form is not returned, the Census Bureau must send someone to the person's house. Even with census takers visiting homes door to door, the Census Bureau was still unable to contact one out of every five of the families who did not return their census form.

Although this may not sound like a lot, consider that in 1990 there were approximately 250 million people in the United States. If a household contains an average of four people, that means that there were 62.5 million forms mailed out. Multiplying that figure by 35 percent (the number of households that did not return the forms) gives the staggering figure of 21.875 million forms that were not returned. Of the 21.875 million households that did not return forms, census takers were unable to track down 20 percent, or 4.375 million households.

Why is this biased sampling? It is believed that of the more than 4 million households not counted, the overwhelming majority was from poorer sections of large cities. This implies that certain parts of the country may be over-represented in Congress and are the recipients of more federal funds than may be deserved.

Achieving a Large Enough Sample.   A second important factor in data collection is whether the chosen sample is large enough. Are one thousand car owners a sufficient number of car owners from which to infer the opinion of all car owners? In order to answer this question, the margin of error needs to be calculated.

The margin of error is a statistic that represents a range in which the surveyor feels confident that the population as a whole will fall. A sufficient sample size needs to have a small margin of error, usually around 5 percent. To determine the margin of error (m), divide one by the square root of the sample size (s): $m = 1 / \sqrt{s}$. Therefore, the sample of one thousand car owners gives us a margin of error of about 3 percent, an allowable margin of error.

Asking the Proper Questions.   Informed citizens who are assessing survey results must consider the type of questions that are asked when a survey is conducted. Were the questions leading? Were they easy or difficult to understand? For example, suppose a study carried out by a local ice cream manufacturer states that 75 percent of Americans prefer ice cream. It seems self-evident that an ice cream company would not report a study that showed Americans do not like ice cream. So perhaps the question in the study was leading: for example, "Do you prefer ice cream or spinach?" It is therefore important to find out exactly what questions were asked and of whom.

Giving a Proper Interpretation.   Data are often interpreted with a bias, and the results can therefore be misleading or incomplete. For example, a bath soap company claims that its soap is 99 percent pure. This statement is misleading because the soap manufacturer does not explain what "pure" is. When reading an unclarified percentage such as in the previous example, one needs to ask such questions. An example of another incomplete or misleading interpretation is that the average child watches approximately 5 hours of television a day. The reader should question what an "average child" is.

Considering Margin of Error.   Margin of error is important to consider when statistics are reported. For example, we might read that the high school dropout rate declined from 18 percent to 16 percent with a margin of error of 3 percent. Because the 2-percentage point decline is smaller than the margin of error (3 percent), the new dropout rate may fall between 13 percent to 19 percent. We cannot be entirely sure that the high school dropout rate actually declined at all.

Confidence intervals, a term usually employed by statisticians, and related to margins of error, is reported by a percentage and is constructed to relay how confident one can be that the sample is representative of the population. The producers of this survey may only be 95 percent confident that their sample is representative of the population. If this is the case then there is a 5 percent chance that this sample data does not typify or carry over to the population of the United States. The margin of error represents the range of this 95-percent confidence interval (the range that represents plus or minus two **standard deviations** from the **mean**).

Understanding and Interpreting Data

Figuring out what data means is just as important as collecting it. Even if the data collection process is sound, data can be misinterpreted. When interpreting data, the data user must not only attempt to discern the differences between causality and coincidence, but also must consider all possible factors that may have led to a result.

After considering the design of a survey, consumers should look at the reported data interpretation. Suppose a report states that 52 percent of all Americans prefer Chevrolet to other car manufacturers. The surveyors want you to think that more than half of all Americans prefer Chevrolet, but is this really the case? Perhaps not all those surveyed were Americans. Also, the 52 percent comes from the sample, so it is important to ask if the sample was large enough, unbiased, and randomly chosen. One also needs to be aware of margins of error and confidence intervals. If the margin of error for this survey is 5 percent than this means that the percentage of car owners in the United States who prefer Chevrolet could actually be between 47 and 57 percent (5 percent higher or lower than the 52 percent).

Similar questions are important to consider when we try to understand **polls**. During the 2000 presidential race, the evening news and newspapers were often filled with poll reports. For example, one poll stated 51 percent of Americans preferred George W. Bush, 46 percent preferred Al Gore, and 3 percent were undecided, with a margin of error of plus or minus 5 percent.

The news anchor then went on to report that *most* Americans prefer George W. Bush. However, given the data outlined above, this conclusion is questionable. Because the difference between George W. Bush and Al Gore is the same as the margin of error, it is impossible to know which

Understanding the nature of particular data sets is critical for anyone who deals with numbers and measurements.

standard deviation a measure of the average amount by which individual items of data might be expected to vary from the arithmetic mean of all data

mean the arithmetic average of a set of data

poll a survey designed to gather information about a subject

candidate was actually preferred. In addition, if we do not know any of the circumstances behind the poll, we should be skeptical about its findings.

As another example, consider census data that shows a radical increase in the number of people living in Florida and Arizona along with a decrease in the number of people living in New York. One could easily (and falsely) conclude that the data "proves" that people are finding New York to be a less desirable place to live and therefore are moving away.

But this hasty conclusion could be missing the big picture. What if the data also reveals that the average age of New Yorkers has dropped since 1990? Further interpretation of the data may reveal that when New Yorkers grow older, they move to warmer climates to retire. This illustrates why data must be thoroughly interpreted before any conclusions can be drawn.

A Data Checklist. When reading any survey, listening to an advertisement, or hearing about poll results, informed consumers should ask questions about the soundness of the data interpretation. A recap of key points follows.

1. Was the sample unbiased (representative of the whole population)?

2. Was the sample large enough for the purpose of the survey (margin of error of the sample)?

3. What type of questions did the surveyor ask? Were they simple and unambiguous? Were they leading (constructed in such a way to get the desired response)?

4. Can the conclusions drawn be justified based on the information gathered?

5. How was the survey done (mail, phone, interview)? Does the survey report mention margins of error or confidence intervals, and, if so, are these such that the conclusions drawn are warranted?

By using these checkpoints and learning to think critically about data collection and interpretation, individuals can become more savvy consumers of information. SEE ALSO Census; Central Tendency, Measures of; Graphs; Mass Media, Mathematics and the; Predictions; Randomness; Statistical Analysis.

Rose Kathleen Lynch and Philip M. Goldfeder

Bibliography

Campbell, Stephen K. *Statistics You Can't Trust: A Friendly Guide to Clear Thinking about Statistics in Everyday Life.* Parker, CO: Think Twice, 1999.

Dewdney, A. K. *200% of Nothing.* New York: John Wiley & Sons, Inc., 1993.

Dorling, Daniel, and Stephen Simpson, eds. *Statistics in Society: The Arithmetic of Politics.* London U.K.: Oxford University Press, 1999.

Moore, David S. *The Basic Practice of Statistics.* New York: Freeman, 2000.

Paulos, John A. *Innumeracy: Mathematical Illiteracy and Its Consequences.* New York: Hill and Wang, 1988.

———. *A Mathematician Reads the Newspaper.* New York: Basic Books, 1995.

Triola, Mario. *Elementary Statistics,* 6th ed. New York: Addison-Wesley, 1995.

Internet Resources

U.S. Census Bureau. <http://www.census.gov>.

Dating Techniques

Movies and television have presented a romantic vision of archaeology as adventure in far-away and exotic locations. A more realistic picture might show researchers digging in smelly mud for hours under the hot sun while battling relentless mosquitoes. This type of archaeological research produces hundreds of small plastic bags containing pottery shards, animal bones, bits of worked stone, and other fragments. These findings must be classified, which requires more hours of tedious work in a stuffy tent. At its best, archaeology involves a studious examination of the past with the goal of learning important information about the culture and customs of ancient (or not so ancient) peoples. Much archaeology in the early twenty-first century investigates the recent past, a sub-branch called "historical archaeology."

What Is Archaeology?

Archaeology is the study of the material remains of past human cultures. It is distinguished from other forms of inquiry by its method of study, excavation. (Most archaeologists call this "digging.") Excavation is not simply digging until something interesting is found. That sort of unscientific digging destroys the archaeological information. Archaeological excavation requires the removal of material layer by layer to expose artifacts in place. The removed material is carefully sifted to find small **artifacts**, tiny animal bones, and other remains. Archaeologists even examine the soil in various layers for microscopic material, such as pollen. Excavations, in combination with surveys, may yield maps of a ruin or collections of artifacts.

artifact something made by a human and left in an archaeological context

Time is important to archaeologists. There is rarely enough time to complete the work, but of even greater interest is the time that has passed since the artifact was created. An important part of archaeology is the examination of how cultures change over time. It is therefore essential that the archaeologist is able to establish the age of the artifacts or other material remains and arrange them in a chronological sequence. The archaeologist must be able to distinguish between objects that were made at the same time and objects that were made at different times. When objects that were made at different times are excavated, the archaeologist must be able to arrange them in a sequence from the oldest to the most recent.

Relative Dating and Absolute Dating

Before scientific dating techniques such as dendrochronology and radiocarbon dating were introduced to archaeology, the discipline was dominated by extensive discussions of the chronological sequence of events. Most of those questions have now been settled and archaeologists have moved on to other issues. Scientific dating techniques have had a huge impact on archaeology.

Archaeologists use many different techniques to determine the age of an object. Usually, several different techniques are applied to the same object. **Relative dating** arranges artifacts in a chronological sequence from oldest to most recent without reference to the actual date. For example, by studying the decorations used on pottery, the types of materials used in the pottery, and the types and shapes of pots, it is often possible to arrange them

relative dating determining the date of an archaeological artifact based on its position in the archaeological context relative to other artifacts

absolute dating determining the date of an artifact by measuring some physical parameter independent of context

superposition the placing of one thing on top of another

into a sequence without knowing the actual date. In **absolute dating**, the age of an object is determined by some chemical or physical process without reference to a chronology.

Relative Dating Methods. The most common and widely used relative dating technique is *stratigraphy*. The principle of **superposition** (borrowed from geology) states that higher layers must be deposited on top of lower layers. Thus, higher layers are more recent than lower layers. This only applies to undisturbed deposits. Rodent burrows, root action, and human activity can mix layers in a process known as bioturbation. However, the archaeologist can detect bioturbation and allow for its effects.

Discrete layers of occupation can often be determined. For example, Hisarlik, which is a hill in Turkey, is thought by some archaeologists to be the site of the ancient city of Troy. However, Hisarlik was occupied by many different cultures at various times both before and after the time of Troy, and each culture built on top of the ruins of the previous culture, often after violent conquest. Consequently, the layers in this famous archaeological site represent many different cultures. An early excavator of Hisarlik, Heinrich Schleimann, inadvertently dug through the Troy layer into an earlier occupation and mistakenly assigned the gold artifacts he found there to Troy. Other sites have been continuously occupied by the same culture for a long time and the different layers represent gradual changes. In both cases, stratigraphy will apply.

correlate to establish a mutual or reciprocal relation between two things or sets of things

A chronology based on stratigraphy often can be **correlated** to layers in other nearby sites. For example, a particular type or pattern of pottery may occur in only one layer in an excavation. If the same pottery type is found in another excavation nearby, it is safe to assume that the layers are the same age. Archaeologists rarely make these determinations on the basis of a single example. Usually, a set of related artifacts is used to determine the age of a layer.

Seriation simply means ordering. This technique was developed by the inventor of modern archaeology, Sir William Matthew Flinders Petrie. Seriation is based on the assumption that cultural characteristics change over time. For example, consider how automobiles have changed in the last 50 years (a relatively short time in archaeology). Automobile manufacturers frequently introduce new styles about every year, so archaeologists thousands of years from now will have no difficulty identifying the precise date of a layer if the layer contains automobile parts.

Cultural characteristics tend to show a particular pattern over time. The characteristic is introduced into the culture (for example, using a certain type of projectile point for hunting or wearing low-riding jeans), becomes progressively more popular, then gradually wanes in popularity. The method of seriation uses this distinctive pattern to arrange archaeological materials into a sequence. However, seriation only works when variations in a cultural characteristic are due to rapid and significant change over time. It also works best when a characteristic is widely shared among many different members of a group. Even then, it can only be applied to a small geographic area, because there is also geographic variation in cultural characteristics. For example, 50 years ago American automobiles changed every year while the Volkswagen Beetle hardly changed at all from year to year.

Cross dating is also based on stratigraphy. It uses the principle that different archaeological sites will show a similar collection of artifacts in layers of the same age. Sir Flinders Petrie used this method to establish the time sequence of artifacts in Egyptian cemeteries by identifying which burials contained Greek pottery vessels. These same Greek pottery styles could be associated with monuments in Greece whose construction dates were fairly well known. Since absolute dating techniques have become common, the use of cross dating has decreased significantly.

Pollen grains also appear in archaeological layers. They are abundant and they survive very well in archaeological contexts. As climates change over time, the plants that grow in a region change as well. People who examine pollen grains (the study of which is known as **pollen analysis**) can usually determine the **genus**, and often the exact species producing a certain pollen type. Archaeologists can then use this information to determine the relative ages of some sites and layers within sites. However, climates do not change rapidly, so this type of analysis is best for archaeological sites dating back to the last ice age.

Absolute Dating Methods.   Absolute dating methods produce an actual date, usually accurate to within a few years. This date is established independent of stratigraphy and chronology. If a date for a certain layer in an excavation can be established using an absolute dating method, other artifacts in the same layer can safely be assigned the same age.

Dendrochronology, also known as tree-ring dating, is the earliest form of absolute dating. This method was first developed by the American astronomer Andrew Ellicott Douglas at the University of Arizona in the early 1900s. Douglas was trying to develop a **correlation** between climate variations and **sunspot activity**, but archaeologists quickly recognized its usefulness as a dating tool. The technique was first applied in the American Southwest and later extended to other parts of the world.

Tree-ring dating is relatively simple. Trees add a new layer of cambium (the layer right under the bark) every year. The thickness of the layer depends on local weather and climate. In years with plenty of rain, the layer will be thick and healthy. Over the lifetime of the tree, these rings accumulate, and the rings form a record of regional variation in climate that may extend back hundreds of years. Since all of the trees in a region experience the same climate variations, they will have similar growth patterns and similar tree ring patterns.

One tree usually does not cover a period sufficiently long to be archaeologically useful. However, patterns of tree ring growth have been built up by "overlapping" ring sequences from different trees so that the tree ring record extends back several thousand years in many parts of the world. The process starts with examination of the growth ring patterns of samples from living trees. Then older trees are added to the sequence by overlapping the inner rings of a younger sample with the outer rings of an older sample. Older trees are recovered from old buildings, archaeological sites, peat bogs, and swamps. Eventually, a regional master chronology is constructed.

When dendrochronology can be used, it provides the most accurate dates of any technique. In the American Southwest, the accuracy and precision of dendrochronology has enabled the development of one of the most

pollen analysis microscopic examination of pollen grains to determine the genus and species of the plant producing the pollen; also known as palynology

genus the taxonomic classification one step more general than species; the first name in the binomial nomenclature of all species

correlation the process of establishing a mutual or reciprocal relation between two things or sets of things

sunspot activity one of the powerful magnetic storms on the surface of the Sun, which causes it to appear to have dark spots; sunspot activity varies on an 11-year cycle

Widely spaced tree rings indicate periods of rapid growth, whereas narrowly spaced rings indicate slow growth.

isotope one of several species of an atom that has the same number of protons and the same chemical properties, but different numbers of neutrons

accurate prehistoric cultural chronologies anywhere in the world. Often events can be dated to within a decade. This precision has allowed archaeologists working in the American Southwest to reconstruct patterns of village growth and subsequent abandonment with a fineness of detail unmatched in most of the world.

Radiometric dating methods are more recent than dendrochronology. However, dendrochronology provides an important calibration technique for radiocarbon dating techniques. All radiometric-dating techniques are based on the well-established principle from physics that large samples of radioactive **isotopes** decay at precisely known rates. The rate of decay of a radioactive isotope is usually given by its half-life. The decay of any individual nucleus is completely random. The half-life is a measure of the probability that a given atom will decay in a certain time. The shorter the half-life, the more likely the atom will decay. This probability does not increase with time. If an atom has not decayed, the probability that it will decay in the future remains exactly the same. This means that no matter how many atoms are in a sample, approximately one-half will decay in one half-life. The remaining atoms have exactly the same decay probability, so in another half-life, one half of the remaining atoms will decay. The amount of time required for one-half of a radioactive sample to decay can be precisely determined. The particular radioisotope used to determine the age of an object depends on the type of object and its age.

Radiocarbon is the most common and best known of radiometric dating techniques, but it is also possibly the most misunderstood. It was developed at the University of Chicago in 1949 by a group of American scientists led by Willard F. Libby. Radiocarbon dating has had an enormous impact on archaeology. In the last 50 years, radiocarbon dating has provided the basis for a worldwide cultural chronology. Recognizing the importance of this technique, the Nobel Prize committee awarded the Prize in Chemistry to Libby in 1960.

The physics behind radiocarbon dating is straightforward. Earth's atmosphere is constantly bombarded with cosmic rays from outer space. Cosmic-ray neutrons collide with atoms of nitrogen in the upper atmosphere, converting them to atoms of radioactive carbon-14. The carbon-14 atom quickly combines with an oxygen molecule to form carbon dioxide. This radioactive carbon dioxide spreads throughout Earth's atmosphere, where it is taken up by plants along with normal carbon-12. As long as the plant is alive, the relative amount (ratio) of carbon-14 to carbon-12 remains constant at about one carbon-14 atom for every one trillion carbon-12 atoms. Some animals eat plants and other animals eat the plant-eaters. As long as they are alive, all living organisms have the same ratio of carbon-14 to carbon-12 as in the atmosphere because the radioactive carbon is continually replenished, either through **photosynthesis** or through the food animals eat.

However, when the plant or animal dies, the intake of carbon-14 stops and the ratio of carbon-14 to carbon-12 immediately starts to decrease. The half-life of carbon-14 is 5,730 years. After 5,730 years, about one-half of the carbon-14 atoms will have decayed. After another 5,730 years, one-half of the remaining atoms will have decayed. So after 11,460 years, only one-fourth will remain. After 17,190 years, one-eighth of the original carbon-14 will remain. After 22,920 years, one-sixteenth will remain.

Radiocarbon dating has become the standard technique for determining the age of organic remains (those remains that contain carbon). There are many factors that must be taken into account when determining the age of an object. The best objects are bits of charcoal that have been preserved in completely dry environments. The worst candidates are bits of wood that have been saturated with sea water, since sea water contains dissolved atmospheric carbon dioxide that may throw off the results. Radiocarbon dating can be used for small bits of clothing or other fabric, bits of bone, baskets, or anything that contains **organic** material.

There are well over 100 labs worldwide that do radiocarbon dating. In the early twenty-first century, the dating of objects up to about 10 half-lives, or up to about 50,000 years old, is possible. However, objects less than 300 years old cannot be reliably dated because of the widespread burning of fossil fuels, which began in the nineteenth century, and the production of carbon-14 from atmospheric testing of nuclear weapons in the 1950s and 1960s. Another problem with radiocarbon dating is that the production of carbon-14 in the atmosphere has not been constant, due to variation in solar activity. For example, in the 1700s, solar activity dropped (a phenomenon called the "Maunder Minimum"), so carbon-14 production also decreased during this period. To achieve the highest level of accuracy, carbon-14 dates must be calibrated by comparison to dates obtained from dendrochronology.

Calibration of Radiocarbon Dates. Samples of Bristlecone pine, a tree with a very long life span, have been dated using both dendrochronology and radiocarbon dating. The results do not agree, but the differences are consistent. That is, the radiocarbon dates were always wrong by the same number of years. Consequently, tree-ring chronologies have been used to calibrate radiocarbon dates to around 12,000 years ago.

When radiocarbon dating was first put into use, it was decided that dates would always be reported as B.P., where B.P. stood for "before present" and

photosynthesis the chemical process used by plants and some other organisms to harvest light energy by converting carbon dioxide and water to carbohydrates and oxygen

organic having to do with life, growing naturally, or dealing with the chemical compounds found in or produced by living organisms

"present" was defined as 1950. That way, dates reported in magazine articles and books do not have to be adjusted as the years pass. So if a lab determines that an object has a radiocarbon age of 1,050 years in 2000, its age will be given as 1000 B.P. Calibrated dates are given using the actual date, such as 950 C.E.

Potassium-Argon Dating. If an object is too old to be dated by radiocarbon dating, or if it contains no organic material, other methods must be used. One of these is potassium-argon dating. All naturally occurring rocks contain potassium. Some of the potassium in rocks is the radioactive isotope potassium-40. Potassium-40 gradually decays to the stable isotope argon-40, which is a gas. When the rock is melted, as in a volcano, any argon gas trapped in the rock escapes. When the rock cools, the argon will begin to build up. So this method can be used to measure the age of any volcanic rock, from 100,000 years up to around 5 billion years old.

This method is not widely used in archaeology, since most archaeological deposits are not associated with volcanic activity. However, Louis and Mary Leakey successfully used the method to determine the ages of fossils in Olduvai Gorge in Tanzania by examining rocks from lava flows above and below the fossils. They were able to establish an absolute chronology for humans and human ancestors extending back two million years. At Laetolli, in Tanzania, volcanic ash containing early **hominid** footprints was dated by this method at 3.5 million years.

hominid a member of family Hominidae; *Homo sapiens* are the only surviving species

fission the splitting of the nucleus of a heavy atom, which releases kinetic energy that is carried away by the fission fragments and two or three neutrons

Other Methods. Uranium-238 is present in most rocks. This isotope of uranium spontaneously undergoes **fission**. The fission fragments have a lot of energy, and they plow through the rock, leaving a track that can be made visible by treating the rock. So by counting fission tracks, the age of the rock can be determined. Like potassium-argon dating, this can only be used to determine the age of the rock, not the age of the artifact itself.

Thermoluminescence is a recently developed technique that uses the property of some crystals to "store" light. Sometimes an electron will be knocked out of its position in a crystal and will "stick" somewhere else in the crystal. These displaced electrons will accumulate over time. If the sample is heated, the electrons will fall back to their normal positions, emitting a small flash of light. By measuring the light emitted, the time that has passed since the artifact was heated can be determined. This method should prove to be especially useful in determining the age of ceramics, rocks that have been used to build fire rings, and samples of **chert** and flint that have been deliberately heated to make them easier to flake into a projectile point.

chert material consisting of amorphous or cryptocrystalline silicon dioxide; fine-grained chert is indistinguishable from flint

Conclusion

Science continues to develop new methods to determine the age of objects. As our knowledge of past chronologies improves, archaeologists will be better able to understand how cultures change over time, and how different cultures interact with each other. As a result, this knowledge will enable us to achieve a progressively better understanding of our own culture. SEE ALSO TIME, MEASUREMENT OF.

Elliot Richmond

Bibliography

Aitken, M. J. *Science-based Dating in Archaeology.* London: Longman, 1990.

Baillie, M. G. L. *A Slice through Time: Dendrochronology and Precision Dating.* London U.K.: Batsford, 1995.

Brennan, Louis A. *Beginner's Guide to Archaeology.* Harrisburg, PA: Stackpole Books, 1973.

Taylor, R. E. *Radiocarbon Dating: An Archaeological Perspective.* Orlando, FL: Academic Press, 1987.

Taylor, R. E., A. Long, and R. Kra. *Radiocarbon after Four Decades: An Interdisciplinary Perspective.* New York: Springer-Verlag, 1994.

Wood, Michael. *In Search of the Trojan War.* New York: New American Library, 1985.

Decimals

The number system most commonly used today is based on the Hindu-Arabic number system, which was developed in what is now India around 300 B.C.E. The Arab mathematicians adopted this system and brought it to Spain, where it slowly spread to the rest of Europe.

The present-day number system, which is called the decimal✶ or **base-10** number system, is an elegant and efficient way to express numbers. The rules for performing arithmetic calculations are simple and straightforward.

Basic Properties

The decimal number system is based on two fundamental properties. First, numbers are constructed from ten **digits**, or numerals—0, 1, 2, 3, 4, 5, 6, 7, 8, and 9—that are arranged in a sequence. Second, the position of a digit in the sequence determines its value, called the place value. Because each digit, by its **place value**, represents a multiple of a **power** of 10, the system is called base-10.

Numbers Greater and Less Than One.   The expansion of numbers greater than 1 consists of sums of groups of tens. Each digit in the expansion represents how many groups of tens are present. The groups are 1s, 10s, 100s, and so on. The groups are arranged in order, with the right-most representing 10^0, or groups of 1s. The next digit to the left in the group stands for 10^1, or groups of 10s, and so on. For example, the expansion of the whole number 3,254 in the decimal system is expressed as:

$$3,254 = (3 \times 10^3) + (2 \times 10^2) + (5 \times 10^1) + (4 \times 10^0)$$
$$= 3000 + 200 + 50 + 4.$$

A number less than 1 is represented by a sequence of numbers to the right of a decimal point. The digits to the right of a decimal point are multiplied by 10 raised to a negative power, starting from negative 1. In moving to the right, the place value decreases in value, each being one-tenth as small as the previous place value. Thus, each successive digit to the right of the decimal point denotes the number of tenths, hundredths, thousandths, and so forth. For example, the expansion of 0.3574 is expressed as:

$$0.3574 = (3 \times 10^{-1}) + (5 \times 10^{-2}) + (7 \times 10^{-3}) + (4 \times 10^{-4})$$
$$= 0.3 + 0.05 + 0.007 + 0.0004.$$

Decimal Fractions.   The example above illustrates standard decimal notation for a number less than 1. But what is commonly referred to as a decimal is actually a decimal fraction. A decimal fraction is a number written in decimal notation that does not have any digits except 0 to the left of the decimal point. For example, .257 is a decimal fraction, which can also be

✶**The prefix "deci" in the word "decimal" means ten.**

base-10 a number system in which each place represents a power of 10 larger than the place to its right

digit one of the symbols used in a number system to represent the multipliers of each place

place value in a number system, the power of the base assigned to each place; in base-10, the ones place, the tens place, the hundreds place, and so on

power the number of times a number is to be multiplied by itself in an expression

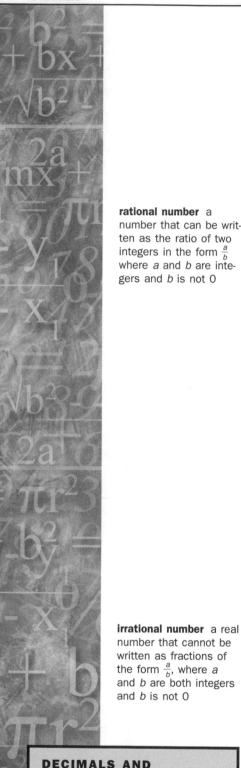

written as 0.257. It is preferable to use 0 to the left of the decimal point when there are no other digits to the left of the decimal point.

Decimal fractions can be converted into a fraction using a power of 10. For example, $0.486 = \frac{486}{1000}$, and $0.35 = \frac{35}{100}$. The fraction may be converted to an equivalent fraction by writing it in its simplest or reduced form. The fraction $\frac{35}{100}$ equals $\frac{7}{20}$, for example.

Decimal Expansion of Rational and Irrational Numbers

Is it possible to convert all fractions into decimals and all decimals into fractions? All fractions, $\frac{a}{b}$, are **rational numbers**, and all rational numbers are fractions, provided b is not 0. So the question is: Can every rational number be converted into a decimal?

Taking the rational number, or fraction $\frac{a}{b}$, and dividing the numerator by the denominator will always produce a decimal. For example, $\frac{1}{4} = 0.25$, $\frac{1}{10} = 0.1$, and $\frac{2}{5} = 0.4$. In each of these examples, the numbers to the right of the decimal point end, or terminate.

However, the conversion of $\frac{1}{3} = 0.333\ldots$, $\frac{2}{9} = 0.222\ldots$, and $\frac{3}{11} = 0.2727\ldots$, results in decimals that are nonterminating. In the first example, the calculation continuously produces 3, which repeats indefinitely. In the second example, 2 repeats indefinitely. In the third example, the pair of digits 2 and 7 repeats indefinitely.

When a digit or group of digits repeats indefinitely, a bar is placed above the digit or digits. Thus, $\frac{1}{3} = 0.\overline{3}$, $\frac{2}{9} = 0.\overline{2}$, and $\frac{3}{11} = 0.\overline{27}$. These are examples of repeating but nonterminating decimals.

It may not always be apparent when decimals start repeating. One interesting example is $\frac{3}{17}$. The division needs to be carried out to sixteen digits before the repeating digits appear:

$$\frac{3}{17} = 0.\overline{1764705882352941}.$$

Nonterminating and nonrepeating decimal numbers exist, and some may have predictable patterns, such as $0.313113111311113\ldots$. However, these numbers are not considered rational, but instead are known as irrational. An **irrational number** cannot be represented as a decimal with terminating or repeating digits, but instead yields a nonterminating, nonrepeating sequence.

A familiar example of an irrational number is $\sqrt{2}$, which in decimal form is expressed as $1.414213\ldots$, where the digits after the decimal point neither end nor repeat. Another example of an irrational number is π, which in decimal form is expressed as $3.141592\ldots$.

Daily Applications of Decimals

In daily use, decimal numbers are used for counting and measuring. Consider a shopping trip to a sporting good store, where a person buys a pair of running shoes, a warm-up jacket, and a pair of socks. The total cost is calculated by aligning at the right all three numbers on top of each other.

$39.95	running shoes
$29.95	warm-up jacket
$ 9.49	socks
$79.39	total

rational number a number that can be written as the ratio of two integers in the form $\frac{a}{b}$ where a and b are integers and b is not 0

irrational number a real number that cannot be written as fractions of the form $\frac{a}{b}$, where a and b are both integers and b is not 0

DECIMALS AND FRACTIONS

Every fraction can be represented by a decimal that either terminates or eventually repeats. Also, every decimal that either terminates or eventually repeats can be represented as a fraction.

As another example, consider a car's gas tank that has a capacity of 18.5 gallons. If the gas tank is full after pumping 7.2 gallons, how much gasoline was already in the tank? The answer is 18.5 minus 7.2, which equals 11.3 gallons. SEE ALSO FRACTIONS; NUMBERS, IRRATIONAL; NUMBERS, RATIONAL; POWERS AND EXPONENTS.

Rafiq Ladhani

Bibliography

Amdahl, Kenn, and Jim Loats. *Algebra Unplugged.* Broomfield, CO: Clearwater Publishing Co., 1995.

Dugopolski, Mark. *Elementary Algebra*, 3rd ed. Boston: McGraw-Hill, 2000.

Dunham, William. *The Mathematical Universe.* New York: John Wiley & Sons, Inc., 1994.

Miller, Charles D., Vern E. Heeren, and E. John Hornsby, Jr. *Mathematical Ideas*, 9th ed. Boston: Addison-Wesley, 2001.

Denominator   *See Fractions.*

Derivative   *See Calculus.*

Descartes and His Coordinate System

Every time you graph an equation on a Cartesian coordinate system, you are using the work of René Descartes. Descartes, a French mathematician and philosopher, was born in La Haye, France (now named in his honor) on March 31, 1596. His parents taught him at home until he was 8 years old, when he entered the Jesuit college of La Flèche. There he continued his studies until he graduated at age 18.

Descartes was an outstanding student at La Flèche, especially in mathematics. Because of his delicate health, his teachers allowed him to stay in bed until late morning. Despite missing most of his morning classes, Descartes was able to keep up with his studies. He would continue the habit of staying late in bed for his entire adult life.

After graduating from La Flèche, Descartes traveled to Paris and eventually enrolled at the University of Poitiers. He graduated with a law degree in 1616 and then enlisted in a military school. In 1619, he joined the Bavarian army and spent the next nine years as a soldier, touring throughout much of Europe in between military campaigns. Descartes eventually settled in Holland, where he spent most of the rest of his life. There Descartes gave up a military career and decided on a life of mathematics and philosophy.

Descartes attempted to provide a philosophical foundation for the new mechanistic physics that was developing from the work of Copernicus and Galileo. He divided all things into two categories—mind and matter—and developed a dualistic philosophical system in which, although mind is subject to the will and does not follow physical laws, all matter must obey the same mechanistic laws.

The philosophical system that Descartes developed, known as Cartesian philosophy, was based on **skepticism** and asserted that all reliable

René Descartes built the foundation for modern philosophical method with a simple catchphrase: "I think, therefore I am." He is also regarded as the founder of analytic geometry.

skepticism a tendency towards doubt

GEOMETRY AND THE FLY

Some mathematics historians claim it may be that Descartes's inspiration for the coordinate system was due to his lifelong habit of staying late in bed. According to some accounts, one morning Descartes noticed a fly walking across the ceiling of his bedroom. As he watched the fly, Descartes began to think of how the fly's path could be described without actually tracing its path. His further reflections about describing a path by means of mathematics led to *La Géometrie* and Descartes's invention of coordinate geometry.

geometry the branch of mathematics that deals with the properties and relationships of points, lines, angles, surfaces, planes, and solids

algebra the branch of mathematics that deals with variables or unknowns representing the arithmetic numbers

analytic geometry the study of geometric properties by using algebraic operations

perpendicular forming a right angle with a line or plane

coordinate plane an imaginary two-dimensional plane defined as the plane containing the x- and y-axes; all points on the plane have coordinates that can be expressed as (x, y)

vertex the point on a triangle or polygon where two sides come together

The Cartesian coordinate system unites geometry and algebra, and is a universal system for unambiguous location of points. Applications range from computer animation to global positioning systems.

knowledge must be built up by the use of reason through logical analysis. Cartesian philosophy was influential in the ultimate success of the Scientific Revolution and provides the foundation upon which most subsequent philosophical thought is grounded.

Descartes published various treatises about philosophy and mathematics. In 1637 Descartes published his masterwork, *Discourse on the Method of Reasoning Well and Seeking Truth in the Sciences*. In *Discourse*, Descartes sought to explain everything in terms of matter and motion. *Discourse* contained three appendices, one on optics, one on meteorology, and one titled *La Géométrie* (The Geometry). In *La Géométrie*, Descartes described what is now known as the system of Cartesian Coordinates, or coordinate geometry. In Descartes's system of coordinates, **geometry** and **algebra** were united for the first time to create what is known as **analytic geometry**.

The Cartesian Coordinate System

Cartesian coordinates are used to locate a point in space by giving its relative distance from **perpendicular** intersecting lines. In coordinate geometry, all points, lines, and figures are drawn in a **coordinate plane**. By reference to the two coordinate axes, any point, line, or figure may be precisely located.

In Descartes's system, the first coordinate value (x-coordinate) describes where along the horizontal axis (the x-axis) the point is located. The second coordinate value (y-coordinate) locates the point in terms of the vertical axis (the y-axis). A point with coordinates (4, −2) is located four units to the right of the intersection point of the two axes (point O, or the origin) and then two units below the vertical position of the origin. In example (a) of the figure, point D is at the coordinate location (4, −2). The coordinates for point A are (3, 2); for point B, (2, −4); and for point C, (−2, −5).

The coordinate system also makes it possible to exactly duplicate geometric figures. For example, the triangle shown in (b) has coordinates A (3, 2), B (4, 5), and C (−2, 4) that make it possible to duplicate the triangle without reference to any drawing.

The triangle may be reproduced by using the coordinates to locate the position of the three **vertex** points. The vertex points may then be connected with segments to replicate triangle ABC. More complex figures may likewise be described and duplicated with coordinates.

A straight line may also be represented on a coordinate grid. In the case of a straight line, every point on the line has coordinate values that must

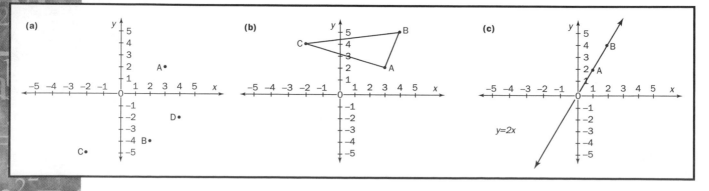

satisfy a specific equation. The line in (c) may be expressed as $y = 2x$. The coordinates of every point on the line will satisfy the equation $y = 2x$, as for example, point A (1, 2) and point B (2, 4). More complex equations are used to represent circles, ellipses, and curved lines.

Other Contributions

La Géometrie made Descartes famous throughout Europe. He continued to publish his philosophy, detailing how to acquire accurate knowledge. His philosophy is sometimes summed up in his statement, "I think, therefore I am."

Descartes also made a number of other contributions to mathematics. He discovered the Law of Angular Deficiency for all **polyhedrons** and was the first to offer a quantifiable explanation of rainbows. In *La Géometrie*, Descartes introduced a familiar mathematics symbol, a raised number to indicate an **exponent**. The expression $4 \times 4 \times 4 \times 4 \times 4$ may be written as 4^5 using Descartes's notation. He also instituted using x, y, and z for unknowns in an equation.

In 1649, Descartes accepted an invitation from Queen Christina to travel to Sweden to be the royal tutor. Unfortunately for Descartes, the queen expected to be tutored while she did her exercises at 5:00 A.M. in an unheated library. Descartes had been used to a lifetime of sleeping late, and the new routine was much too rigorous for him. After only a few weeks of this regimen, Descartes contracted pneumonia and died on February 11, 1650. SEE ALSO COMPUTER ANIMATION; COORDINATE SYSTEM, POLAR; COORDINATE SYSTEM, THREE-DIMENSIONAL; GLOBAL POSITIONING SYSTEM; NAVIGATION.

Arthur V. Johnson II and J. William Moncrief

Bibliography

Boyer, Carl B. *History of Mathematics*. New York: John Wiley & Sons, Inc., 1968.

Burton, David. *The History of Mathematics: An Introduction*. New York: Allyn and Bacon, 1985.

Eves, Howard. *In Mathematical Circles*. Boston: Prindle, Webber & Schmidt, Inc., 1969.

Johnson, Art. *Classic Math: History Topics for the Classroom*. Palo Alto, CA: Dale Seymour Publications, 1994.

Internet Resources

MacTutor History of Mathematics Archive. University of St Andrews. <http://www-groups.dcs.st-and.ac.uk/~history/Mathematicians.html>.

Differential Equation *See Calculus.*

Dimensional Relationships

Usually, when mathematicians compare the size of two-dimensional objects, they compare their areas. For example, how many times larger is a larger square than a smaller one? One way to answer this question is to determine the lengths of the sides of the squares, and use this information to find the respective areas.

WHO USES COORDINATES?

The system of coordinates that Descartes invented is used in many modern applications. For example, on any map the location of a country or a city is usually given as a set of coordinates. The location of a ship at sea is determined by longitude and latitude, which is an application of the coordinate system to the curved surface of Earth. Computer graphic artists create figures and computer animation by referencing coordinates on the screen.

polyhedron a solid formed with all plane faces

exponent the symbol written above and to the right of an expression indicating the power to which the expression is to be raised

Use the formula for the area of a square, $A = S^2$, where A represents area and S represents the side length of the square. Suppose two squares have side lengths of 2 and 6, respectively. Hence, the respective areas are 4 and 36. Thus the area of the larger square is nine times that of the smaller square. Therefore, a square whose side length is three times that of a second square will have an area nine times as great.

Use the notation S_1 to denote the side of the smaller square and S_2 to denote the side of the larger square. With this notation, $S_2 = 3S_1$. The area of the larger square then becomes $(3S_1)^2 = 3S_1 \times 3S_1 = 9S_1^2$. This can be generalized further by letting one side of the square be k times the side of another, also known as the ratio of similitude (k) between the figures. Then $(kS_1)^2 = kS_1 \times kS_1 = k^2S_1^2$. From this, it is evident that if the side lengths of one square are k times the side lengths of another, the area of the first is k^2 that of the other.

This principle is true for any two-dimensional object. Suppose two circles have radii that are in the ratio of 2:1. Letting $R_2 = 2R_1$, the area of the larger circle can be represented by $A = \pi(2R_1)^2 = 4\pi R_1^2$.

As another example, suppose the sides and altitude of the larger triangle are twice those of a smaller triangle. Thus the area of the larger triangle can be written as $A = \frac{1}{2}(2b_1)(2h_1) = 2b_1h_1 = 4(\frac{1}{2}b_1h_1)$.

For three-dimensional objects, volumes of similar figures relate to each other in a manner akin to areas of two-dimensional figures. A cube, for example, with a side length twice that of another cube, will have a volume $2^3 = 8$ times as great. A sphere with a radius five times that of a smaller sphere will have a volume $5^3 = 125$ times as great.

ratio of similitude the ratio of the corresponding sides of similar figures

If k represents the **ratio of similitude** of two similar objects, then the areas of the two objects will be in the ratio of k^2, and the volumes of the two objects will be in the ratio of k^3. SEE ALSO DIMENSIONS.

Albert Goetz

Dimensions

A dimension is a measurement of space. In a three-dimensional world, we usually think of three different directions as we measure the space in which we exist—length, width, and height. To indicate a certain location in space, we would provide three different coordinates on three different axes (x, y, and z).

The understanding of different dimensions is crucial in understanding much of mathematics. The ability to visualize and a flexibility in adjusting to n-dimensional worlds is a skill worth pursuing.

Portraying Three Dimensions

Even though most everyday experience is in three dimensions, most high school mathematics takes place in a two-dimensional world in which there is only length and width. Part of this is because traditional learning is largely communicated through books or on a chalkboard. Book pages or the planes of chalkboards have primarily two dimensions. Even if there is a picture in a book of a three-dimensional object, the object is "flattened" so that its likeness can be communicated through a two-dimensional medium. This can cause differences between what we see in a three-dimensional object and how the object is portrayed in two dimensions.

For example, consider a cube. In real life, a **vertex** of a cube is formed when three 90° angles from three different square faces intersect at a point. However, in a two-dimensional representation of a cube, the right angles may measure other than 90° on the page. For example, in the picture of the cube below, each angle around the center vertex measures close to 120°. The image of the three-dimensional object must be altered this way in order for it to give us the perception that it is really three-dimensional.

vertex the point on a triangle or polygon where two sides come together

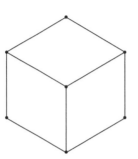

Portraying three dimensions in two-dimensional representations can also play tricks with our sense of perception. Many optical illusions are created by taking an impossible figure in three dimensions and drawing a two-dimensional picture of it.

Artist M. C. Escher was a master of communicating impossible ideas through two-dimensional drawings. In many of his engravings, the scene is impossible to construct in three dimensions, but by working with angles and making a few simple alterations, Escher fools our normally reliable sense of perception.

Imagining Dimensions

Points, lines, and planes are theoretical concepts typically modeled with three-dimensional objects in which we learn to ignore some of their dimensions. For example, earlier it was stated that a piece of paper or a plane is primarily two-dimensional. Although a piece of paper clearly has a thickness (height), albeit small, we think of it as being two-dimensional. So when considering objects with different dimensions, we must be able to visualize and think abstractly.

When we think of a plane, we start with a sheet of paper, which has length, width, and a very small height. Then we imagine that the height slowly disappears until all that remains is a length and a width. Similarly, when we draw lines on a chalkboard, we know that the chalkdust has length, a small width, and even an infinitesimal thickness. However, a mathematician imagines the line as having only one dimension: length. Finally when we consider a point in space, we must imagine that the point is merely a position or a location in space: that is, it has no size. To imagine a point, begin with an image of a fixed atom in space that is slowly

melting or disappearing until all that remains is its location. That location is a true mathematical image of a point.

A college professor gave the following way to think about dimensions. Start with a figure of zero dimensions: that is, a point. Set two of these items next to each other and connect them with a line segment. You now have a new entity of one dimension called a line segment. Again set two of these line segments next to each other and connect them with line segments. You now have a two-dimensional entity called a square. Connect two squares, and you have a three-dimensional entity called a cube. Connect the vertices of two cubes and you have a four-dimensional entity sometimes known as a hypercube or **tesseract**.✶

tesseract a four-dimensional cube, formed by connecting all of the vertices of two three-dimensional cubes separated by the length of one side in four-dimensional space

✶A tesseract has 16 vertices, 32 edges, 24 squares, and 8 cubes.

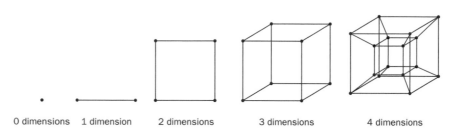

0 dimensions 1 dimension 2 dimensions 3 dimensions 4 dimensions

If you are having trouble visualizing a tesseract (as shown above), keep in mind that you are looking at a two-dimensional picture of something that is four-dimensional! Even if you build a three-dimensional physical model of a tesseract, you will still need to imagine the missing dimension that would bring us from three dimensions into four.

Abbott's *Flatland*

Imagining worlds of different dimensions is the premise of Edwin A. Abbott's book, *Flatland*. He describes an entire civilization that lives in a world with only two dimensions. All of its inhabitants are either lines, or polygons such as triangles, squares, and pentagons. These individuals cannot perceive of anything but length and width. Imagine, for example, living in a blackboard and only being able to move from side to side or up and down. Depth would be an unknown quantity.

Abbott's book describes a day when a sphere visits a family in Flatland. Because Flatlanders are unable to perceive a third dimension of depth, they are only able to perceive first a point (as the sphere first entered their world), then a small circle which increases in area until it reaches the very middle of the sphere, and then a circle of decreasing area until it becomes a point again. Then it disappears. Imagine trying to communicate to these Flatlanders anything about the third dimension when they had never experienced anything in that realm.

Use a similar analogy when thinking about what four dimensions might be like. Even if a creature from the fourth dimension visited us here in three-dimensional "Spaceland," and tried to describe the fourth dimension to us, we would not be equipped to understand it fully. SEE ALSO COORDINATES, THREE-DIMENSIONAL; ESCHER, M. C.; MATHEMATICS, IMPOSSIBLE.

Jane Keiser Krumpe

Bibliography

Abbott, Edwin A. *Flatland.* New York: Penguin Books USA, Inc., 1984.

Berger, Dionys. *Sphereland.* New York: Crowell, 1965.

Escher, M. C. *M. C. Escher, 29 Master Prints.* New York: Harry N. Abrams, Inc., Publishers, 1983.

Rucker, Rudolf v. B. *Geometry, Relativity and the Fourth Dimension.* New York: Dover Publications, Inc., 1977.

Distance, Measurement of

In the twenty-first century, societies need to make a wide range of measurements, from economic indicators and population trends to the times of sporting events and various standardized tests. Despite all of the varied measurement that is performed, modern societies still focus attention on the same two subjects, time and distance. In this entry, the focus will be on the measurement of distance.

Early Attempts to Measure Distance

Early civilizations used various crude instruments to measure distance, ranging from a simple **pace** to measuring rods and marked cords. The accuracy that was achieved with such basic devices can be astonishing. For example, the Great Pyramid of Egypt, built about 2400 B.C.E., has four base edges that are each within 0.01 percent of 751 feet in length.

pace an ancient measure of length equal to normal stride length

Most societies developed random units of measure that became standardized over time. The Egyptians used the *cubit*, which varied in length from 15 inches to 19 inches, depending on the ruling dynasty. To measure longer distances, some societies employed individuals to pace off the distance. In Egypt, these individuals were called "rope stretchers." They tied a specific length of rope to their two ankles and then paced off the distance so that each and every stride stretched the rope to its full length. The Egyptians used other crude measuring devices, such as marked cords and wooden rods. Each of the four faces of the Great Pyramid is positioned exactly on one of the four points of the compass. A *groma* was used to establish right angles for such measuring purposes. The groma was a wooden cross that pivoted and had plumb lines hanging from each arm to ensure proper positioning.

Distance measurement remained static for centuries after the Egyptians, with few advancements. About 500 B.C.E., Greek mathematician Thales demonstrated how to use the geometric principles of similarity to measure distances indirectly. For example, Thales used shadows to measure the height of the Great Pyramid. Still, the data needed for such indirect measurements had to be found using cords and measuring rods.

Two hundred years later, Greek mathematician Eratosthenes determined the circumference of Earth to within a few hundred miles by using geometric principles and data from rope stretchers. About 200 B.C.E., the astrolabe was invented to measure the **angle of elevation** of various stars. These data were used to find the time of day, which in turn was used by sailors for navigation. Later developments led to its replacement by the **sextant**. In the 1600s, the theodolite was invented, which is a device that measures angles of

angle of elevation the angle formed by a line of sight above the horizontal

sextant a device for measuring altitudes of celestial objects

theodolite a surveying instrument designed to measure both horizontal and vertical angles

celestial body any natural object in space, defined as above Earth's atmosphere; the Moon, the Sun, the planets, asteroids, stars, galaxies, nebula

aerial photography photographs of the ground taken from an airplane or balloon; used in mapping and surveying

elevation and horizontal angles simultaneously. The **theodolite** is essentially a telescope that pivots around horizontal and vertical axes. Modern theodolites can measure angles to an accuracy of 1/3600 of a degree.

In 1620, Edmund Gunther (1581–1626) invented a chain to survey land. It was 66 feet long and not subject to humidity, fraying, or other irregularities that might affect a rope or cord. The chain was the precursor to the modern steel tape measure. At about the same time, the telescope was invented. This made it possible to see great distances across the heavens and to see stars that had previously been beyond human sight. The distances between **celestial bodies** remained unknown, but advances in telescopes gave rise to the ability to measure distances across the heavens. During the same time period, Anthony Leeuwenhoek invented the first modern microscope, opening up a new world of discovery at the opposite end of the measurement spectrum.

Modern Advances in Distance Measurement

The early twentieth century saw great advancements in distance measurements. First, **aerial photography** made accurate measurements of distances across difficult terrain easily possible. This was followed by satellite photography, making it feasible to survey great tracts of land easily. In the twenty-first century, modern theodolites employ electromagnetic distance measurement processes. These instruments measure the time a laser or ultra high radiation (either microwave for longer distances or infrared radiation for shorter distances) needs to pass over a specific distance. Modern surveying instruments send out a laser pulse to a target on location. The target reflects the laser beam back to the surveyor. The time required to travel out and back is measured by a computer, which then calculates the distance. At the other end of measurable distances, powerful electronic microscopes enable scientists to see increasingly smaller objects.

Modern precision instruments have even affected standard measurement units like the meter. Originally the standard meter was a length of platinum that was exactly one meter long. However, a metallic object can grow or shrink according to atmospheric conditions. The effects of dust and handling can also affect such an object, although only at a microscopic level. To avoid such effects, a meter is now defined as the distance that light in a vacuum travels in 1/229,792,458 of a second.

Modern precision has made it possible to measure extremely large and small distances. The longest distance measurement is for galaxies that are 14 billion light years from Earth. (Light travels approximately 186,000 miles per second. A light year is how far light travels in a year.) This distance is referred to as 10^{25} meters. At the other end of the scale, scientists use scanning electron microscopes to see molecular particles that are 10^{-16} meters long, or 0.1 Fermi in length. (One Fermi is 10^{-15} meter.) How much more precision is still possible to achieve is difficult to predict. Most scientists agree that there are objects in the universe that are even farther away from Earth. Newer, more powerful telescopes will likely be able to detect them and measure their distance from Earth. Scientists also envision a time when objects as small as an individual atom or even subatomic particles will be "visible" and thus can be measured. SEE ALSO ASTRONOMY, MEASUREMENTS IN;

Measurement, English System of; Measurement, Metric System of; Mile, Nautical and Statute; Navigation; Telescope; Time, Measurement of.

Arthur V. Johnson II

Bibliography

Dilke, O. A. W. *Reading the Past: Mathematics and Measurement.* London U.K.: British Museum Press, 1987.

Morrison, Philip, and Phylis Morrison. *Powers of Ten.* New York: Scientific American Books, Inc., 1982.

Strauss, Stephen. *The Sizesaurus: from Hectares to Decibels, a Witty Compendium of Measurements.* New York: Kondasha America, Inc., 1995.

Division by Zero

The number 0 has unique properties, including when a number is multiplied or divided by 0. Multiplying a number by 0 equals 0. For example, $256 \times 0 = 0$. Dividing a number by 0, however, is undefined.

Why is dividing a number by 0 undefined? Suppose dividing 5 by 0 produces a number x:

$$\frac{5}{0} = x.$$

From $\frac{5}{0} = x$ it follows that $0 \times x$ must be 5. But the product of 0 and any number is always 0. Therefore, there is no number x that works, and division by 0 is undefined.

A False Proof

If division by 0 were allowed, it could be proved—falsely—that $1 = 2$. Suppose $x = y$. Using valid properties of equations, the above equation is rewritten

$x^2 = xy$ (after multiplying both sides by x)

$x^2 - y^2 = xy - y^2$ (after subtracting y^2 from both sides)

$(x - y)(x + y) = y(x - y)$ (after factoring both sides)

$(x + y) = y$ (after dividing both sides by $(x - y)$)

$2y = y$ ($x = y$, based on the original supposition)

$2 = 1$ (after dividing both sides by y)

This absurd result ($2 = 1$) comes from division by 0. If $x = y$, dividing by $(x - y)$ is essentially dividing by 0 because $x - y = 0$.

Approaching Limits

It is interesting to note that dividing a number such as 5 by a series of increasingly small numbers (0.1, 0.01, 0.001, and so on) produces increasingly large numbers (50, 500, 5000, and so on). This division sequence can be written as $\frac{5}{x}$ where x approaches but never equals 0. In mathematical language, as x approaches 0, $\frac{5}{x}$ increases without limit or that $\frac{5}{x}$ approaches **infinity**. SEE ALSO Consistency; Infinity; Limit.

Frederick Landwehr

infinity a quantity beyond measure; an unbounded quantity

Bibliography

Amdahl, Kenn, and Jim Loats. *Algebra Unplugged.* Broomfield, CO: Clearwater Publishing Co., 1995.

Miller, Charles D., Vern E. Heeren, and E. John Hornsby, Jr. *Mathematical Ideas*, 9th ed. Boston: Addison-Wesley, 2001.

Dürer, Albrecht

German Painter, Printmaker, and Engraver
1471–1528

Albrecht Dürer was born in 1471 in Nuremberg, Germany, and died there in 1528. He is regarded as one of the leading artists of the Renaissance. His use of mathematical methods in artistic composition influenced subsequent development of art.

Dürer first worked with his father, who was an accomplished goldsmith, then broadened his artistic training by assisting artist Michel Wohlgemuth. Developing his expertise quickly, Dürer was soon able to go out on his own as a painter and printmaker. He became widely known, traveling throughout Europe while studying and producing works of art, and was a particular favorite of Emperor Maximilian I.

Dürer attempted to portray nature realistically in his works, paying close attention to the appearance of animals, plants, and the human body and trying to reproduce them accurately. He was even known to have dissected **cadavers** to better understand the human body. Dürer's realistic paintings of plants influenced botanists to use drawings that more closely resembled the plants portrayed.

To improve his paintings and etchings, Dürer sought a mathematical formulation for the ideal human body and for beauty in general. He studied the problems of space, **perspective**, and **proportion** and constructed his forms on the canvas, using arithmetic and geometric techniques. The results of his studies were published posthumously in 1528 as *The Four Books on Human Proportions,* a work that has had a significant effect on succeeding generations of artists. SEE ALSO HUMAN BODY.

J. William Moncrief

Bibliography

Dürer, Albrecht. *The Complete Engravings, Etchings and Drypoints of Albrecht Dürer.* Mineola, NY: Dover Publications, 1972.

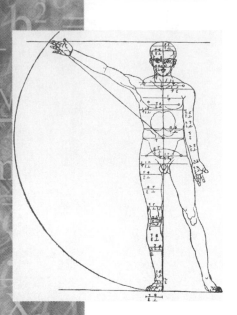

Albrecht Dürer's engraving "Proportion of Man" is both a mathematical and artistic representation of the human body.

cadaver the term used to refer to a corpse intended for medical research or training

perspective the point of view; a drawing constructed in such a way that an appearance of three dimensionality is achieved

proportion the mathematical relation between one part and another part, or between a part and the whole; the equality of two ratios

Earthquakes, Measuring

Earthquakes happen every day. Thousands occur across the world every week. Most are not felt, but throughout history there have been many earthquakes that have been very strong and caused extensive destruction. Mathematics skills are invaluable to earthquake scientists, and with them they can sometimes predict when and where earthquakes will happen, and make measurements of earthquakes when they do occur.

Earthquakes happen when the **tectonic plates** of the Earth shift. As this movement happens, pressure builds on the plates and faults. Eventually this pressure is released through an earthquake. During an earthquake seismic waves radiate out from a central point in all directions. There are four basic types of seismic waves, two that travel through the Earth, and two that are felt at the surface. These waves are recorded on a seismograph, which is an instrument made up of sensitive detectors that produce a permanent recording.

tectonic plates large segments of Earth's crust that move in relation to one another

Size of Earthquakes

To determine the magnitude or size of an earthquake, scientists use the Richter scale. Developed by Charles Richter in 1934, this scale is based on a logarithmic increase of magnitude. With a scale such as this, for every whole number increase on the scale, the amplitude of the earthquake goes up ten times. For example, an earthquake with a reading of 5.0 on the Richter scale has a magnitude 10^5 (or 100,000) times as great as an earthquake with a magnitude of zero.

There are more than 1,000 earthquakes a day with recorded magnitudes of two or greater. An earthquake measuring between 6.1 and 6.9 can cause destruction in an area up to 100 kilometers in diameter. The San Francisco earthquake of 1906 measured 7.8 on the Richter scale.

Another way to measure an earthquake is to use the Mercalli Intensity Scale. This scale measures the intensity or energy of an earthquake. Though each earthquake has a fixed magnitude, the effects of it are different depending on location. This measurement is based on criteria such as structural damage and the observations of people who felt the earthquake. From these types of observations, the intensity of an earthquake can be estimated.

The Mercalli scale is not considered as scientific as the Richter scale, since it is based on factors that can change depending on where the infor-

Large sections of a major expressway collapsed during a 1995 earthquake in Kobe, Japan, where thousands of people perished.

mation is derived. After an earthquake, for example, witnesses may exaggerate or not agree on what they saw. In addition damage does not always accurately measure the strength of an earthquake.

Depth and Location of Earthquakes

Earthquakes occur between the Earth's surface and about 700 kilometers below the surface. The way to determine the depth of an earthquake is to look at wave characteristics on a seismogram, which is a graph of seismic waves. For example, an indication of a large earthquake with a deep focus would be surface waves with small amplitudes, and uncomplicated deep waves.

The point on Earth's surface directly above the origin of an earthquake is called its **epicenter**. To find out where an earthquake is located, scientists must examine its waves. The simplest method is to look at the different arrival times of wave types at multiple seismograph stations. Scientists then use standard travel-time tables and travel-time curves to find the distance to the earthquake from each station. Arcs are then drawn, with the distance from each station to the earthquake used as a radius. The point where all the arcs intersect is the epicenter of the earthquake.

epicenter the point on Earth's surface directly above the site of an earthquake

✴**When predicting earthquakes, some scientists study the behavior of animals, which can become very erratic before a quake strikes.**

Calculating Earthquake Odds

Earthquakes are naturally recurring events, and scientists continue to develop better methods to predict when and where earthquakes might happen.✴ Earthquake probabilities are based on balancing the continual motions of the Earth's plates with the slip on faults, which occurs primarily during earthquakes. Scientists must also look at the history of a given fault to know when it last ruptured, potential quake sizes, and the rate at which the plate is moving. By combining geology, physics, and statistics, scientists continue to become more accurate in their earthquake predictions. SEE ALSO LOGARITHMS; PROBABILITY, THEORETICAL.

Brook E. Hall

MAJOR QUAKE LIKELY TO STRIKE BETWEEN 2000 AND 2030

Scientists believe that there is an 80-percent probability of at least one earthquake with a Richter magnitude between 6.0 and 6.6 striking the San Francisco Bay region before 2030. By keeping aware of earthquake threats, people can make informed decisions on how to prepare for future quakes.

Bibliography

Bolt, Bruce A. *Earthquakes.* New York: W. H. Freeman, 1999.

Lay, Thorne, and Terry C. Wallace. *Modern Global Seismology.* San Diego: Academic Press, 1995.

Internet Resources

Calculating the Earthquake Odds. United States Geological Survey. <http://geopubs .wr.usgs.gov/fact-sheet/fs152-99/calcodds.html>.

How Are Earthquake Magnitudes Measured? UPSeis. <http://www.geo.mtu.edu/UPSeis/ intensity.html>.

The Science of Seismology. United States Geological Survey. <http://earthquake.usgs .gov/4kids/science.html>.

Economic Indicators

Individuals and families have checking accounts, savings accounts, credit cards, and bills, so people make budgets to determine how much money they are making and spending. Businesses do the same thing. Countries, such as the United States, also use a budget to keep close track of their finances. The study of money and where it is going and where it came from is called economics. The economy is the system through which money circulates. Economists are the people who study the movement of money through the economy. By looking at economic indicators (which are features of the economy that are represented in numbers) economists make predictions about the potential strengths and weaknesses in the economy. Economic indicators give economists valuable insights into a country's financial standing.

Leading Indicators

Leading economic indicators are those that have the ability to forecast the probable future economy. An example of a leading indicator is the length of the workweek; that is, the average number of hours employees work in a week. As business increases, employers generally increase the number of hours that current employees work instead of immediately hiring new employees. A longer workweek tells economists that businesses are doing well. If business is increasing, the economy is doing well. If, on the other hand, the economy is doing poorly, employers will shorten their employees' workweek before laying off employees, a measure which is, for most employers, used only as a last effort to save money. Since the workweek lengthens or shortens before any effects on the economy are seen, a change in the length of the workweek in either direction can be used as a forecasting tool for economists.

Lagging Indicators

Other economic indicators result from changes in various features of the economy. An example of a lagging indicator is the unemployment rate, which is the number that represents the percentage of the labor force that is not employed. The labor force is defined as all people over 16 years of age who are able to work. However, it does not include stay-at-home mothers or fathers, students, people who cannot work because of their health, or people who are not looking for jobs. If many people are unemployed, the economy is doing poorly. If few people are unemployed, the economy is doing well. Since change in the unemployment rate tells how many people either lost or gained jobs, it simply describes what has already happened; it does not predict what might happen.

Numbers in the Economy

Most of the numbers used to calculate economic indicators come from the U.S. Census Bureau, which is the division of the U.S. Department of Commerce that keeps statistics, such as the unemployment rate, the workweek length, the number of new houses being built, the number of building permits being given out, the number of new jobs being created, as well as many other figures. All of these statistics are used to provide economists with the data they need to study the economy. Economists are most concerned with changes in these statistics, which raises questions such as "Are there more new jobs being created this year than last year?" or "Are people working fewer hours this month than last month?"

The numbers for economic indicators are often put into indexes. Indexes are combinations of data from different economic indicators. The index numbers provide a broader view of the economy. One of the most frequently used numbers is the index of leading economic indicators (LEI).

Interest rates on credit cards vary from lender to lender and from person to person, depending on one's credit history. Smart consumers shop around to find the best rates available.

This index measures changes in several leading economic indicators. An increase in the LEI for 3 or more months signals that the economy is improving; a decrease in the LEI for 3 or more months suggests a possible recession. A recession is a temporary decrease in business and therefore a downturn in the economy.

Gross Domestic Product

One of the best indicators of the economy is the gross domestic product (GDP). This dollar figure is the value of all goods and services produced within a nation in a calendar year. The gross national product (GNP) is also a dollar figure, but differs in that it is the value of all goods and services produced by a nation's citizens within a year. For example, the profits from an American-owned business operating in Germany would be included in the GNP, but not in the GDP because the business is not within the United States. The gross domestic product (GDP) is more commonly used as an economic indicator.

Goods that are included in the GDP must be newly manufactured items, and they must be finished products. In making an automobile, first a manufacturer makes the steel and sells it to the auto manufacturer. At this stage the steel is not counted in the GDP because it is not a finished product. The steel is counted in the GDP only as part of the value of the finished automobile.

The goods and services counted in the GDP consist not only of the things that people buy: They can be things that people produce that get consumed without ever being sold. One example is a farmer who milks cows. If the farmer then drinks some of the milk he or she produces, it is still counted in the GDP, even though it was never sold. Economists will guess at its market value (its worth) and add it to the total GDP. If milk sells for $2.50 per gallon at the time and it is estimated that the farmer's family drank 100 gallons of milk during the year, $250 would be added to the GDP. In this sense, the GDP is not a precise measurement.

Information for calculating the GDP is collected every quarter (i.e., every 3 months). The GDP in each quarter is multiplied by 4 to calculate an "annual GDP." Economists often adjust the GDP even further. Since seasonal changes affect the economy, economists often make adjustments for the seasons of the year. In the summer, for example, tourism increases and more money is spent. Instead of saying that the GDP is higher in the summer, economists adjust it so it is standard throughout the year. They do this by looking at the change in the GDP over several summers. For example, if the average change every summer is an increase of 3 percent, but one summer it increased 5 percent, it will only be said to have increased 2 percent above "normal."

fluctuate to vary irregularly

Because prices **fluctuate** from year to year, another adjustment must be made to the GDP in order to allow economists to compare GDPs from different years. Most products, such as cars, homes, and clothing cost more now than they did 20 years ago. Therefore a dollar today purchases a different amount of product than it did in the past. To account for this, economists calculate each year's GDP in constant dollars. Constant dollars measure the value of products in a given year based on the prices of products in some base year. For example, in the early-1990s, economists used 1983 as a base year to convert to constant dollars. When economists refer

to constant dollars, the base year is often stated. By doing this, the change in the GDP from year to year is due to the change in the amount of goods and services being produced.

Inflation

Economists use the inflation rate to help them adjust the GDP to constant dollars. Inflation is the rate, expressed as a percentage, at which prices of goods and services are increasing each year. It may be reported on the news that "in March prices increased 1 percent, an annual inflation rate of 12 percent." The annual rate is calculated by multiplying the rate for the month times 12. But the annual rate of inflation for that year will only be 12 percent if prices continue to increase 1 percent per month for the rest of the year. Inflation rates may also be given as "the year's inflation." This does not mean an annual rate but a rate since January of that year. In the preceding example, the months included would be January, February, and March. It is important to understand the concept of inflation as well as the means by which it is reported.

The following example converts the GDP in 1980 to constant 1972 dollars. First, think of the base year (1972) prices as 1.0. By 1980, prices in the United States had increased to 1.8, an 80 percent increase since 1972. The GDP (in 1980 dollars) in 1980 was $2.62 trillion dollars. To change this to 1972 dollars, divide it by 1.8. This gives the constant dollar GDP of $1.45 trillion. This number is significantly lower than the current dollar GDP of 1980. However, it allows economists to compare the economy from year to year more accurately.

Consumer Price Index

Inflation is determined by the Consumer Price Index, which is a measurement of price increase. Surveyors from the U.S. Labor Department collect information from households around the country about what goods are being purchased and consumed. Beyond knowing how much a household is spending, for example, on groceries or entertainment, analysts determine how much is being spent on specific items, such as eggs, milk, and movie rentals. All of the information collected from the surveyors is then averaged. The result provides the Labor Department with a representative budget for an average household.

The surveyors then price all of the items that are in that representative budget every month. They can compare the prices each month to find out how much they have changed. The rate at which they change is inflation. It is important to recalculate the consumer price index periodically because of the changing habits of consumers.

These economic indicators are only a few of the many that economists study every day. However, these indicators are the ones that are most often reported to the public and the ones that most directly affect consumers. For example, inflation rates, which may affect the interest rate a consumer must pay on a car loan or mortgage, are used to adjust interest rates. As inflation rates rise, so do interest rates, thus affecting consumers' purchasing power. A basic understanding of economics and economic indicators is essential in sound financial management. SEE ALSO AGRICULTURE; STOCK MARKET.

Kelly J. Martinson

Bibliography

Greenwald, Douglas, Ann Gray, Kirk Sokoloff, and Nancy Warren, eds. *Encyclopedia of Economics.* New York: McGraw-Hill, Inc., 1982.

Levi, Maurice. *Economics Deciphered: A Layman's Survival Guide.* New York: Basic Books, Inc., 1981.

Sommers, Albert T. *The U.S. Economy Demystified: What the Major Economic Statistics Mean and Their Significance in Business.* Lexington, MA: D.C. Heath and Company, 1985.

Einstein, Albert

American Physicist and Mathematician
1879–1955

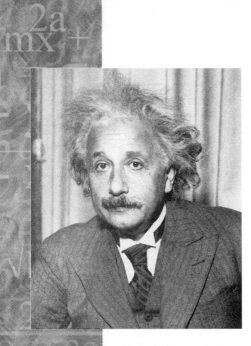

Although he attended school in both Germany and Switzerland, Albert Einstein was disinterested in the formalities of education, which led him to teach himself calculus, higher mathematics, and physics. He was awarded the Nobel Prize for Physics in 1921.

relativity the assertion that measurements of certain physical quantities such as mass, length, and time depend on the relative motion of the object and observer

quantum describes a small packet of energy (matter and energy are equivalent)

Albert Einstein is perhaps the best-known scientist who ever lived. His contributions include the special and general theories of **relativity**, the assertion of the equivalence of mass and energy, and the **quantum** explanation of the behavior of electromagnetic radiation, including light. Einstein was born in Ulm, Germany, in 1879 and died in Princeton, New Jersey, in 1955.

Einstein showed little academic ability before entering the Federal Polytechnic Academy in Zurich, Switzerland, in 1896, where he studied both mathematics and physics. After graduating in 1900, he briefly taught school and then took a position in the patent office. During this time, he wrote articles on theoretical physics in his spare time.

Einstein's ability to apply advanced mathematics in the solution of complex physical problems led to the publication of a group of momentous papers in 1905. A doctorate from the University of Zurich and world fame soon followed.

The subjects of the 1905 publications included special relativity, the equivalence of matter and energy, and the quantum nature of radiation. These revolutionary publications, in combination with the general theory of relativity, which he published in 1915, and the development of quantum mechanics, to which he made significant contributions, transformed science and again demonstrated the indispensability of mathematics in the scientific endeavor.

The atomic age, the space age, and the electronic age owe much to Einstein's contributions to physics, changing human civilization more dramatically in the twentieth century than in previous centuries combined.

J. William Moncrief

Bibliography

Hoffmann, Banesh. *Albert Einstein: Creator and Rebel.* New York: Viking, 1972.

Electronics Repair Technician

Modern life is powered by electricity, but electrical equipment sometimes breaks down. Electronics repair technicians can troubleshoot a piece of malfunctioning equipment and repair it. They can also test and maintain equipment to keep it from breaking down at all.

"Electronics" is a broad category, and electronics repair technicians find jobs in a number of settings and can pursue any range of specializations, including heating and air conditioning, home appliances, computers, and telecommunications, among others. Some electronics repair technicians even specialize in musical instruments such as electric guitars. While hands-on experience is important, most electronics repair technicians find that entry and advancement in the job market are easier if they have a strong math and science background in high school from classes such as physics, algebra, trigonometry, and calculus. It is also helpful to have a two-year degree in electronics technology from a community college or vocational-technical college. Such a program emphasizes not only electronics, but also applied mathematics and geometry. Although it is not mandatory, many pass an exam to be become certified.

Good electronics repair technicians have a firm grasp of the mathematics and physics of electricity. They have to measure and understand electrical charges, currents and amps, voltage, and resistance. They must be familiar with Ohm's law, which is the relationship between current, voltage, and resistance. An electronic repair technician should understand the structure and operation of electrical components, including resistors, capacitors, diodes, transistors, integrated circuits, and switches. In addition, they need to read and understand **schematic diagrams**, which visually present "outlines" of circuits, showing how electrical components connect. SEE ALSO BOOLE, GEORGE.

Michael J. O'Neal

Electronics repair technicians must be able to use mathematics to troubleshoot a wide range of problems.

schematic diagram a diagram that uses symbols for circuit elements and arranges these elements in a logical pattern rather than a practical physical arrangement

Bibliography

Keller, Peter A. *Electronic Display Measurements: Concepts, Techniques, and Instrumentation.* New York: Wiley, 1997.

Nasar, Syed A. *3,000 Solved Problems in Electrical Circuits.* New York: McGraw-Hill, 1992.

Encryption *See Cryptology.*

End of the World, Predictions of

Keeping track of time has been an integral activity of every civilization, no matter how primitive. There are ample indications that even civilizations in pre-historic times made concerted attempts to measure time. Many civilizations, including the Mayan, and individuals, such as Stifel in sixteenth-century Germany, used measurements of time to predict the end of the world.

Keeping Track of Time

For early civilizations, keeping track of time involved two distinct pursuits: food and religion. The cycles for planting and harvesting could be anticipated and planned for with a calendar. Primitive societies could also plan for bird and animal migrations in advance of their arrival. In both cases, even a primitive calendar could help communities grow crops and hunt game in a better, more organized manner.

Stonehenge a large circle of standing stones on the Salisbury plain in England, thought by some to be an astronomical or calendrical marker

base-10 a number system in which each place represents a power of 10 larger than the place to its right

*The last month in the Mayan calendar was a special month of bad luck and danger.

The religious aspect of keeping time was tied to the worship of the heavens. Ancient peoples viewed the motions of heavenly bodies and related phenomena, such as an eclipse of the moon, as acts of the gods that were important to predict. Archeologists think the standing stones of **Stonehenge** in England were a massive observatory that ancient peoples used to track the rising and setting of the sun on the summer and winter solstice. It also appears that they used Stonehenge to keep track of lunar eclipses. The ability to keep time and predict heavenly phenomena strengthened the hold that the religious class had over its followers.

Today's calendar is derived, in part, from the calendar used by ancient Sumerians and Babylonians. In approximately 3000 to 4000 B.C.E., these Middle Eastern peoples invented a written alphabet and a fairly accurate calendar. The Babylonians used a lunar calendar, which consisted of twelve lunar months of 29 or 30 days each, depending on the motion of the moon. The total number of days in their year was only 354 days. Religious feast days were added to some of the months to bring the total to 360 days.

This total of 360 days fit in well with the Babylonian mathematics of the times. Their number system was based on the number 60, in contrast to the modern-day number system, which is a decimal, or **base-10**, system. The 360-day year also accommodated Babylonian astrology.

In Babylonian astrology, the year was divided into twelve parts, each devoted to a god who was personified by the movement of various constellations in the heavens. The 360-day year was still 5 days shorter than the actual length of a year, so the Babylonians added a festival of 5 days at the end of the year to bring the total to 365 days.

Many cultures that followed the Babylonians adopted their 365-day year. This was still incorrect because a year is now known to be 365.2422 days. As a result, calendars descended from the Babylonian calendar required frequent adjustments, and the calendar for many cultures was constantly being revised to make up for lost or gained days.

The present calendar went through several refinements from its beginning during the Roman Empire. It was not until 1582 that a commission under Pope Gregory IX developed our present-day calendar, with an accuracy that will not need any revision for at least 3,000 years.

Around the year 500 C.E. the Mayas of Central America were using a calendar that is still more accurate than our calendar of today. The Mayan calendar* was used exclusively by the priestly classes and consisted of a ritual cycle of 260 individually named days and a yearly calendar of 365 days. The ritual cycle lasted 20 months, each month containing 13 days (20 × 13 = 260). The yearly calendar, or *tun*, contained 18 months of 20 days each (18 × 20 = 360), with a final month of 5 days added at the end of the year.

The Mayas also adjusted their calendar periodically, according to solar eclipses and observations of Venus. The two Mayan calendar cycles ran at the same time, and a named day would fall on the same day of the year every 18,980 days or every 52 years. This 52-year cycle is called a calendar round.

The calendar round was not used to indicate the specific year during which an event took place. Instead, the event was placed in a "long count."

A long count consists of 20 *tuns* making a *katun*, in turn 20 *katuns* make a *baktun*, and finally 13 *baktuns* make a "Great Cycle" of 1,872,000 days, or about 5,130 years.

According to Mayan tradition, the present creation is the fifth such creation of the gods. The gods were dissatisfied with their first four attempts to create mankind and destroyed each of the first four creations after a period of time called a long count. The fifth creation took place in 3133 B.C.E., and the present long count started at that time. This long count will expire on December 24, 2011. At that time, the gods will declare themselves either pleased with mankind or will destroy the world and begin again, starting the clock for a new long count.

Predicting the End of the World

Since the time of the ancient Babylonians, many individuals and cultures have looked to the heavens and to astrology to predict the future. Many mathematicians earned their living by casting horoscopes, including Jerome Cardano (1501–1576) and Johann Kepler (1571–1630).

During the sixteenth century, several mathematicians applied their knowledge of mathematics to questionable Bible scholarship and dubious Biblical interpretation to predict the exact date for the end of the world. After a careful study of the Bible and mathematics, German mathematician Michael Stifel (1486–1567) predicted a date for the end of the world.

Stifel was an educated man, who graduated with a degree in mathematics from the University of Wittenberg. He was a monk at a Catholic monastery for a time after graduation but eventually joined Protestant leader Martin Luther, even staying at Luther's house in Wittenberg. Soon after joining with Luther, Stifel began to apply his mathematics to the Bible. After some careful study, Stifel determined that a hidden message in the Bible revealed that the world would end on October 3, 1533.

When the fateful day arrived, Stifel gathered his small group of believers from the town of Lochau to the top of a hill to await the end of the world and their deliverance into heaven. As the morning wore on and nothing happened, some of the believers began to get worried. Soon most of the believers were anxiously questioning Stifel. At about midday, Stifel excused himself and hurried to town where he was put into a jail cell for protection against his now angry believers, many of whom sold houses and farms in expectation of the world's end. Eventually Stifel was able to leave town safely. In time, he gained Luther's forgiveness in return for a promise to never again apply mathematics to Biblical matters.

A more famous mathematician from the same time period also predicted a date for the world's end. Scottish mathematician John Napier (1550–1617) was a nobleman who spent nearly all his life in Scotland. Napier was an able mathematician, who was also active in religious controversies of the times. In fact, he devoted more time to his religious studies than to his mathematics. He was a zealous supporter of the Protestant cause.

After 27 years of writing, Napier published *The Plaine Discovery of the Whole Revelation of St. John*. In it, he identified the Pope as the Antichrist. In *Discovery*, he also predicted that the end of the world would happen between 1688 and 1700. In this prediction, Napier had the good fortune to select a

day far beyond his life span. When his prediction failed to come true, he avoided the humiliation that had come to Stifel some 75 years earlier.

More recently, William Miller predicted the world would end on October 22, 1844. Thousands of believers were disappointed when the prophesied end did not come, but many shifted their belief to a future, unspecified time when the end would come.

While most predictions of the world's end today come from religious groups, there are scientists who are making such predictions about the world's end. Their predictions are based on our present knowledge of stars, such as the Sun. Our Sun has a finite life and eventually will burn out. When might such an event occur? The best estimates are that the core of the Sun will collapse in approximately 5 billion years. The resulting increase in temperature of the Sun's core will ultimately end all life on Earth. However, like Napier, the scientists making these estimates will not live to see whether their predictions come true. SEE ALSO CALENDAR, NUMBERS IN THE; TIME, MEASUREMENT OF.

Arthur V. Johnson II

Bibliography

Burton, David. *The History of Mathematics: An Introduction.* New York: Allyn and Bacon, 1985.

Eves, Howard. *In Mathematical Circles.* Boston: Pridle, Webber & Schmidt, Inc., 1969.

James, Peter, and Nick Thorpe. *Ancient Inventions.* New York: Ballantine Books, 1994.

Johnson, Art. *Famous Problems and Their Mathematicians.* Englewood, CO: Teacher's Ideas Press, 1999.

McLeish, John. *The Story of Numbers: How Mathematics Shaped Civilization.* New York: Fawcett Columbine, 1991.

Internet Resources

MacTutor History of Mathematics Archive. University of St Andrews. <http://www-groups.dcs.st-and.ac.uk/~history/Mathematicians.html>.

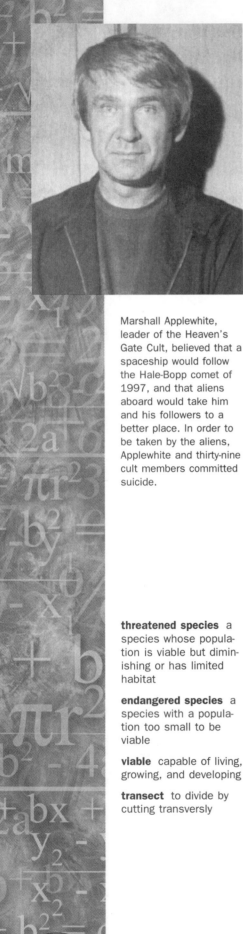

Marshall Applewhite, leader of the Heaven's Gate Cult, believed that a spaceship would follow the Hale-Bopp comet of 1997, and that aliens aboard would take him and his followers to a better place. In order to be taken by the aliens, Applewhite and thirty-nine cult members committed suicide.

threatened species a species whose population is viable but diminishing or has limited habitat

endangered species a species with a population too small to be viable

viable capable of living, growing, and developing

transect to divide by cutting transversly

Endangered Species, Measuring

The U.S. Endangered Species Act (ESA) is one of the most important and controversial legislative acts in recent years. This law requires the use of specific measures to protect certain species of plants or animals that are listed as **threatened species** or **endangered species**. Before a species is listed as threatened or endangered, biologists must determine if a **viable** population of the plant or animal in question exists in the wild. This usually means determining the number of existing individuals, the sex of each, the number within breeding age, the breeding success rate, mortality rates, birth rates, whether sufficient genetic diversity exists, and many other factors. To answer these questions, the number of plants or animals must be counted.

Study Methods Used to Estimate Population Size

Study methods include observation and photography, live trapping, and **transect** sampling. All of the methods result in an estimate of the number of individuals in the population. This number is then compared with what is considered a minimum viable population, which is the smallest number of individuals of a species in a particular area that can survive and maintain genetic diversity.

Observation and Photography. These are the simplest study methods. Observation and photography involve going into an area known to contain individuals from the population in question and simply counting how many can be found. This method works well for species that are not very mobile. For example, there is a species of snail that inhabits a small area on one mountain slope. This area is so small that one person can count the number of individuals present. In other cases, the number of individuals is so small that the entire population can be counted. Whooping cranes exist in such small numbers that the entire population is known from yearly censuses made on both the cranes's wintering grounds and their breeding grounds. Whooping cranes can be counted from observation towers, or they can be photographed from low flying airplanes or helicopters.

Observation can involve senses other than vision. Estimates of bird populations are often made by listening to singing males. The songs are distinctive enough that the species can be identified from their song. Knowledge of their breeding success, the number of offspring per pair, and mortality rates can then be used to determine if the population is viable.

Live Trapping. Sometimes population estimates are made by placing traps in the area being studied. The number of animals captured is then related back to the total number of animals in the area. Live trapping generally does not harm the animals, and it has the advantage of allowing the researcher to gather other information about the species, such as age, sex, and health. Individuals can also be marked so that their movements can be followed. Birds trapped in this way are commonly banded. Bird banding has given biologists and wildlife managers extensive information about bird migration patterns.

Transect Sampling. Transect sampling is a standard statistical technique for determining the population in an area. The researcher or surveyor walks along a straight line (called a transect) through the area of interest and counts every individual that can be seen. Alternatively, the researcher may observe other evidence of the presence of an animal (such as droppings). Under ideal conditions, the number of individuals observed within the transect area has the same proportion to the total number of individuals within the total area.

Suppose a surveyor walks across the area A along the transect L. At some time, the surveyor will be at point Z, and may see an individual at X. The width of the strip that can be seen by the surveyor is 2W, and the distance of the animal or plant from the surveyor is r_i. The angle from the transect line to the observed animal or plant is θ_i. The **perpendicular** distance from the transect line to the observed individual is y_i. Note that $y_i = r_i \sin \theta_i$.

When one thinks of endangered or threatened species, one often thinks first of animals such as pandas or eagles. However, plants—like this species of fringed orchid—may also fall under the protection of the Endangered Species Act.

perpendicular forming a right angle with a line or plane

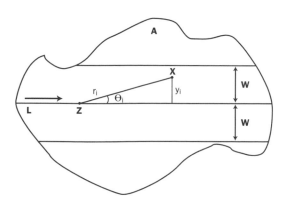

parameter an independent variable, such as time, that can be used to rewrite an expression as two separate functions

probability density function a function used to estimate the likelihood of spotting an organism while walking a transect

Fourier series an infinite series consisting of cosine and sine functions of integral multiples of the variable each multiplied by a constant; if the series is finite, the expression is known as a Fourier polynomial

exponential power series the series by which *e* to the *x* power may be approximated; $e^x = 1 + x + x^{2/2!} + x^{3/3!} + \ldots$

negative exponential an exponential function of the form $y = e^{-x}$

The mathematical model for estimating the size of a population from transect data depends on two assumptions: (1) not all individuals will be detected and (2) the probability of detecting an individual decreases as its perpendicular distance from the transect line increases. These two assumptions are generally expressed as a detection function, $g(y)$, which represents the probability that an individual will be observed at a distance x from the transect line. The function $g(y)$ decreases as y increases. Generally, estimating detection functions requires calculus. However, the result is an *effective* width, a, of the transect area that is different from the actual width. Once a is known, the population density is given by $D = \dfrac{n}{2La}$ where n is the number of individuals observed, and L is the length of the transect. The basic problem in estimating population density is estimating the **parameter *a***. The parameter a can be estimated accurately by choosing an appropriate **probability density function** $f(y) = \dfrac{g(y)}{a}$. Division by a makes the probability density function equal to one, which is what is expected of probability functions. Candidate choices for $f(y)$ include **Fourier series**, **exponential power series**, and **negative exponentials**.

The critical assumption permitting estimation from distance data is that all objects located directly on the line (distance = 0) are certain to be detected, so $g(0) = 1$. If $g(0) = 1$, then $f(0) = \dfrac{1}{a}$. The equation for estimating population density can now be rewritten in terms of $f(0)$: $D = \dfrac{nf(0)}{2L}$. The estimator function $f(0)$ can usually be determined by trial and error or by one of several different mathematical models available. Wildlife managers commonly use computer programs that have the various mathematical models and estimator functions included.

Determining if a Species Has a Minimum Viable Population

Once the size of the population has been estimated, researchers must then decide if the population is healthy and can survive on its own, or if it is too small to be viable and requires protection. There are various methods of estimating viability of a population.

One method often used by biologists to estimate the viability of a population of vertebrates is the 50/500 rule. The minimum number of individuals in a breeding population required to prevent an unacceptable level of inbreeding is 50. The number of breeding individuals required for the long-term genetic variability necessary for a healthy population is 500. This rule is established by assuming that a mature male and a mature female are randomly drawn and randomly paired. However, in many populations, one male may dominate a large group of females, excluding other males from the genetic pool. In this and similar cases, a larger population is needed for viability.

Since not all individuals in a population are active breeders, the census population must be at least twice as large as the breeding population. Many researchers use a census population of 1,000 to 10,000 individuals as the minimum necessary for long-term genetic viability.

Other Factors Affecting Minimum Viable Population. When rules such as the 50/500 method are not applicable or when greater precision is desired, one of several analytic approaches to calculating the Minumum Viable Population may be used. One analytic factor to be considered is the sex ratio. If the percentage of males is 50 percent, then the sex ratio is not skewed. However, in many populations the fraction of males can be larger or smaller than 50 percent. In these groups, larger census populations are necessary.

Another factor affecting the size of the census population is the average number of offspring. If a certain species typically produces many offspring, the census population can increase quite rapidly. Relative birth and death rates can also be used to predict population increase or decrease.

Simulations. None of the preceding approaches has been completely satisfactory in estimating populations and as a result, simulations have been suggested as an alternative. Simulations are computer programs that attempt to model population dynamics. Some are applicable to many different populations, while others have been developed for specific situations, such as a program to estimate the population of the grizzly bears of Yellowstone National Park.

The Endangered Species Act

The ultimate goal of counting specific species may be to determine if they should be listed as threatened or endangered. The first endangered species legislation was enacted in 1966. This act established a list of animals that were threatened with extinction. However, federal agencies were limited in their ability to protect these species. The most significant part of this first act was the establishment of the National Wildlife Refuge System, which was designed to protect the habitats of endangered species.

In 1969 the U.S. Congress passed the Endangered Species Conservation Act. This act included invertebrates as well as vertebrates. It also restricted interstate commerce in illegally taken animals. In 1973 the Endangered Species Act (ESA) was passed. The ESA has been called the most comprehensive legislation for the preservation of endangered species ever enacted by any nation. Since 1973, the ESA has been reauthorized and amended twice.

Under the ESA, two departments have the sole authority to list species: The National Marine Fisheries Service is authorized to list marine mammals and fish, and the U.S. Fish and Wildlife Service lists all other species. This division of responsibility between the U.S. Department of Commerce and the U.S. Department of the Interior has caused some difficulties in the consistent application of rules and criteria for listing species. The act was amended in 1982 to state that listing should be based solely on biological criteria.

The ESA identifies two different population conditions related to the viability of species. "Threatened" species are those whose populations are still viable, but may be declining or have a limited habitat, and therefore be in danger of becoming threatened. "Endangered" species have populations that are too small to be considered viable and thus are in danger of becoming extinct. SEE ALSO STATISTICAL ANALYSIS.

Elliot Richmond

Bibliography

Norton, B. G. *Why Preserve Natural Variety?* Princeton, NJ: Princeton University Press, 1987.

Robinson, M. H. "Global Change, the Future of Biodiversity, and the Future of Zoos." *Biotropica* 24 (1992): 345–352.

Rohlf, D. J. *The Endangered Species Act: A Guide to Its Protections and Implementation.* Stanford, CT: Stanford Environmental Law Society, 1989.

Tarpy, C. "Zoos: Taking Down the Bars." *National Geographic* 184 (July 1993): 237.

U.S. Office of Technology Assessment. *Technologies to Maintain Biological Diversity.* U.S. Government Printing Office, Washington, DC, 1987.

Internet Resources

U.S. Fish and Wildlife Service. "Box Score of Endangered Species." Endangered Species Home Page, 2000. <http://endangered.fws.gov/wildlife.html>.

Escher, M. C.

Dutch Artist
1898–1972

Maurits Cornelis Escher was born in Leeuwarden, Holland, in 1898. He enrolled in the School for Architecture and Decorative Arts in Haarlem because his father, a civil engineer, wanted him to become an architect. Escher, however, left school in 1922 to pursue his interest in art. He married in 1924 and moved to Rome where he lived until 1934. Growing political tension in Europe caused him to move his family first to Switzerland, then to Belgium, and finally back to the Netherlands in 1941. He remained there until his death in 1972.

Mathematics in Art

Escher's art is of particular interest to mathematicians because, although he received no mathematical training beyond his early years, he used a variety of mathematical principles in unique and fascinating ways. Escher's artwork encompasses two broad areas: the geometry of space, and the so-called "logic" of space.

On a visit to the Alhambra in Spain, Escher was inspired by the colorful geometrical patterns of tiles. He began to explore the various ways of filling two-dimensional space with symmetrically repeated arrangements of images known as tessellations. In the process, he discovered the same principles that had been developed previously, unknown to Escher, within the branch of mathematics known as group theory. When mathematicians and scientists became aware of his work, they helped popularize his art, and he soon gained an international reputation.

Subsequent interactions with mathematicians introduced Escher to other mathematical concepts that he explored in his art. Among the results are his so-called impossible constructions that appear reasonable but prove to be impossible to construct in three-dimensional space. He also employed **non-Euclidean geometry**, representations of infinite space, and various aspects of **topology**.

Although Escher completed his final graphic work in 1969, the popularity of his images continues today. Several Internet sites are dedicated to providing information about Escher and selling renditions of his art. SEE

M. C. Escher's lithographs and woodcuts of geometric distortions and mathematical impossibilities made him famous throughout the world.

non-Euclidean geometry a branch of geometry defined by posing an alternate to Euclid's fifth postulate

topology the study of those properties of geometric figures that do not change under such nonlinear transformations as stretching or bending

ALSO DIMENSIONS; EUCLID AND HIS CONTRIBUTIONS; MATHEMATICS, IM-
POSSIBLE; TESSELLATIONS; TOPOLOGY.

J. William Moncrief

Bibliography

Escher, M. C. *The Graphic Work of M. C. Escher.* New York: Meredith Press, 1967.

MacGillavry, Caroline H. *Symmetry Aspects of M. C. Escher's Periodic Drawings.* Utrecht: A. Oosthoek's Uitgeversmaatschappij NV, 1965.

Estimation

Adding, multiplying, and performing similar mathematical operations in one's head can be difficult tasks, even for the most skilled mathematics students. By estimating, however, basic operations are easier to calculate mentally. This can make daily calculation tasks, from figuring tips to monthly budgets, quickly attainable and understandable.

How to Estimate

Although the core of estimation is **rounding**, *place value* (for example, rounding to the nearest hundreds) makes estimating flexible and useful. For instance, calculating $2.4 + 13.7 - 10.8 + 8 - 124.2 - 32$ to equal -142.9 in one's head may be a daunting task. But if the equation is estimated by 10s, that is, if each number is rounded to the nearest 10, the problem becomes $0 + 10 - 10 + 10 - 120 - 30$, and it is easier to calculate its value at -140. Estimating to the 1s makes the equation $2 + 14 - 11 + 8 - 124 - 32 = -143$, which is more accurate but more difficult to calculate mentally. Note that the smaller the place value used, the closer the estimation is to the actual sum.

rounding process of giving an approximate number

Estimation by Tens

Multiplication and division can be estimated with any place value, but estimating by 10s is usually the quickest method. For example, the product $8 \times 1,294 = 10,352$ can be estimated by 10s as $10 \times 1,290 = 12,900$, which is calculated with little effort. Division is similar in that estimating by 10s allows for the quickest calculation, even with decimals. For instance, $1,232.322 \div 12.2 = 101.01$ is quicker to estimate by 10s as $1,230.0 \div 10.0 = 123.0$.

Regardless of the ease of estimating by 10s, there is a greater degree of inaccuracy as compared to estimating by 1s. However, this estimation method need not be abandoned in order to gain accuracy; instead, it can be used to obtain estimations that are more accurate, as the following example illustrates.

Suppose a couple on a date enjoys a dinner that costs $24.32. The customary tip is 15 percent, but the couple does not have a calculator, tip table, or pencil to help figure the amount that should be added to the bill. Using the estimating-by-10s method, they figure that 15 percent of $10 is $1.50; if the bill is around $20, then the tip doubles to $3. However, a $3 tip is not enough because they have not included tip for the $4.32 remaining on the bill. Yet if $1.50 is the tip for $10, then $0.75 would be an appropriate tip for $5, which is near enough to $4.32. A total estimated tip of $3.75 is

close (in fact, an overestimation) to 15 percent of $24.32, which is $3.65 (rounded to the nearest cent).

Conservative Estimation

As seen in several of the examples, estimations tend to be more (an overestimation) or less (an underestimation) than the actual calculation. Whether this is important depends upon the situation. For example, overestimating the distance for a proposed trip may be a good idea, especially in figuring how much gas money will be needed.

This property of rounding and estimation is the foundation of conservative estimation found in financial planning. When constructing a monthly budget, financial planners will purposely underestimate income and overestimate expenses, usually by hundreds. Although an accurate budget seems ideal, this estimating technique creates a "cushion" for unexpected changes, such as a higher water bill or fewer hours worked. Furthermore, financial planners will round down (regardless of rounding rules) for underestimation and round up for overestimation.

The following table represents a sample budget for an individual. The first column includes amounts expected to pay; the second is a conservative estimate of the next month's budget; the third is a list of the actual amounts incurred; and the fourth is the difference between actual and budgeted amounts. Note that negative numbers, or amounts that take away from income, are written in parentheses.

The table shows that the individual earned less than expected and in some cases spent more than expected. Nevertheless, because the budget is conservative, there is a surplus (money left over) at the end of the month.

ESTIMATING A MONTHLY BUDGET			
	Expected Amount	Budget	Actual Amount	Difference
Income	$3,040	$3,000	$2,995	($5)
Tax	(578)	(600)	(579)	21
Rent	(575)	(600)	(575)	25
Utilities	(40)	(100)	(62)	38
Food	(175)	(200)	(254)	(54)
Insurance	(175)	(200)	(175)	25
Medical	(45)	(100)	(97)	3
Car Payments	(245)	(300)	(245)	55
Gas	(85)	(100)	(133)	(33)
Student Loans	(325)	(400)	(325)	75
Savings	(300)	(300)	(300)	0
Fun Money	(49)	(100)	(175)	(75)
Surplus (Deficit)	$28	$0	$75	$75

Estimation by Average

Counting the number of words on a page can be a tedious task. Therefore, writers often estimate the total by averaging the number of words on the first few lines and then multiplying that average by the number of lines on the page.

Another application of estimation by average is the classic game of guessing how many jellybeans are in a jar. The trick is to average the number of beans on the top and bottom layers and then to multiply that average by the number of layers in the jar. Because it is customary to declare a winner who guessed the closest but not over the actual count, it is best to estimate conservatively.

Estimation is a powerful skill that can be applied to tasks from proofing arithmetic to winning a counting game. However, the use of estimation is not always appropriate to the task. For example, estimating distance and direction of space debris and ships is unwise, since even the smallest decimal difference can mean life or death. In addition, technology makes it possible to add and multiply large groups of numbers faster than it may take to estimate the total. Nevertheless, estimation is an important tool in managing the everyday mathematics of life. SEE ALSO FINANCIAL PLANNER; ROUNDING.

Michael Ota

Bibliography

Pappas, Theoni. *The Joy of Mathematics: Discovering Mathematics All Around You.* San Carlos, CA: World Wide Publishing, 1989.

Euclid and His Contributions

Euclid was an ancient Greek mathematician from Alexandria who is best known for his major work, *Elements*. Although little is known about Euclid the man, he taught in a school that he founded in Alexandria, Egypt, around 300 B.C.E.

For his major study, *Elements*, Euclid collected the work of many mathematicians who preceded him. Among these were Hippocrates of Chios, Theudius, Theaetetus, and Eudoxus. Euclid's vital contribution was to gather, compile, organize, and rework the mathematical concepts of his predecessors into a consistent whole, later to become known as Euclidean geometry.

In Euclid's method, **deductions** are made from premises or axioms. This deductive method, as modified by Aristotle, was the sole procedure used for demonstrating scientific certitude ("truth") until the seventeenth century.

At the time of its introduction, *Elements* was the most comprehensive and logically rigorous examination of the basic principles of geometry. It survived the eclipse of classical learning, which occurred with the fall of the Roman Empire, through Arabic translations. *Elements* was reintroduced to Europe in 1120 C.E. when Adelard of Bath translated an Arabic version into Latin. Over time, it became a standard textbook in many societies, including the United States, and remained widely used until the mid-nineteenth century. Much of the information in it still forms a part of many high school geometry curricula.

Axiomatic Systems

To understand Euclid's *Elements*, one must first understand the concept of an **axiomatic system**. Mathematics is often described as being based solely on logic, meaning that statements are accepted as fact only if they can be logically deduced from other statements known to be true.

What does it mean for a statement to be "known to be true?" Such a statement could, of course, be deduced from some other "known" statement. However, there must be some set of statements, called axioms, that are sim-

Euclid, the best-known mathematician of classical antiquity, is considered by many to be the founder of geometry.

deduction conclusion arrived at through reasoning

axiomatic system a system of logic based on certain axioms and definitions that are accepted as true without proof

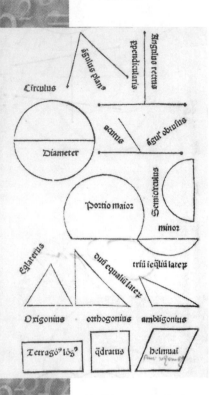

Euclidean geometry is based on Euclid's thirteen-volume *Elements*. An excerpt is shown here from an early Latin translation.

theorem a statement in mathematics that can be demonstrated to be true given that certain assumptions and definitions (called axioms) are accepted as true

ply assumed to be true. Without axioms, no chain of deductions could ever begin. Thus even mathematics begins with certain unproved assumptions.

Ideally, in any axiomatic system, the assumptions are of such a basic and intuitive nature that their truth can be accepted without qualms. Yet axioms must be strong enough, or true enough, that other basic statements can be proved from them.

Definitions are also part of an axiomatic system, as are undefined terms (certain words whose definitions must be assumed in order for other words to be defined based on them). Thus an axiomatic system consists of the following: a collection of undefined terms; a collection of definitions; a collection of axioms (also called postulates); and, finally, a collection of **theorems**. Theorems are statements that are proved by the logical conclusion of a combination of axioms, definitions, and undefined terms.

Euclid's Axioms

In the *Elements*, Euclid attempted to bring together the various geometric facts known in his day (including some that he discovered himself) in order to form an axiomatic system, in which these "facts" could be subjected to rigorous proof. His undefined terms were point, line, straight line, surface, and plane. (To Euclid, the word "line" meant any finite curve, and hence a "straight" line is what we would call a line segment.)

Euclid divided his axioms into two categories, calling the first five postulates and the next five "common notions." The distinction between postulates and common notions is that the postulates are geometric in character, whereas common notions were considered by Euclid to be true in general.

Euclid's axioms follow.

1. It is possible to draw a straight line from any point to any point.

2. It is possible to extend a finite straight line continuously in a straight line. (In modern terminology, this says that a line segment can be extended past either of its endpoints to form an arbitrarily large line segment.)

3. It is possible to create a circle with any center and distance (radius).

4. All right angles are equal to one another. (A right angle is, by Euclid's definition, "half" of a straight angle: that is, if a line segment has one of its endpoints on another line segment and divides the second segment into two angles that are equal to each other, the two equal angles are called right angles.)

5. If a straight line falling on (crossing) two straight lines makes the interior angles on the same side less than two right angles, the two straight lines, if produced indefinitely, meet on that side on which the angles are less than the two right angles.

6. Things which are equal to the same thing are equal to each other.

7. If equals are added to equals, the wholes (sums) are equal.

8. If equals are subtracted from equals, the remainders (differences) are equal.

9. Things that coincide with one another are equal to one another.

10. The whole is greater than the part.

It was Euclid's intent that all the remaining geometric statements in the *Elements* be logical consequences of these ten axioms.

In the two millennia that have followed the first publication of the *Elements*, logical gaps have been found in some of Euclid's arguments, and places have been identified where Euclid uses an assumption that he never explicitly states. However, although quite a few of his arguments have needed improvement, the great majority of his results are sound.

Euclid's Fifth Postulate

The axioms in Euclid's list do seem intuitively obvious, and the *Elements* itself is proof that they can, as a group, be used to prove a wide variety of important geometric facts. They also, with one exception, seem sufficiently basic to warrant axiom status—that is, they need not be proved by even more basic statements or assumptions. The one exception to this is the fifth postulate. It is considerably more complicated to state than any of the others and does not seem quite as basic.

Starting almost immediately after the publication of the *Elements* and continuing into the nineteenth century, mathematicians tried to demonstrate that Euclid's fifth postulate was unnecessary. That is, they attempted to upgrade the fifth postulate to a theorem by deducing it logically from the other nine. Many thought they had succeeded; invariably, however, some later mathematician would discover that in the course of his "proofs" he had unknowingly made some extra assumption, beyond the allowable set of postulates, that was in fact logically equivalent to the fifth postulate.

In the early nineteenth century, after more than 2,000 years of trying to prove Euclid's fifth postulate, mathematicians began to entertain the idea that perhaps it was not provable after all and that Euclid had been correct to make it an axiom. Not long after that, several mathematicians, working independently, realized that if the fifth postulate did not follow from the others, it should be possible to construct a logically consistent geometric system without it.

One of the many statements that were discovered to be equivalent to the fifth postulate (in the course of the many failed attempts to prove it) is "Given a straight line, and a point P not on that line, there exists at most one straight line passing through P that is parallel to the given line." The first "non-Euclidean" geometers took as axioms all the other nine postulates of Euclidean geometry but replaced the fifth postulate with the statement "There exists a straight line, and a point P not on that line, such that there are two straight lines passing through P that are parallel to the given line." That is, they replaced the fifth postulate with its negation and started exploring the geometric system that resulted.

Although this negated fifth postulate seems intuitively absurd, all our objections to it hinge on our pre-conceived notions of the meanings of the undefined terms "point" and "straight line." It has been proved that there is no logical incompatibility between the negated fifth postulate and the

other postulates of Euclidean geometry; thus, non-Euclidean geometry is as logically consistent as Euclidean geometry.

The recognition of this fact—that there could be a mathematical system that seems to contradict our most fundamental intuitions of how geometric objects behave—led to great upheaval not only among mathematicians but also among scientists and philosophers, and led to a thorough and painstaking reconsideration of what was meant by words such as "prove," "know," and above all, "truth." SEE ALSO POSTULATES; THEOREMS AND PROOFS; PROOF.

Naomi Klarreich and J. William Moncrief

Bibliography

Heath, Sir Thomas L. *The Thirteen Books of Euclid's Elements*. 1908. Reprint, New York: Dover Publications, 1956.

Kline, Morris. *Mathematical Thought from Ancient to Modern Times*, vol. 1. New York: Oxford University Press, 1972.

Trudeau, Richard J. *The Non-Euclidean Revolution*. Boston: Birkhäuser, 1987.

Euler, Leonhard

Swiss Geometer and Number Theorist
1707–1783

Leonhard Euler is a name well known in many academic fields: philosophy, **hydrodynamics**, astronomy, optics, and physics. His true fame comes, however, through his prolific work in pure mathematics. He produced more scholarly work in mathematics than have most other mathematicians. His abilities were so great that his contemporaries called him "Analysis Incarnate."

Euler (pronounced "oiler") was born in Switzerland in 1707. He had originally intended to follow the career path of his father, who was a Calvinist clergyman. Euler studied theology and Hebrew at the University of Basel.

Johann Bernoulli, however, tutored Euler in mathematics on the side. Euler's facility in the subject was so great that his father, an amateur mathematician himself, soon favored the decision of his son to pursue mathematics rather than join the clergy.

Euler first taught at the Academy of Sciences in St. Petersburg, Russia, in 1727. He married and eventually became the father of thirteen children. His children provided him with great joy, and children were often playing in the room or sitting on his lap while Euler worked. It was in Russia that he lost sight in one eye after working for three days to solve a mathematics problem that Academy members urgently needed but had predicted would take months to solve.

Euler was a very productive writer, completing five hundred books and papers in his lifetime and having four hundred more published posthumously. The Swiss edition of his complete works is contained in seventy-four volumes. He wrote *Introductio in Analysin Infinitorum* in 1748. This book introduces much of the material that is found in modern algebra and trigonometry textbooks.

Leonhard Euler developed integral calculus, introduced the concept of function, and created much mathematical notation. His devotion to solving difficult equations caused him to suffer from eye trouble.

hydrodynamics the study of the behavior of moving fluids

Euler wrote the first treatment of **differential calculus** in 1755 in *Institutiones Calculi Differentialis* and in 1770 explored determinate and **indeterminate algebra** in *Anleitung zur Algebra*. Three-dimensional surfaces and **conic sections** were also extensively treated in his writings.

Euler introduced many of the important mathematical symbols that are now in standard usage, such as Σ (for summation), π (the ratio of the circumference of a circle to its diameter), $f(x)$ (function notation), e (the base of a natural logarithm), and i (square root of negative one). He was the first to develop the calculus of variations. One of the more notable equations that he developed was $\cos\theta + i\sin\theta = e^{i\theta}$, which shows that exponential and trigonometric functions are related. Another important equation he developed establishes a relationship among five of the most significant numbers, $e^{\pi i} + 1 = 0$.

All of Euler's work was not strictly academic, however. He enjoyed solving practical problems such as the famous "seven bridges of Königsberg" problem that led to Euler circuits and paths. He even performed calculations simply for their own sake.

Euler later went to Berlin to become the director of Mathematics at the Academy of Science under Frederick the Great and to enjoy a more free political climate. However, Euler was viewed as being rather unsophisticated, and Frederick referred to him as a "mathematical Cyclops." He returned to Russia when a more liberal leader, Catherine the Great, came to rule.

By 1766, Euler was completely blind but continued to dictate his work to his secretary and his children. His last words, uttered as he suffered a fatal stroke in 1783, imitated his work in eloquence and simplicity: "I die."
SEE ALSO BERNOULLI FAMILY; NETS.

Laura Snyder

Bibliography

Ball, W. W. Rouse. *A Short Account of the History of Mathematics*, 4th ed. New York: Dover Publications, 1960.

Bell, E. T. *Men of Mathematics*. New York: Simon and Schuster, 1986.

Benson, Donald C. *The Moment of Proof: Mathematical Epiphanies*. New York: Oxford University Press, 1999.

Hollington, Stuart. *Makers of Mathematics*. London: Penguin Books, 1994.

Motz, Lloyd, and Jefferson Hane Weaver. *The Story of Mathematics*. New York: Avon Books, Inc., 1993.

Parkinson, Claire L. *Breakthroughs: A Chronology of Great Achievements in Science and Mathematics*. Boston: G. K. Hall & Co., 1985.

Exponential Growth and Decay

An exponential function is a function that has a **variable** as an **exponent** and the base is positive and not equal to one. For example, $f(x) = 2^x$ is an exponential function. Note that $f(x) = x^2$ is *not* an exponential function (but instead a basic **polynomial** function), because the exponent is a constant and not a variable. Exponential functions have graphs that are continuous curves and approach but never cross a horizontal **asymptote**. Many real-

differential calculus the branch of mathematics primarily dealing with the solution of differential equations to find lengths, areas, and volumes of functions

indeterminate algebra study and analysis of solution strategies for equations that do not have fixed or unique solutions

conic sections the curves generated by an imaginary plane slicing through an imaginary cone (circles, ellipses, parabolas, hyperbolas)

variable a symbol, such as letters, that may assume any one of a set of values known as the domain

exponent the symbol written above and to the right of an expression indicating the power to which the expression is to be raised

polynomial an expression with more than one term

asymptote the line that a curve approaches but never reaches

Graphs of a two exponential functions.

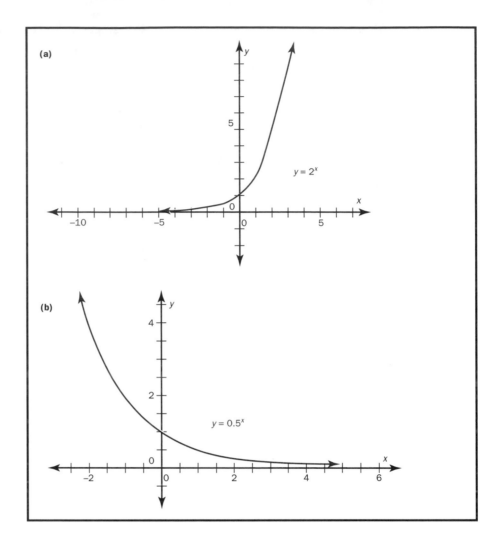

world processes follow exponential functions or their inverses, logarithmic functions.

Exponential Change

Exponential growth is a mathematical change that increases without limit based on an exponential function. The change can be in the positive or negative direction. The important concept is that the rate of change continues to increase. Exponential decay is found in mathematical functions where the rate of change is decreasing and thus must reach a limit, which is the horizontal asymptote of an exponential function. In the figure above, the asymptote is the x-axis where the rate of change approaches zero. Exponential decay may also be either decreasing or increasing; the important concept is that it progresses at a slower and slower rate.

Exponential growth and decay are modeled in many real-world processes. Populations of growing microbes, and indeed a growing population of any life when not constrained by environmental factors such as available space and nutrition, can be modeled as a function showing exponential growth. The growth of a savings account collecting compound interest is another example of an exponential growth function.

Exponential decay is seen in many processes as well. The decrease in radioactive material as it undergoes fission and decays into other atoms fits a curve of exponential decay. The discharge of an electric capacitor through a resistance can be calculated using exponential decay. A warm object as it cools to a constant surrounding temperature, or a cool object as it warms, will exhibit a curve showing exponential decay.

A Sample Problem

The following is an example of how the mathematics of exponential growth and decay can be used to solve problems. Suppose that a radioactive sample, measured after 2 days, had only 60 percent as much of the sample as it had initially. How much of the sample could be expected to remain after 5 days?

To solve this problem, it must be understood that the sample is reducing in size by exponential decay and the rate at which it is reducing must first be determined. Formulas for this exponential decay are as follows:

$$N = N_o e^{kt} \quad \text{and} \quad \ln\left(\frac{N}{N_o}\right) = kt$$

where N_o is the original value, N is the new value, k is decay constant or rate of change, and t is time. Using the second formula we see that N_o is 100 and N is 60, and t (in days) is 2, we get $\ln(\frac{60}{100}) = k2$ which is $-0.5108 = k2$ or $-0.2554 = k$. So the decay rate is -0.2554. Now that we know the decay rate, to find out what happens in 5 days we use the first formula $N = N_o e^{kt}$ where $N = 100e^{5(-0.2554)}$ and so $N = 27.89$. Thus we will have 27.89 percent of the sample after 5 days. SEE ALSO Logarithms; Powers and Exponents.

Harry J. Kuhman

Bibliography

Dykes, Joan, and Ronald Smith. *Finite Mathematics with Calculus.* New York: Harper Perennial, 1993.

Trivieri, Lawrence A. *Precalculus Mathematics, Functions and Graphs.* New York: Harper Perennial, 1993.

Factorial

The pattern of multiplying a positive **integer** by the next lower consecutive integer occurs frequently in mathematics. Look for the pattern in the following expressions.

$7 \times 6 \times 5 \times 4 \times 3 \times 2 \times 1$

$4 \times 3 \times 2 \times 1$

$(n + 5) \times (n + 4) \times (n + 3) \times (n + 2) \times (n + 1) \times n$

The mathematical symbol for this string of factors is the familiar exclamation point (!). This pattern of multiplied whole numbers is called *n* factorial and is written as *n*! So, starting with the greatest factor, *n*, the factorial pattern is as follows:

$$n! = n(n - 1)(n - 2)(n - 3)\ldots(1).$$

So,

3! is $3 \times 2 \times 1 = 6$

5! is $5 \times 4 \times 3 \times 2 \times 1 = 120$

and

$1! = 1$.

Zero factorial (0!) is arbitrarily defined to be 1.

Most scientific calculators have a key (such as *x*!) that can be used to find factorial values. As *n* becomes larger, the value of its factorials increases rapidly. For example, 13! is 6,227,020,800.

How Factorials Are Used

Many mathematical formulas use factorial notation, including the formulas for finding **permutations** and **combinations**. For example, the number of permutations of *n* elements taken *n* at a time is *n*!, and the number of permutations of *n* elements taken *r* at a time is equal to $\frac{n!}{(n - r)!}$.

There is also a problem that involves prime and **composite numbers** which uses a formula containing factorial notation. Mathematicians have, for many years, puzzled over the question of how **prime numbers** were distributed. Notice that, in the **whole numbers** less than 20, there are eight

integer a positive whole number, its negative counterpart, or zero

permutation arrangement of a set of objects

combinations a group of elements from a set in which order is not important

composite number a number that is not prime

prime number a number that has no factors other than itself and 1

whole numbers the positive integers and zero

prime numbers (2, 3, 5, 7, 11, 13, 17, and 19). But from 20 to 40, there are only four prime numbers (23, 29, 31, and 37).

No one has yet found a formula that will generate all the prime numbers. However, the following sequence will give a string of n consecutive composite numbers (numbers that are *not* prime) for any positive integer n.

$$(n + 1)! + 2, (n + 1)! + 3, (n + 1)! + 4, (n + 1)! + 5, (n + 1)! + 6,$$
$$\text{and so on up to } (n + 1)! + (n + 1).$$

When n is 2, notice that this sequence only has two terms:

$$(n + 1)! + 2, (n + 1)! + (n + 1)$$

which is

$$(2 + 1)! + 2, (2 + 1)! + (2 + 1)$$

For the first term, $(2 + 1)! + 2$ is $3! + 2$ or $(3 \times 2 \times 1) + 2$, giving a value of 8. The second term has a value of 9.

When $n = 2$, this sequence gives two consecutive numbers that are *not* prime numbers: 8, 9. When $n = 3$, this sequence gives three consecutive numbers that are *not* prime numbers: 26, 27, 28. This relationship between the value of n and the number of consecutive numbers that are not prime numbers continues in this sequence for any whole number value for n. For a greater n, such as 300, a sequence of 300 composite numbers (that is, a list of 300 consecutive numbers with no prime number in the list) can be found. SEE ALSO Factors; Primes, Puzzles of; Permutations and Combinations.

Lucia McKay

Bibliography

Stephens, Larry. *Algebra for the Utterly Confused.* New York: McGraw-Hill, 2000.

Factors

Factors can be thought of as the multiplying building blocks for integers. A factor is an **integer** that divides another integer without leaving a remainder. In general, an integer x is a factor of the integer y if $\frac{y}{x}$ is also an integer.

integer a positive whole number, its negative counterpart, or zero

Because 8 divides 24 evenly (as 3), with no remainder, 8 is a factor of 24. Eight factors into $2 \times 2 \times 2$. Hence, the integer 24 is made up of the factors 2, 2, 2, and 3 multiplied together.

Every integer is a factor of itself, because it divides itself evenly, with no remainder. Also, 1 is a factor of every number. All integers therefore have factors, because each integer (except 0) has at least two factors—1 and itself.

prime number a number that has no factors other than itself and 1

When an integer has only two factors, then it is a **prime number**. Because the only factors of 5 are 1 and 5, 5 is a prime number. When a number has more than two factors, then it is a composite number. Besides 1 and 15, 15 has two more factors—3 and 5; hence, 15 is a composite number.

All even numbers, 2, 4, 6, 8,. . . have 2 as a factor. By definition, an even number is a multiple of 2 and can be written as $2n$, where n is a positive integer. Odd numbers, 1, 3, 5, 7,. . . are of the form $2n + 1$. Therefore, by definition, 2 cannot be a factor of an odd number.

A factor that is a prime number is called a prime factor. For instance, 3 and 5 are prime factors of 15, and $3 \times 5 = 15$. The "fundamental theorem of arithmetic" states that every integer can be expressed as a unique product of prime factors. In other words, every whole number can be expressed as a product of primes (and 1) unique to it. For example, the prime factors of 20 are 2, 2, and 5, since $2 \times 2 \times 5 = 20$, and no other set of prime factors will yield the number 20.

The Greatest Common Factor

What is the greatest common factor of 16 and 8? This question asks which factors 16 and 8 have in common and which of those factors is the greatest. For instance, 4 is a common factor of both 8 and 16. Eight is also a common factor of 8 and 16. But 8 is the greatest common factor of 8 and 16. As the name suggests, the greatest common factor of two or more numbers is the largest factor shared by them. What is the greatest common factor of 12, 8, and 4? It is 4 because 4 is the largest number that divides all three numbers. SEE ALSO PRIMES, PUZZLES OF.

Rafiq Ladhani

Bibliography

Amdahl, Kenn, and Jim Loats. *Algebra Unplugged.* Broomfield, CO: Clearwater Publishing Co., 1995.

Miller, Charles D., Vern E. Heeren, and E. John Hornsby, Jr. *Mathematical Ideas*, 9th ed. Boston: Addison-Wesley, 2001.

number theory the study of the properties of the natural numbers, including prime numbers, the number theorem, and Fermat's Last Theorem

analytic geometry the study of geometric properties by using algebraic operations

probability theory the branch of mathematics that deals with quantities having random distributions

loci sets of points, lines, or surfaces that satisfy particular requirements

Fermat, Pierre de

French Lawyer and Mathematician
1601–1665

Pierre de Fermat was born in 1601 in Beaumont-de-Lomagne, France, and died in 1665 in Castres, France. He was the founder of modern **number theory**, one of the initiators of **analytic geometry**, and co-founder of **probability theory**. He also invented important mathematical methods that anticipated differential and integral calculus.

Little is known of Fermat's early life. He received his law degree from the University of Orleans and served as councilor to parliament beginning in 1634. His real passion, however, was mathematics. Throughout his life he attacked difficult problems, many times with remarkable success. Unfortunately, he did not publish his results, which were known only through correspondence. Had Fermat published, his contributions would have been more influential during his lifetime.

Fermat applied the methods of algebra to geometry using a coordinate system in his study of **loci**. Descartes's equivalent approach earned him, not Fermat, credit for founding analytic geometry because Fermat's work was not published until after his death.

Blaise Pascal contacted Fermat in 1654, and through the ensuing correspondence in which they tried to mathematically predict the numbers that dice would show in gambling, they co-founded probability theory. In developing a method of finding tangents to curves and determining the area

Pierre de Fermat's disagreements with Descartes over principles of analytic geometry hurt Fermat's reputation as a mathematician, but it was Descartes who admitted in the end that Fermat's methods were correct.

bounded by curves, Fermat laid the groundwork for both differential calculus and integral calculus.

Fermat developed numerous theorems involving **prime numbers** and **integral numbers** and, consequently, is regarded as the founder of modern number theory. The best known of these theorems, Fermat's Last Theorem, was not proved until 1994. SEE ALSO FERMAT'S LAST THEOREM; PROBABILITY, THEORETICAL.

J. William Moncrief

Bibliography

Bell, E. T. *Men of Mathematics.* New York: Simon and Schuster, 1986.

Mahoney, Michael S. *The Mathematical Career of Pierre de Fermat.* Princeton, NJ: Princeton University Press, 1994.

Fermat's Last Theorem

The proof of Fermat's Last Theorem involves two people separated by over 350 years. The first is the French lawyer and mathematician Pierre de Fermat, who, in about 1637, left a note written in the margin of a book. His note said that the equation $a^n + b^n = c^n$ has no solutions when a, b, and c are whole numbers and n is a whole number greater than 2. The note went on to say that he had marvelous proof of this statement, but the book margin was too narrow for him to write out his proof.

In the twentieth century, a 10-year-old British boy named Andrew Wiles read about this problem and was intrigued and challenged by it. No wonder: Fermat's Last Theorem has been called the world's greatest and hardest mathematical problem. Wiles's childhood dream became "to solve it myself . . . such a challenge . . . such a beautiful problem."

Andrew Wiles worked secretly and mostly alone to solve Fermat's Last Theorem. Despite his proof offered in 1994, no one has yet found the proof that Pierre de Fermat claimed to possess because no one has found a proof that used the mathematics and mathematical tools available to Fermat in the seventeenth century.

The Challenge

Before finding out how Wiles proved Fermat' Last Theorem, consider the equation $a^n + b^n = c^n$. Working with the Pythagorean theorem and right triangles reveals that, in every right triangle, $a^2 + b^2 = c^2$. There are also certain whole number values for a, b, and c that are called Pythagorean triples, such as 3, 4, and 5; 5, 12, and 13; 27, 36, and 45; or 9, 40, and 41. Many such triples can be found, and there are formulas that can be used to grind them out endlessly.

Notice, however, that the exponent (n) for these Pythagorean triples is 2. Fermat's Last Theorem says that such triples cannot be found for any whole number greater than 2. By the 1980s, mathematicians using computers had proven that Fermat's Last Theorem was correct for all the whole number values of n less than 600, but that is not the same as a general proof that the statement must always be true. Fermat's statement—that the equation $a^n + b^n = c^n$ has no solutions when a, b, and c are whole numbers and n is a whole number greater than 2—may be fairly simple to state, but it has not been so simple to prove.

The Solution

After 7 years of working on the problem in complete secrecy, Andrew Wiles used modern mathematics and modern methods to prove Fermat's Last Theorem. The modern mathematics and methods he used did not, in general, entail making long and elaborate calculations with the aid of computers. Instead, Wiles, while a researcher at Princeton, used modern **number theory** and thousands of hours of writing by hand on a chalkboard as he thought, tried, and failed, and thought some more about how to prove Fermat's Last Theorem.

As Wiles worked on finding a proof, he looked for patterns; he tried to fit in his ideas with previous broad conceptual ideas of mathematics; he modified existing work; he looked for new strategies. He used the work of many mathematicians, reading their papers to see if they contained ideas or methods he could use. It took him 3 years to accomplish the first step. In spring of 1993, he felt that he was nearly there, and in May of 1993, he believed he had solved the problem.

Wiles asked a friend to review his work, and, in September of 1993, a fundamental error was found in his proof. He worked until the end of November 1993 trying to correct this error, but finally he announced that there was a problem with part of the argument in the proof. Wiles worked almost another whole year trying to correct this flaw. After months of failure while working alone, he was close to admitting defeat. He finally asked for help from a former student, and together they worked for 6 months to review all the steps in the proof without finding a way to correct the flaw.

In September of 1994, a year after the error was originally found, Wiles went back one more time to look at what was not working. On Monday morning, September 19, 1994, Andrew Wiles saw how to correct the error and complete his proof of Fermat's Last Theorem. He called the insight that completed this proof "indescribably beautiful—so simple and elegant."

The solution of Fermat's Last Theorem involves the very advanced mathematical concepts of elliptic curves and modular forms. Wiles's subsequent paper on the proof, "Modular Elliptic Curves and Fermat's Last Theorem," was published in 1995 in the *Annals of Mathematics*. SEE ALSO FERMAT, PIERRE DE.

Lucia McKay

Bibliography

Eves, Howard. *An Introduction to the History of Mathematics.* New York: Holt, Rinehart, and Winston, 1964.

vos Savant, Marilyn. *The World's Most Famous Math Problem.* New York: St. Martin's Press, 1993.

Internet Resources

"What Is the Current Status of FLT?" <http://www.cs.unb.ca/~alopez-o/math-faq/node24.html>.

WHY IS IT CALLED THE "LAST" THEOREM?

Fermat's Last Theorem was not called so because it was his last work. (He apparently wrote the marginal note about this theorem in 1637, and he died in 1665.) Rather, this statement came to be called Fermat's Last Theorem because it was the last remaining statement from Fermat's mathematical work that had not yet been proved.

number theory the study of the properties of the natural numbers, including prime numbers, the number theorem, and Fermat's Last Theorem

---

Fibonacci, Leonardo Pisano

Italian Number Theorist
1175–1240

Leonardo Pisano Fibonacci (c. 1175–c. 1240) is considered by many to be the greatest number theorist of the Middle Ages. The following sequence

Leonardo Pisano Fibonacci is credited with introducing the Hindu-Arabic numbering system to Western Europe, but his fame is more often associated with the development of the Fibonacci sequence of numbers.

✱**Today, the Fibonacci Association publishes a journal, *The Fibonacci Quarterly,* whose primary focus is to promote interest in Fibonacci and related numbers.**

Pythagorean triple any set of three numbers obeying the Pythogorean relation such that the square of one is equal to the sum of the squares of the other two

square a quadrilateral with four equal sides and four right angles

1, 1, 2, 3, 5, 8, 13, 21, 34, 55, 89, 144,

233, 377, 610, 987, 1597, 2584, 4181, . . .

defined by $F_1 = 1$, $F_2 = 1$, and for $n \geq 3$, $F_n = F_{n-1} + F_{n-2}$ is called the Fibonacci sequence in his honor. The Fibonacci sequence evolved from the following problem in Fibonacci's book *Liber abbaci.*

> A certain man put a pair of rabbits in a place surrounded by a wall. How many pairs of rabbits can be produced from that pair in a year if it is supposed that every month each pair begets a new pair which from the second month on becomes productive?

The answer is $F_{12} = 377$.

It is worth noting that Fibonacci did not name the Fibonacci sequence; the sequence was given the name by the nineteenth-century French mathematician, Edouard Lucas. Lucas also found many important applications of the Fibonacci sequence.✱

Fibonacci made many other contributions to mathematics. He is credited with introducing the Hindu-Arabic numerals to Europe. This is the positional number system based on the ten digits 0, 1, 2, 3, 4, 5, 6, 7, 8, 9 and a decimal point.

In *Liber quadratorum* ("The Book of Squares"), Fibonacci described a method to construct **Pythagorean triples**. If he wanted to find two **squares** whose sum was a square, he took any odd square as one of the two squares. He then found the other square by adding all the odd numbers from 1 up to but not including the odd square. For example, if he took 9 as one of the two squares, the other square is obtained by adding all the odd numbers up to 9—that is, 1, 3, 5, and 7, whose sum is 16, a square. And $9 + 16 = 25$, another square. Also, in this book Fibonacci proved that there are no positive integers m and n, such that $m^2 + n^2$ and $m^2 - n^2$ are both squares.

Curtis Cooper

Bibliography

Horadam, A. F. "Eight Hundred Years Young," *The Australian Mathematics Teacher* 31 (175) 123–134.

Internet Resources

Biography of Leonardo Pisano Fibonacci. <http://www-groups.dcs.st-and.ac.uk/~history/Mathematicians/Fibonacci.html>.

The Fibonacci Association. <http://www.mscs.dal.ca/Fibonacci/>.

The Fibonacci Quarterly. <http://www.sdstate.edu/~wcsc/http/fibhome.html>.

Field Properties

David Hilbert, a famous German mathematician (1862–1943), called mathematics the rules of a game played with meaningless marks on paper. In defining the rules of the game called mathematics, mathematicians have organized numbers into various sets, or structures, in which all the numbers satisfy a particular group of rules. Mathematicians call any set of numbers that satisfies the following properties a *field*: closure, commutativity, associativity, distributivity, identity elements, and inverses.

Determining a Field

Consider the set of non-negative even numbers: {0, 2, 4, 6, 8, 10, 12,. . .}. To determine whether this set is a field, test to see if it satisfies each of the six field properties.

Closure. When any two numbers from this set are added, is the result always a number from this set? Yes, adding two non-negative even numbers will always result in a non-negative even number. The set of non-negative even numbers is therefore *closed under addition.*

Is the set of even non-negative numbers also closed under multiplication? Yes, multiplying two non-negative even numbers will also always result in a non-negative even number. The *closure property* applies to the set of non-negative even numbers under the two operations of addition and multiplication.

Commutativity. Notice also that, with any two numbers from this set (a, b), $a + b = b + a$ and $ab = ba$. Therefore, the *commutative property for addition and for multiplication* applies also.

Associativity. It is also true that $(a + b) + c = a + (b + c)$ and $(ab)c = a(bc)$. The *associative property for addition and for multiplication* thus applies for the set of non-negative even numbers.

Distributivity. If the *distributive property* applies to the set of non-negative even numbers, $a(b + c) = ab + ac$. Since this is true for any non-negative even numbers, the set does satisfy this property.

Identity Elements. Within this set of non-negative even numbers, is there an identity element for addition? That is, is there a number n such that adding that number leaves a non-negative even number unchanged in value? Does the set contain an n such that $a + n = a$? Yes, n can be 0, so 0 is the identity element for addition in this set.

Is there a corresponding identity element for multiplication in this set? No. Here the set of non-negative even numbers fails the test. There is no number p in this set such that $ap = a$. The number p could be 1 because 1 is an identity element for multiplication, but 1 is not in the set of non-negative even numbers.

Because the *identity property* is not satisfied by the set of non-negative even numbers, the set does *not* form a field.

Inverses. The set of non-negative even numbers also does not satisfy the sixth property for a field. This set does not contain additive and multiplicative inverses for each number in the set. An additive inverse for 2 might be -2, since $2 + (-2) = 0$, but -2 is not in this set. A multiplicative inverse for 2 might be $\frac{1}{2}$, since $2 \left(\frac{1}{2}\right) = 1$, but $\frac{1}{2}$ is also not in this set.

Numbers Sets that Are Fields

Are there sets of numbers that are fields—that is, that satisfy all six of the field properties—closure, commutativity, associativity, distributivity, identity elements, and inverses? If the set of non-negative even integers is expanded to include the negative integers (to supply the additive inverses), all the integers (so that 1 is the multiplicative identity), and all the rational numbers (such as $\frac{1}{2}$, to supply all the multiplicative inverses, or reciprocals), then the result is the set of all **rational numbers**.

rational numbers numbers that can be written as the ratio of two integers in the form a/b where a and b are integers and b is not zero

The set of rational numbers is a field because it satisfies all six properties. This set is closed because adding or multiplying any two rational numbers results in a rational number. It is commutative, associative, and distributive. It contains an additive identity, 0, and a multiplicative identity, 1. Every number in the set (except 0) has an additive inverse and a multiplicative inverse in the set.

Notice that the rules for a field do not require that 0 have a reciprocal; division by 0 is undefined.

Another set of numbers that form a field, because they satisfy all six of the field properties, is the set of all numbers on the real number line. This set of all real numbers is formed by joining the rational numbers to all the irrational numbers. Recall that an irrational number cannot be expressed as the ratio of two integers.

A third set of numbers that forms a field is the set of complex numbers. Complex numbers are all the numbers that can be written in the form $a + bi$ where a and b are real numbers, and i is the square root of -1.

There are other sets of numbers that form a field. For example, consider this set of numbers: {0, 1, 2, 3}. The operation of addition is defined in the following way. Add the two numbers in the set and, if the result is 4 or more, subtract the number 4 until a number, called the sum, remains that is in the set. This method of arithmetic is called modular arithmetic (in this case, mod 4).

Thus, $2 + 3$, for example, yields 1 (since $5 - 4 = 1$); and $1 + 3$ yields 0 (since $4 - 4 = 0$). When addition is defined in this way (in this case, as mod 4), then this set is closed under addition. The identity element for addition is 4 because, for example, $2 + 4$ yields 2, so that adding 4 leaves a number from this set unchanged.

Notice that each number in the set (other than 0) does have a multiplicative inverse, since, using mod 4 arithmetic, $1 \times 1 = 1$, and $2 \times 3 = 2$, and $3 \times 1 = 3$. The set is also closed under multiplication, using mod 4 arithmetic. It also shows associativity, commutativity, and distributivity under these definitions of addition and multiplication. There are many other finite sets that are finite fields when this kind of modular arithmetic is used. SEE ALSO INTEGERS; NUMBERS, REAL.

Lucia McKay

Bibliography

Hogben, Lancelot. *Mathematics in the Making.* London: Rathbone Books Limited, 1960.

National Council of Teachers of Mathematics. *Historical Topics for the Mathematics Classroom.* Reston, VA: NCTM, 1989.

Financial Planner

Financial planners help individuals and businesses invest money. They provide financial advice based on their knowledge of tax and investment strategies, stocks and bonds, insurance, retirement plans, and real estate.

Financial planners interview their clients to help them define their financial needs and goals and to determine how much money clients have available for investment. Whether the goal is long-term investing (for example, retirement) or short-term investing, financial planners use information provided by a client to develop a financial plan tailored to the client's needs. Additionally, a financial planner often sells stocks, bonds, mutual funds, and insurance.

Financial planners can work for credit unions, credit counseling companies, banks, and companies that specialize in offering financial advice. The vast majority of financial planners have bachelor's or master's degrees. A college degree in business administration or finance is useful.

Financial planners often use mathematics on the job. They calculate which proportion of a client's money may go into a particular investment. For example, does the client want half of his money to be invested in stocks and half in real estate?

Financial planners review stocks and bonds to determine which have the best profits. For example, a stock that is bought for $10 a share and becomes worth $15 a share shows a 50 percent return on the investment. They must calculate how much a purchase of multiple shares of a stock will cost. Four shares at $20 per share will cost $80.

For long-term investments, a financial planner may need to calculate compound interest. He or she must project and add all the investments over time to assess if enough money will be available for the client's retirement. SEE ALSO ECONOMIC INDICATORS; STOCK MARKET.

Denise Prendergast

Financial planners often discuss investment strategies with clients over the telephone. Their pay, or commission, is often a percentage of the dollar amount of the financial product sold.

Bibliography

Career Information Center, 8th ed. New York: Macmillan Reference USA, 2002.

Internet Resources

Occupational Outlook Handbook, 2000–2001 Edition. <http://stats.bls.gov/ocohome .htm>.

Flight, Measurements of

Piloting an aircraft requires constant scanning and verifying of measurements. Pilots develop a sense of reasonable measurements for routine situations. For non-routine situations, pilots practice in simulators so they can quickly make sense of the measurements they see on the aircraft's instrument panel. When necessary, they can make rapid decisions to correct for unanticipated conditions. The U.S. customary system of measurement is used, because that is the system used by most pilots in the United States and worldwide.

Level Flight

On an aircraft, a propeller or jet engine provides thrust, which moves the plane forward through the air. Thrust acts parallel to the direction of flight. The weight of the aircraft is the force of gravity acting toward the center of Earth. The aerodynamic forces of lift and drag result from air pressure. Lift, the vertical component, acts to oppose gravity. Drag acts opposite to the flight path of the aircraft.

MATHEMATICS AND FLYING

High school students who plan to attend a college with a strong flight program should complete 4 years of high school mathematics, including trigonometry and pre-calculus. Some students will have taken calculus in high school, but students may take calculus in their first year of college. Good grades in trigonometry and pre-calculus, in which vectors are studied, meet the prerequisites for enrolling in aerodynamics and simultaneously beginning flight training. Soon after beginning, first-year college students in aviation programs become accustomed to the many measurements critical to flying and to using mathematics to make sense of the measurements.

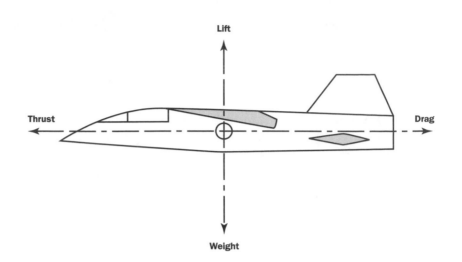

An aircraft in level flight must be in a condition of equilibrium, meaning the forces (vector quantities) acting upon the aircraft (thrust, drag, weight, and lift) are in balance. To be in balance, lift must equal weight and engine thrust (power) must equal drag.

During flight, pilots continuously scan the cockpit instrument panel. They pay particular attention to the instruments that display measurements of altitude, speed, attitude, and direction.

Altitude

Pilots are concerned with three types of altitude: true-altitude, pressure-altitude, and absolute-altitude. They read true-altitude (height above mean sea level) and pressure-altitude (height above a standard reference plane) from a pressure-altimeter, which is an instrument dependent upon air pressure. A pilot uses a radar-altimeter to read absolute altitude, which is the height above the terrain directly below the aircraft.

Prior to takeoff, pilots set local barometric pressure into the pressure-altimeter to monitor true-altitude during takeoff and climb. For flight below 18,000 feet, pilots continue to monitor true-altitude. Every 100 miles, they obtain local pressure from air controllers on the ground and update their altimeter. For flight above 18,000 feet pilots reset their altimeter to the standard pressure of 29.92 inches of mercury and monitor pressure-altitude. Consistent use of standard air-pressure at high altitudes by all aircraft permits maintenance of necessary vertical separation.

Altimeter readings do not provide pilots with information about how high they are above terrain features. Instead, pilots monitor their position using a variety of electronic aids, including the global positioning system (GPS). Below 5,000 feet they can monitor their ground height using a radar altimeter. For example, if the altimeter reads 3,000 feet and the aircraft is over a 2,000-foot plateau, the pilot can "ping" Earth with a radar signal. The radar altimeter translates the return signal to an altitude above ground level of 1,000 feet.

Airspeed

knot nautical mile per hour

The airspeed indicator converts airflow to an airspeed reading in **knots**. The airspeed indicator receives information about airflow from a device that is mounted on the outside of the aircraft. Pilots or computers correct for the air density at altitude to determine true airspeed. As altitude increases, air density decreases. At 18,000 feet the air density is about one-half of sea-level density and creates considerably less impact on the aircraft.

To determine true airspeed, pilots must make corrections for the airspeed indicator reading. If an airspeed indicator reads 100 knots in an aircraft that is traveling at an altitude of 5,000 feet with outside air temperature of 10 degrees Celsius, a pilot can consult a conversion chart that shows the indicated airspeed should be multiplied by 1.09 to obtain true airspeed. In this example, the computed true airspeed would be 109 knots using the conversion chart, or 110 knots using a rule of thumb. For quick mental estimations, pilots use a rule of thumb in which they add 2 percent of indicated airspeed for each 1,000 feet of altitude to get true airspeed. Pilots can compute groundspeed, critical for determining flight time and fuel needs, by adding **tailwind** or subtracting **headwind** from true airspeed.

Attitude

Attitude refers to the position of an aircraft with reference to the horizon. Attitude measurements of pitch, roll, and yaw are measured on a right hand, three-dimensional axis system, with the origin representing the center of gravity for the aircraft. Attitude is measured in degrees from level flight.

tailwind a wind blowing in the same direction as that of the course of a vehicle

headwind a wind blowing in the opposite direction as that of the course of a vehicle

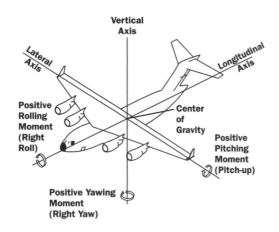

An attitude indicator on the control panel provides pitch and roll information by displaying a symbol that represents aircraft wings on a "moveable horizon." The moveable horizon is an equator-like horizontal line drawn on the sphere in the horizon indicator. The sphere is attached to a spinning **gyroscope**, which remains in a vertical position relative to Earth. The hemispherical region above the horizon line represents the sky, and below represents the ground. A symbol of an aircraft is drawn on the clear circular case over the sphere. When the aircraft changes attitude, the aircraft symbol changes position relative to the horizon on the sphere. Pilots can determine the amount of pitch or roll by comparing the position of the wing of the aircraft symbol with the horizon line.

Pitch is rotation about the y-axis or lateral axis. A nose-up aircraft position results in positive degrees of pitch. To determine the pitch of the aircraft, pilots consult the position of the aircraft symbol with respect to the

gyroscope a device typically consisting of a spinning wheel or disk, whose spin-axis turns between two low-friction supports; it maintains its angular orientation with respect to inertial conditions when not subjected to external forces

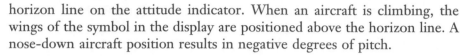

horizon line on the attitude indicator. When an aircraft is climbing, the wings of the symbol in the display are positioned above the horizon line. A nose-down aircraft position results in negative degrees of pitch.

Roll is rotation about the positive *x*-axis or longitudinal axis. If a pilot causes the left wing to roll downward 30 degrees about the longitudinal axis, the aircraft is said to be in a 30 degree left bank.

Direction

Yaw is the term for rotation about the vertical or *z*-axis. An aircraft is said to yaw when it changes direction. Pilots fly a magnetic heading that they read from the heading indicator. This tool consists of a flat circular card that is mounted underneath a clear cover with an aircraft drawn on it. The circular card is marked with 360 degrees similar to a circular protractor, with 0 degrees representing north.

The heading indicator illustrated above shows the aircraft's heading in degrees from magnetic North. Here the aircraft is headed due North. Note that each number must be multiplied by 10 to yield the actual degree reading.

As an aircraft (and the aircraft symbol) turns and rotates, a gyroscope attached to the circular card keeps the card stabilized and fixed in space. The nose of the aircraft symbol continually points in the direction the aircraft is heading.

A gyroscope does not "know" the direction of magnetic north: therefore, pilots initially read a magnetic heading from a magnetic compass and set the heading indicator. Gyroscopic drift causes heading indicators to become inaccurate during flight. Therefore, heading indicators must be periodically corrected with information from a magnetic compass.

Take-off

During take-off, engine thrust accelerates the aircraft to the critical velocity necessary for lift to overcome drag, rolling friction, and the weight of the plane. Pilots continually monitor airspeed during take-off, aware that once the aircraft exceeds what is termed "refusal speed" there is no longer enough runway to stop the aircraft and the pilot is committed to take-off.

Gross weight of an aircraft is a critical factor in take-off. Runway distance required for take-off varies with the square of the gross weight of the aircraft. For example, consider a Boeing 707 taking off at sea level at standard temperature and barometric pressure. If the aircraft weighs 172,500 pounds without cargo or passengers, it requires a take-off speed of 112 knots and 1,944 feet of runway distance to take-off. If the aircraft were loaded with 100,000 pounds of cargo and passengers, the aircraft would then weigh 272,500 pounds, require a 156 knot take-off speed, and 5,500 feet of runway to take-off. The 58 percent increase in weight required a 39 percent increase in take-off speed and a 183 percent increase in take-off distance.

At take-off, the pilot guides the aircraft to the intended altitude. To maintain a steady **velocity** climb, forces must be in equilibrium. During the climb, the weight vector (W) is resolved into a vector perpendicular to the flight path (Wcosγ) and a vector parallel to the flight path (Wsinγ), where γ is the climb angle, and cos and sin are two trigonometric functions.

velocity distance traveled per unit of time in a specific direction

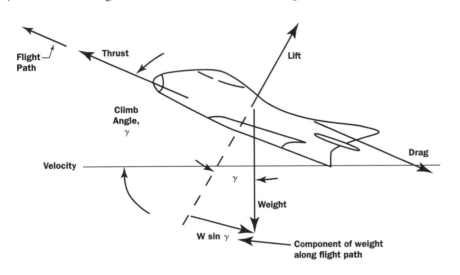

To balance the forces along the flight path, the thrust force must equal the drag force plus Wsinγ. A reasonable climb angle for a Boeing 707 aircraft is 6 degrees. A take-off weight of 172,500 pounds and a 6-degree angle of climb requires approximately 78,100 pounds of jet engine thrust. The four engines on a Boeing 707 each can supply 22,000 pounds of thrust. The take-off angle is the result of optimizing the pounds of fuel needed for climb and the time and ground distance traveled before the aircraft reaches its desired flight altitude. During take-off the pilot monitors the vertical velocity indicator to assure that the aircraft maintains the climb angle. Ascending at 4,325 feet per minute results in an approximate climb angle of 6 degrees.

Landing

When pilots travel, Federal Aviation Agency (FAA) air traffic controllers monitor their flight. Pilots fly between points on airways, which can be thought of as highways in the sky. When an aircraft comes within a specified radius of the airport at which the pilot plans to land, FAA controllers pass the aircraft to an approach controller. Approach controllers "vector the aircraft" for approach and landing. This means they give pilots an airspeed and direction to fly toward the glide slope. The glide slope is an angle, with direction, on which the aircraft descends for its landing. It is generally about 3 degrees.

In a ground directed approach, approach controllers direct pilots with heading corrections and rates of descent in feet per minute so the aircraft will stay on the glide slope. In an instrument landing approach, pilots monitor direction, attitude, and vertical-velocity indicators to maintain the aircraft on the glide slope until touch down. SEE ALSO ANGLES, MEASUREMENT OF; GLOBAL POSITIONING SYSTEM; MAGNETIC AND GEOGRAPHIC POLES; NAVIGATION; VECTORS.

A. Darien Lauten and Edward L'Hommedieu

Bibliography

Dole, Charles E. *Flight Theory for Pilots*, 4th ed. Jeppesen Sanderson Training Products, 1994.

Hurt, H. H., Jr. *Aerodynamics for Naval Aviators*. Issued by the Office of the Chief of Naval Operations Aviation Training Division, U.S. Navy, 1960, NAVWEPS 00-80T-80. Revised January, 1965.

Machado, Rod. *Rod Machado's Private Pilot Handbook*. The Aviation Speakers Bureau, 1996.

Form and Value

Two mathematical expressions may take different form and yet have the same value. For example, $\sqrt{4}$ and 2 look different but are the same number. Likewise, the number 1 can be expressed as 3^0 or $\frac{5}{5}$.

In the decimal system, for example, the fraction $\frac{1}{2}$ is also expressed as 0.5. The word "fraction" refers to the form of a number. The form of $\frac{8}{2}$ is a fraction, but its value is 4, which is an integer. Similarly, $2\frac{1}{2}$ has the form of a mixed fraction, but it can be expressed as the fraction $\frac{5}{2}$, or the decimal number 2.5.

monomial an expression with one term

binomial an expression with two terms

Algebraic expressions also have form and value. The value of $3(x + 2)$ and $3x + 6$ is the same, but $3(x + 2)$ is in the **monomial** form, and $3x + 6$ is in the **binomial** form. Numbers can be also written using both monomial and binomial form.

In monomial form, even numbers are expressed as $2x$ for $x = 1, 2, 3, \ldots$ generating all even numbers $2, 4, 6, \ldots$. In binomial form, even numbers are expressed as $2x + 2$ for $x = 0, 1, 2, \ldots$, which again generates all the even numbers $2, 4, 6, \ldots$.

Rafiq Ladhani

Bibliography

Amdahl, Kenn, and Jim Loats. *Algebra Unplugged*. Broomfield, CO: Clearwater Publishing Co., 1995.

Miller, Charles D., Vern E. Heeren, and E. John Hornsby, Jr. *Mathematical Ideas*, 9th ed. Boston: Addison-Wesley, 2001.

Fractals

The term "fractal" was coined by Benoit Mandelbrot to describe a "self-similar" geometrical object that looks much the same on many different scales of measurement. This property contrasts with the property of a circle, for example, which loses its structure when viewed on a different scale and becomes almost a straight line when any arc is greatly magnified.

Fractals are representations of objects with an **infinite** amount of detail. When magnified, fractals do not become simpler, but instead remain as complex as they were without magnification. This is why fractals seem to describe natural objects in a better way than simple geometric figures like triangles, rectangles, or circles.

A coastline is a classical example of self-similarity in nature. From the air, a sea coast looks irregular by virtue of its bays and headlands. A closer look will reveal the same structure yet on a different scale. Each bay has its own bays and headlands. An even closer look will show even more bays and promontories within the larger bays. Even a beach will have small bays, capes, and peninsulas. On a much smaller scale in nature, a microscope will reveal a self-similar structure even within a grain of sand, which will have indentations and extrusions.

Constructing Geometric Fractals

Any mathematically created fractal can be made by the iteration, or repetition, of a certain rule. There are three basic types of iteration:

- generator iteration, which is repeatedly substituting certain geometric shapes with other shapes;

- IFS (Iterated Function System) iteration, which is repeatedly applying geometric **transformations** (such as rotation and reflection) to points; and

- formula iteration, which is repeating a certain mathematical formula or several formulas.

The property of self-similarity holds true for the majority of mathematically created fractals.

The figure below illustrates the geometric construction of the Koch Curve, named after Helge von Koch, a Swedish mathematician who introduced this curve in a 1904 paper. First, begin with a straight line, as shown in (a). This initial object can be called the initiator. Partition this into three equal parts, then replace the middle third by an **equilateral** triangle and take away its base, as shown in (b). These steps are repeated with each resulting segment, as shown in (c). The repetition of steps is known as iteration. The curve shown in (d) is the result after three iterations, and the curve in (e) is after four iterations. The actual Koch Curve cannot be shown because it is theoretical, resulting from an infinite number of iterations.

infinite a quantity beyond measure; an unbounded quantity

transformation changing one mathematical expression into another by translation, mapping, or rotation according to some mathematical rule

equilateral having the property that all sides are equal; a square is an equilateral rectangle

(a)

(b)

(c)

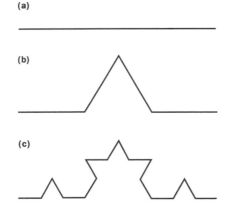

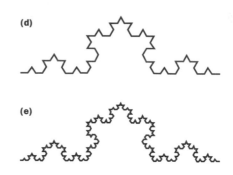

(d)

(e)

Other geometric fractals can be created using the same method. Using a triangle as the initiator, the Sierpinski Gasket✳ is constructed as shown below. With each iteration, the figure becomes more complex as scaled copies build upon identical scaled copies, as shown by the small triangles on the left. The large image on the far right shows the results after six iterations.

✳**The Sierpinski Gasket is named after Polish mathematician Waclaw Sierpinski (1882–1969).**

Characteristics of Fractals

finite having definite and definable limits; countable

When showing images of fractal figures, approximations given by a **finite** number of steps are displayed because these approximations—as in the case of the Koch Curve—will yield a curve with finite length. The actual fractal curve will have infinite length.

Because actual fractal figures like the Koch Curve have infinite length, they have interesting properties uncommon in simpler geometric figures. For example, a fractal closed curve such as the Koch Snowflake can enclose a figure with infinite **perimeter** and finite area. Although not shown here, the Koch Snowflake is constructed from an equilateral triangle, using a Koch Curve to initiate each of its sides. The snowflake has an infinite perimeter because the geometric pattern in (d) of the previous unnumbered figure comprises the snowflake's outer border and can be repeated an infinite number of times at increasingly smaller scales.

perimeter the distance around an area

Fractal Dimensions. Because of their complexity, fractal objects cannot be assigned a dimension as can a line or a square. For example, the Koch Curve cannot have dimension 1, as a line, nor can it have dimension 2, as a square. So there must be other ways of calculating its fractal dimension.

The calculation of fractal dimensions is related to (1) the number of pieces into which a structure can be divided and (2) the reduction factor. The Koch Curve, in general, has 4^k pieces with a reduction factor of $\frac{1}{3^k}$. So when it has four pieces, the reduction factor is $\frac{1}{3}$, and when it has sixteen pieces the reduction factor is $\frac{1}{9}$. Similarly, the Sierpinski Gasket, in general, has 3^k pieces with a reduction factor $\frac{1}{2^k}$. So with three pieces the reduction factor is $\frac{1}{2}$, and with nine pieces the reduction factor is $\frac{1}{4}$.

This idea was used in 1919 by the German mathematician Felix Hausdorff to define a fractal dimension that agrees with the usual dimension on the usual spaces. Although it is too complicated to be presented here, it is interesting to know that the dimension of the Koch Curve is approximately 1.2619 (or $\frac{\log 4}{\log 3}$) and the Sierpinski Gasket has a dimension close to 1.585 (or $\frac{\log 3}{\log 2}$).

For shapes that are not as regular as the Koch Curve or the Sierpinski Gasket, such as clouds or coastlines, this method of determining the fractal dimension does not work. Fractals that are not composed of a certain number of identical versions of itself require other methods for determining the fractal dimension.

Julia and Mandelbrot Sets

Complex numbers are numbers of the form $a + bi$, where $i = \sqrt{-1}$. By representing the complex number $a + bi$ with the point (a, b) in the **Cartesian plane**, a graphical representation of the complex numbers known as the **complex plane** is obtained. Complex numbers can be added, multiplied, and divided, just as **real numbers**. However, it is important to bear in mind that $i^2 = -1$. So functions can be defined using complex numbers as input, and the output of these functions will be, in general, complex numbers.

Gaston Julia (1893–1978) investigated what happens when functions in the complex plane are iterated. Consider, for example, the function $f(z) = z^2 + c$, where c is a complex number. For real numbers, it is not difficult to evaluate this function. If $c = 1 + i$, and one wants to evaluate the function for $z = 2$, then $f(2) = 2^2 + 1 + i = 4 + 1 + i = 5 + i$. Squaring complex numbers is just a little bit more difficult, but it is enough to realize that when a function like this takes a complex number as input, it yields another complex number as output. If this function is iterated (that is, if the output becomes the input), and the function is evaluated again and again, one of two things can happen. Either the output numbers will begin to grow and to go farther from the origin, or somehow they will stay close to the origin, even if the function is iterated many times.

For example, select $c = -0.125 + 0.75i$, and evaluate f for $z = 0$. Evaluating the function again using as the input the output of $f(0)$, and continuing this repetition of using each output value as the next input value yields a sequence of complex numbers different than the sequence of complex numbers that would result from evaluating the same function with an initial value of $z = -0.5 + 0.5i$. The difference is that for the initial value $z = 0$, the resulting sequence of complex numbers remains bounded; that is, the sequence remains close to the origin. On the other hand, the sequence given by $z = -0.5 + 0.5i$ quickly goes far away from the origin.

The collection of complex numbers, represented as points on the complex plane, that lead to sequences that stay always close to the origin is called the prisoner set for c, whereas the collection of points that lead to unbounded sequences is called the escape set for c. The Julia Set is the boundary between the two sets.

Cartesian plane a mathematical plane defined by the x and y axes or the ordinate and abscissa in a Cartesian coordinate system

complex plane the mathematical abstraction on which complex numbers can be graphed; the x-axis is the real component and the y-axis is the imaginary component

real number a number that has no imaginary part; member of a set composed of all the rational and irrational numbers

The elegance of the Mandelbrot Set (top left) becomes evident in three magnifications, starting at a very small portion of the set's border in the center of the first frame. Between the top right and lower left frames, the magnification increases by a factor of 5. The lower right frame is a much greater magnification of the edge of the spiral in the middle of the previous frame. Note the miniature Mandelbrot Set (in white) embedded in this final magnification.

Although not shown here, the prisoner set for $c = -0.125 + 0.75i$ and its bordering Julia Set is considered connected because it appears in one piece. On the other hand, the Julia Set for $c = -0.75 + 0.125i$ is disconnected because it consists of pieces that are separated from each other. If all those values c in the complex plane that have connected Julia Sets are colored black, the result is known as the Mandelbrot Set, named in honor of

Benoit Mandelbrot. It is not surprising that this set has a complexity that placed it beyond the reach of mathematicians until computers were used to study it. Mandelbrot studied Julia's work extensively and used computer graphics to render the Julia Sets and the Mandelbrot Set.

Self-similarity in the Mandelbrot Set is of a different nature than in the Koch Curve and Sierpinski Gasket because it arises from iterations of quadratic functions rather than from generator iterations or IFS iterations, as described above. In the Mandelbrot Set, identical pictures cannot be seen right away. But as the four-frame image shows, under increasing magnifications, the borders will reveal hidden complexities and even tiny copies of the Mandelbrot Set.

Fractals in Science and Art

Before Mandelbrot, none of the mathematical pioneers thought that their theoretical speculations about iterative processes and their relation to extremely unusual sets would end up being the best tools to describe nature. And yet fractals have proven to be a rich subject of study. They have been used to describe nature and are used frequently by scientists of different disciplines to explore very diverse phenomena. Fractal structures can be found in the leaves of a tree, in the course of a river, in the shape of a broccoli, in our arterial system, and on the surface of a virus.

The earliest applications of fractals, and perhaps the most widely seen by nonscientists, occur in the arts and in the film industry, where **fractal forgery** has been used to create landscapes for science fiction movies. Using fractals, convincing simulations of clouds, mountains, and surfaces of alien worlds have been created for our amusement.

In the 1970s, a young scientist, Loren Carpenter, made a computer movie of a flight over a fractal landscape. This brought him to the attention of Lucasfilm Ltd, whose graphic division, Pixar, immediately hired him. His work with fractals was used to create the geography of the moons of Endor and the outline of the Death Star in the movie *Return of the Jedi*. Fractals were also used to generate the landscape of the Genesis planet in the movie *Star Trek II: Wrath of Khan*. Carpenter has received awards for his contributions to the film industry, and his work in these two movies triggered the extended use of fractals for special effects and to simulate landscapes and other irregular shapes in three-dimensional (3-D) computer games.

The study of fractals is still a young branch of mathematics, and more applications are yet to be revealed. SEE ALSO MANDELBROT, BENOIT B.; NUMBERS, COMPLEX.

Óscar Chávez and Gay A. Ragan

This image entitled "Futuristic Heads" illustrates the creative use of fractals. The irregular patterns on the surface of each head would reveal tiny details and complexities if magnified.

fractal forgery creating a natural landscape created by using fractals to simulate trees, mountains, clouds, or other features

Bibliography

Mandelbrot, Benoit B. *The Fractal Geometry of Nature*. New York: W.H. Freeman and Company, 1982.

Peitgen, Heinz-Otto, Hartmut Jürgens, and Dietmar Saupe. *Fractals for the Classroom*. New York: Springer Verlag, 1992.

Peitgen, Heinz-Otto, and Peter H. Richter. *The Beauty of Fractals*. New York: Springer Verlag, 1986.

Stewart, Ian. "Does God Play Dice?" *The Mathematics of Chaos*. Malden, MA: Blackwell Publishers, Inc., 1999.

Internet Resources

Burbanks, Andy. *Zoom on the Mandelbrot Set.* <http://www.lboro.ac.uk/departments/ma/gallery/mandel/index.html>.

"Fractals Unleashed." *ThinkQuest.* <http://library.thinkquest.org/26242/full/>.

Julia and Mandelbrot Set Generation. Mathematics and Computer Science Dept. Clark University. <http://aleph0.clarku.edu/~djoyce/julia/juliagen.html>.

Fraction Operations

A fraction compares two numbers by division. To conduct basic operations, keep in mind that any number except 0 divided by itself is 1, and 1 times any number is itself. That is, $\frac{5}{5} = 1$, and $1 \times 5 = 5$. Thus, any number divided or multiplied by a fraction equal to one will be itself. For example, $5 \times \frac{3}{3} = 5$ and $5 \div \frac{481}{481} = 5$.

When multiplying fractions, the numerators (top numbers) are multiplied together and the denominators (bottom numbers) are multiplied together. So $\frac{5}{7} \times \frac{8}{9} = \frac{(5 \times 8)}{(7 \times 9)} = \frac{40}{63}$. And $\frac{4}{5} \times 6 = \frac{4}{5} \times \frac{6}{1} = \frac{24}{5}$.

To divide fractions, rewrite the problem as multiplying by the reciprocal (multiplicative inverse) of the divisor. So $\frac{5}{7} \div \frac{8}{9} = \frac{5}{7} \times \frac{9}{8} = \frac{45}{56}$.

To add fractions that have the same, or a common, denominator, simply add the numerators, and use the common denominator. The figure below illustrates why this is true.

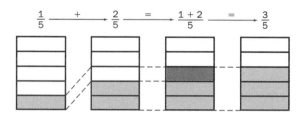

However, fractions cannot be added until they are written with a common denominator. The figure below shows why adding fractions with different denominators is incorrect.

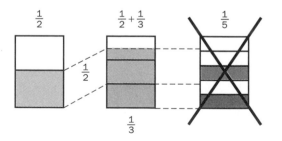

To correctly add $\frac{1}{2}$ and $\frac{1}{3}$, a common denominator must first be found. Usually, the least common multiple of the denominators (also called the least common denominator) is the best choice for the common denominator. In the example below, the least common multiple of the two denominators—2 and 3—is 6, so the least common denominator is 6. To convert the fractions, multiply $\frac{1}{2}$ by $\frac{3}{3}$ (which is equivalent to 1) to get $\frac{3}{6}$. Similarly, multiply $\frac{1}{3}$ by $\frac{2}{2}$ (which is equivalent to 1) to get $\frac{2}{6}$.

First $\frac{1}{2} \times \frac{3}{3} = \frac{3}{6}$

And $\frac{1}{3} \times \frac{2}{2} = \frac{2}{6}$

So $\frac{3}{6} + \frac{2}{6} = \frac{5}{6}$, or $\frac{1}{2} + \frac{1}{3} = \frac{5}{6}$

To model this problem visually, divide a rectangle into halves horizontally, then into thirds vertically, creating six equal parts (see the figure below). Shade one-half in color to show $\frac{1}{2}$, and then shade one-third in gray to show $\frac{1}{3}$. Since, as the figure shows, the upper left square has been shaded twice, it must be "carried" (see arrow). Now five of six squares are shaded; therefore, $\frac{1}{2} + \frac{1}{3} = \frac{5}{6}$.

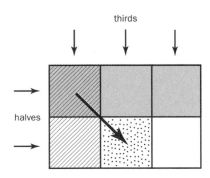

thirds

halves

Subtraction of fractions is similar to addition, in that the fractions being subtracted must have a common denominator. So $\frac{1}{2} - \frac{1}{3} = \frac{3}{6} - \frac{2}{6} = \frac{1}{6}$. SEE ALSO FRACTIONS.

Stanislaus Noel Ting

Fractions

Fractions are usually thought of as $\frac{1}{2}$, $\frac{3}{4}$, or maybe the decimal fraction 0.5. Perhaps some think of a fraction as a part of a circle or 5 parts out of 10 parts. The word "fraction" itself is related to a word meaning broken, as in "fracture."

Historically, fractions have been thought of and written in many different ways. Apparently the Babylonians, about 4,000 years ago, wrote fractions in a way similar to our decimal fractions, but instead of our **base-10**, they used **base-60**. They also used a space instead of a decimal point. This relatively simple system, however, does not reappear in common usage until about 3,600 years later in Europe.

Understanding Fractions

One mathematics dictionary defines a fraction as "a number less than 1." But this definition is too simple. The number $\frac{5}{3}$ is certainly not "less than one," but most people would still call it a fraction. Indeed, this same dic-

base-10 a number system in which each place represents a power of 10 larger than the place to its right

base-60 a number system used by ancient Mesopotamian cultures for some calculations in which each place represents a power of 60 larger than the place to its right

tionary calls $\frac{5}{3}$ an improper fraction or "a fraction whose numerator is larger than the denominator."

Another book defines a fraction as "a numeral representing some part of a whole." But what whole is $\frac{5}{3}$ representing part of, according to this definition? If a circle or a rectangle is divided into three equal parts, the denominator, or bottom, of the fraction is 3. But how many of those parts, or thirds, are represented by the fraction $\frac{5}{3}$? The numerator, or top, of the fraction tells you that $\frac{5}{3}$ represents five of the parts, each of which is one-third of a whole.

Another way to define a fraction is as a number that can be expressed in the form $\frac{a}{b}$, where a and b are **whole numbers** and b is not equal to 0. But this definition, taken from another mathematics dictionary, has problems too. The whole numbers are 0, 1, 2, 3, 4, 5. . . .. So does this definition mean that $-\frac{2}{3}$ is not a fraction? Although -2 is not a whole number, clearly $-\frac{2}{3}$ is a fraction.

A better definition—and one that holds up under scrutiny—is that a fraction is a numeral written in the form $\frac{a}{b}$ where a can represent any number and b can represent any number except 0. By this definition, $\frac{4.5}{-6.2}$ is a fraction, as are $\frac{(2.5)}{7}$, $\frac{100}{3}$, and $\frac{6}{2}$, as well as $\frac{\pi}{2}$. This definition names a fraction according to the form. This means that $\frac{100}{2}$ is a fraction, and 50 is not a fraction. The values of the two numerals are the same, but the form of the numerals is not.

However, it is useful to be able to talk about the numbers that can be expressed as the ratio, or quotient, of two **integers**, such as $\frac{2}{3}$, $\frac{6}{3}$, and $-\frac{8}{9}$. These numbers, which can be negative, are called **rational numbers**. All rational numbers can be written in the form of fractions; however, not all fractions are rational numbers. For example, the fraction $\frac{\pi}{2}$ is not a rational number because π is not an integer. SEE ALSO DECIMALS; FORM AND VALUE; FRACTION OPERATIONS; NUMBERS, IRRATIONAL; NUMBERS, RATIONAL; RATIO, RATE, AND PROPORTION.

Lucia McKay

Bibliography

Eves, Howard. *An Introduction to the History of Mathematics.* New York: Holt, Rinehart and Winston, 1964.

Hogben, Lancelot. *Mathematics in the Making.* London: Crescent Books, 1960.

———. *The Wonderful World of Mathematics.* New York: Garden City Books, 1955.

Functions and Equations

In mathematics, function is a central idea. Imagine a machine that takes numbered balls from 1 through 26 and labels them with the English alphabet letters A through Z. This machine mimics a mathematical function. A function takes an object from one set **A** (the input) and maps it to an object in another set **B** (the output). In mathematics, **A** and **B** are usually sets of numbers. In symbols, this relationship is written as $f: A \rightarrow B$.

So, a function f is the name of a relationship between two sets. Functions are usually denoted by the letters f, g, or h. **A** is called the **domain** (input), and **B** is called the **range** (output). If the elements of the domain

---

WHOLES AND PARTS

The Greek mathematicians (around 600 B.C.E. to 600 C.E.) had some problem working with fractions because the number 1 had a mystical significance as an indivisible unity. They did not want to break unity into parts, so they used ratios instead.

---

whole numbers the positive integers and zero

integer a positive whole number, its negative counterpart, or zero

rational number a number that can be written in the form *a/b* where *a* and *b* are integers and *b* is not 0

domain the set of all values of a variable used in a function

range synonymous with range, the set of all values of a variable in a function mapped to the values in the domain of the independent variable

are denoted by x, and the elements of the range are denoted by y, then a function can also be written as $y = f(x)$. This is read as "y is a function of x." Notice that this notation does not mean that f is multiplied by x. Instead, the value of f depends on the value of x.

Examples of Functions

A simple example of a function is $y = f(x)$, where $f(x) = x + 2$. To each number x, add 2 to get y. When x is 3, y is 5, and when x is 4, y is 6. The value y of the function, $f(x)$, depends on the choice of x. The input, or x, is called the independent variable, and the output, or y, is called the dependent variable.

Another example is a relationship between the positive **integer** set (domain) and the even number set (range). To each positive integer n, the function $f(n)$ assigns a value of $2n$. In symbols, $f(n) = 2n$.

In a function, each element of the domain must map to exactly one element of the range. However the opposite is not true. For example, $f(x) = |x|$ is a function. Each value of $f(x)$ corresponds to two values of x.

Now consider a function g with the **real number set** as the domain set. To each number x, g assigns 3 times x. That is, $g(x) = 3x$.

Function Notation and Graphs

Functions are visualized geometrically by plotting their graphs on a **Cartesian plane**. You can plot a function by taking a few numbers from the domain sets and finding their functional values. For example, $g(x) = 3x$ would yield the points $(-1, 3)$, $(0, 0)$, and $(1, 3)$. These points can be connected by a straight line.

In functions such as $f(x) = 3x$, $g(x) = x + 2$, or $h(x) = (\frac{1}{2})x$, the **power** of the independent variable, x, is 1. Such functions are called **linear functions**. Plotting the graph of linear functions always produces straight lines. In contrast, consider the function $f(x) = x^2$; its graph is not a straight line but rather a **parabola**. SEE ALSO MAPPING; MATHEMATICAL.

Rafiq Ladhani

Bibliography

Amdahl, Kenn, and Jim Loats. *Algebra Unplugged*. Broomfield, CO: Clearwater Publishing Co., 1995.

Miller, Charles D., Vern E. Heeren, and E. John Hornsby, Jr. *Mathematical Ideas*, 9th ed. Boston: Addison-Wesley, 2001.

integer a positive whole number, its negative counterpart, or zero

real number set the combined set of all rational and irrational numbers; the set of numbers representing all points on the number line

Cartesian plane a mathematical plane defined by the x and y axes or the ordinate and abscissa in a Cartesian coordinate system

power the number of times a number is to be multiplied by itself in an expression

linear function a function whose graph on the x-y plane is a straight line or a line segment

parabola a conic section; the locus of all points such that the distance from a fixed point called the focus is equal to the perpendicular distance from a line

Galileo Galilei

Italian Astronomer, Physicist, and Mathematician
1564–1642

Galileo Galilei is a pivotal figure in intellectual and scientific history. His ideas and activities were integral to the Scientific Revolution, which resulted in world-changing advances in science and technology, and in fundamental changes in the way reality is perceived.

Galileo was born in Pisa, Italy, in 1564. In 1581, he entered the University of Pisa, where his father wanted him to study medicine. But Galileo was interested in mathematics and philosophy, and he left the university without a degree. In 1589, he taught mathematics at the university, but lost his job by challenging Aristotelian teachings held by the university and the Catholic Church. However, he immediately became professor of mathematics at the University of Padua.

Galileo was among the first to perceive that the natural world acts in a regular manner that can be interpreted and understood mathematically. Applying this approach, he developed the concept of acceleration and discovered the law of falling bodies, explaining the movement of projectiles, pendulums, and objects moving on an inclined plane.

Galileo accepted the Sun-centered model of the solar system that had been proposed by Copernicus. This model was in opposition to the Earth-centered model of Ptolemy that was accepted by scholars and the Catholic Church. Soon after the first telescope was invented, Galileo built his own version in 1609 and improved its magnification power. He was the first to use a telescope to study the heavens, obtaining, through these investigations, proof of the Copernican system. He discovered sunspots, valleys and mountains on the Moon, satellites circling Jupiter, and the phases of Venus.

In 1610, Galileo published his observations and interpretations in *The Starry Messenger*, refuting Aristotle and Ptolemy and supporting Copernicus. Opposition came immediately from scholars and churchmen, who accused him of heresy.

In 1612, Galileo published a book on hydrostatics based on observations, measurements, and mathematical analysis. He was again attacked by churchmen and university scholars for not adhering to the accepted Aristotelian approach. He openly argued that physical evidence and mathemat-

Galileo's many important discoveries put him in direct opposition to the Catholic Church, the ruling body of the time. Only centuries later would Galileo be cleared of heresy.

ical proofs should not be made dependent on interpretations of scripture but that such interpretations should be subject to change when new evidence becomes available. Not surprisingly, the Catholic Church issued an edict in 1616 banning Copernicanism and censored Galileo's writings.

Undaunted, in 1632 Galileo published *Dialogue on the Two Chief World Systems* contrasting the planetary models of Ptolemy and Copernicus, with clear preference for Copernicus. He was called to Rome and tried for heresy. Convicted, he was forced to publicly retract his ideas and placed on permanent house arrest. His works were banned, but this order was essentially ignored outside of Italy. His ideas spread rapidly, gaining support throughout Europe.

Galileo continued his work, and his last book, *Discourses Concerning Two New Sciences*, was published in Leiden in 1638. This classic volume presented a mechanical mathematical physics that eventually led to the development of what would be called Newtonian physics. Galileo died in 1642, the year of Isaac Newton's birth. In 1992, the Catholic Church rescinded its 1633 conviction of Galileo as a heretic—350 years after his death. SEE ALSO NEWTON, SIR ISAAC; SOLAR SYSTEM GEOMETRY, HISTORY OF.

J. William Moncrief

Bibliography

Gamow, George. *The Great Physicists from Galileo to Einstein.* New York: Dover Publications, Inc., 1988.

Santillana, Giorgio de. *The Crime of Galileo.* Chicago: University of Chicago Press, 1955.

Games

Have you ever played Tic-Tac-Toe? Did you win? Did you know that each Tic-Tac-Toe game will always end in a tie unless one player makes a mistake?

There are nine squares on a Tic-Tac-Toe game board, so the first player has nine choices for the first move. The second player has eight choices for the second move (one square is taken), which makes a total of 72 possible arrangements after the first two turns. After five turns, there are 15,120 possible arrangements.

Someone could possibly win on the sixth turn if the other player played really badly, so the nine possible winning positions must be subtracted from the total, leaving 60,471 arrangements after only six moves. No one can keep track of that many combinations, but that is not necessary. The successful Tic-Tac-Toe strategy is simply to block the other player's moves while hoping the other player makes a mistake.

A good chess player must use a sequence of opening moves that will yield the best possible position. In chess, the player in control of the white pieces (White) always moves first. Since only the eight pawns and two knights can move on the first move, there are twelve possible first moves for White. (The two knights can each move to two different positions).

There are also twelve different opening moves for the player controlling the black pieces (Black), so after only two moves, there are 144 different possible arrangements of pieces on the board. Each move opens up other pieces that can move, so after only four moves, there are about 70,000 different possible arrangements of pieces on the chessboard. Not every arrangement is of equal value, but with 70,000 different positions to consider, it is difficult for even good players to keep track of all possibilities. So good chess players remember patterns of pieces and learn to recognize certain patterns that give them an advantage over their opponents.

A great deal of mathematics is therefore involved in most games. Poker players must calculate the probabilities of certain card arrangements in order to win. (Never draw to an inside straight!) Bridge players must use probability to calculate the possible arrangements of cards in their opponents' hands in order to decide which strategy to use in playing winningly.

Bridge Strategies

Bridge players use mathematics in evaluating their hands. In one popular system, an ace is worth four points, a king is worth three points, a queen is worth two points, and a jack is worth only one point. Players also count distribution points. Having no cards of one suit is worth three points, a singleton is worth two points, and only two cards of a suit is worth one point. Evaluating the hand this way allows a player to determine if a hand is "biddable."

Once play starts, math is used to determine how best to play the cards. For example, in a typical hand, one side may have nine cards of the trump suit, which means the other side has four trump cards. Suppose the missing cards are the queen, 8, 6, and 3. How are those cards likely to be distributed between the opponents' two hands? One opponent could have all four trump cards, one could have three cards, and the other opponent one card, or each opponent might have two cards. The mathematics of probabilities shows that the most likely arrangement is for one opponent to have three of the missing trump cards. So a player cannot depend on capturing the missing queen by simply leading the ace and king. SEE ALSO PROBABILITY, THEORETICAL.

Elliot Richmond

Bibliography

McGervey, John D. *Probabilities in Everyday Life.* Chicago: Nelson-Hall, 1986.

Card games such as bridge and poker use arithmetic and probabilities.

Gaming

Recent years have indicated a change in the locality of legalized casino gambling across the United States. Until 1978 gaming, as it is commonly called, was available only in Nevada. Today, however, the casino business has expanded to other states. One reason for the increase in the number of gambling places is that many people enjoy playing these games of chance. Another critical factor is the profit margins realized by entrepreneurs in the casino industry.

Casinos offer a wide range of games to meet the interests of their clientele. Blackjack, roulette, baccarat, and craps are among the popular games. All casino games share two important characteristics that are critical to their

The gaming industry continues to grow because the odds are in favor of the house.

continued success. On the one hand, each game is exciting because the unpredictable nature of probabilistic outcomes makes it possible for a player to be lucky and win in the short run. On the other hand, the significant "house edge" associated with each of these games ensures that in the long run the bettor will lose and the casino will win money. To better understand the risks of casino gambling, consider the chances of winning in roulette and blackjack.

Roulette

The simplest of casino games to analyze from the perspective of theoretical probability is roulette. In this game a small ball is rolled onto a revolving tray containing thirty-eight numbered compartments. The ball randomly comes to rest in one of these thirty-eight compartments. In addition to the compartments numbered from 1 to 36, there are two extras numbered 0 and 00. It is these last two numbers that provide the casino with their edge.

The bettor has several options when playing roulette. If a particular number is chosen, the player will win $35 for every dollar bet if that number occurs. In this case, if a winning bet of $2 is placed the bettor will receive $72 in return, 35 to 1 on each dollar bet, plus the original $2 bet. The bettor may also choose to bet on the color of the number hit (eighteen are red and eighteen are black), whether the number is even or odd (0 and 00 are considered neither even nor odd), or whether the number hit will be 1 through 18, or 19 through 36.

In each of these bets, the probability of winning is 18/38 because in each case there are eighteen favorable results out of the total number of thirty-eight possible outcomes. Finally, the player can get 2 to 1 odds by betting that the number will be from 1 to 12, 13 to 24, or 25 to 36.

One interesting aspect of roulette is that the "strategy" used in choosing from the aforementioned betting options has absolutely no effect on the expected value of the win or loss on that bet. To show this, the expected value of each of these options can be calculated. In a nutshell, the expected value is the average amount that a player would win or lose on a bet. A positive expected value indicates that the game is favorable and that on average the player will win money, whereas a negative expected value indicates that the player will on average lose money.

If 0 and 00 were not included on the roulette wheel, the expected value on any wager would be 0, indicating that in the long run, the average win or loss for the bettor would be zero. To calculate the expected value, multiply the probability of each of the expected outcomes by the amount won or lost by the player given that outcome. Thus without 0 and 00, a player betting on even or odd would expect to win 50 percent of the time and lose the other 50 percent of the time.

If a bet of X dollars is made, the expected value is $(0.5)(-X) + (0.5)(+X) = 0$. Similarly, on the 36 number wheel, the expected win or loss on a bet of \$X on an individual number is 0. The player wins $\frac{1}{36}$th of the time and loses $\frac{35}{36}$ths of the time, making the expected value $(\frac{35}{36})(-X) + (\frac{1}{36})(+35X) = 0$. Any game with an expected value of 0 is referred to as a fair game and will not be found in any casino!

The green numbers 0 and 00 provide the casino with its edge. If a bet is made on an individual number, the probability of winning is $\frac{1}{38}$, since there are now 38 equally likely outcomes that can occur. Calculating the expected value for betting \$X on an individual number yields the following equation: $(\frac{37}{38})(-X) + (\frac{1}{38})(+35X) = (-\frac{2}{38})X = (-\frac{1}{19})X$. Thus the expected value is approximately -0.053 times the amount of the wager. This means that the player on average will lose a little more than 5 cents on every dollar bet.

An even or odd bet has a probability of $\frac{18}{38}$ of winning since 0 and 00 are considered neither even nor odd. Calculating the expected value for the player betting \$X on even or odd yields the following equation: $(\frac{20}{38})(-X) + (\frac{18}{38})(+X) = (-\frac{2}{38})X = (-\frac{1}{19})X$. Thus the expected value on this type of bet is exactly the same as that of betting on an individual number. The reader is encouraged to perform the appropriate calculations to verify that betting on 1 through 12 also yields an expected value of -0.053 multiplied by the amount of the bet. In roulette, therefore, no matter what strategy is used, the disadvantage to the player remains constant.

Some gamblers, however, feel they can win by trying to determine what is "due" to happen on a particular trial. For example, if the previous four numbers have been red, some feel that black is more likely to occur the next time. They reason that because attaining red five times in a row is extremely unlikely, the next result is more likely to be black. The fallacy here is that although the probability of red occurring five times in a row is indeed very unlikely, the unlikely event of four consecutive reds has already occurred.

Because successive trials of a roulette wheel are independent of one another, the next number has the same chance of being red or black as in previous trials, $\frac{18}{38}$. Thus playing this "hunch" strategy does not make the player any more (or less) likely to win as the expected value for each trial remains -0.053 times the amount bet.

Blackjack

Blackjack is perhaps the most complex of casino games and for this reason has been the subject of considerable analysis by gamblers. Calculating the

expected value of a hand of blackjack is an extremely difficult task for several reasons. First, there are many ways in which a hand can be dealt to the player and the dealer. Second, almost every casino offers slightly different rule variations of the game. Finally, unlike roulette, the decisions made by the player throughout the course of a hand dramatically affect the chances of winning.

In the game of blackjack, picture cards have a value of 10, aces can be counted as 1 or 11, and all other cards take on the value of the card. The game begins with the player and the dealer each being dealt two cards. The player's goal is to come closer to 21 than the dealer without going over, known as busting. After seeing both of their cards and one of the dealer's cards (commonly called the "dealer's up card"), the player must decide how to proceed. The player can "stay" with the present total, take another card ("hit"), double the wager and be given one and only one more card, or split a pair by placing another bet equal to the original and then proceeding with two separate hands.

In the majority of cases, the only reasonable decision is to take a hit or stand with the current total. Should the player take a hit, he or she can take additional hits until either the total of the cards exceeds 21 or the player does not want any more cards. The player loses immediately if the sum of the cards exceeds 21. If the player stops taking cards without exceeding 21, it is the dealer's turn to act. In casino versions of blackjack, the dealer does not make decisions but instead the dealer's play is fixed. The dealer must hit whenever her total is 16 or less and must stay when her total is 17 or more.

Many books on blackjack provide a basic strategy that is considered optimal for the player. Optimal basic strategy is determined by considering every possible combination of the player's hand and the dealer's up card and making the play that yields the best expected value in each case. Depending on the rule variations, most authors claim that by playing a sound basic strategy the house advantage will only be about 2 to 3 percent. Although this disadvantage is less than that of roulette, we must keep in mind that it is based on the player making the correct decisions at all times. Unlike roulette, the quality of the decisions made in the course of playing has a dramatic effect on the chances of winning. In practice, most players do not consistently make the optimal decisions and for this reason, many blackjack players lose at a much faster rate than they otherwise should.

How the House Stays Ahead

A simple example will show how the casino gains its advantage as the number of games played increases. Suppose we consider a situation in which the player has a 40 percent chance of winning and a 60 percent chance of losing each game with the amount won or lost in each game being equal. If three games are played, the player must win two or three games in order to be ahead. The probability of this occurring is $3(.4)(.4)(.6) + 1(.4)(.4)(.4) = 35$ percent, because there are three ways in which the player can win two out of three games. That is, the probability of this occurring is $(.4)(.4)(.6)$ for each of the three ways, and there is one way of winning all three games, the probability of which is $(.4)(.4)(.4)$. Similarly, the probability of winning three or more games in five is

$$10(.4)(.4)(.4)(.6)(.6) + 5(.4)(.4)(.4)(.4)(.6) + 1(.4)(.4)(.4)(.4)(.4) = 32 \text{ percent.}$$

Further analysis of more games played can be done using the **binomial distribution**. The successive probabilities of the player winning when the game is played 7, 9, 11, 13, 15, 17 and 19 times are 0.29, 0.266, 0.246, 0.228, 0.212, 0.198, and 0.187, respectively.

The probability of winning decreases with the duration that a gambler plays. In a casino, a gambler may play hundreds of hands of blackjack or games of roulette consecutively, yet the chances of the player being ahead after a lengthy session are extremely small. Furthermore, from the casino's perspective, thousands of hands of blackjack and games of roulette are being played every hour by their numerous patrons, nearly around the clock. Given this huge number of trials, the casinos are assured of making large profits. SEE ALSO PROBABILITY AND THE LAW OF LARGE NUMBERS; PROBABILITY, THEORETICAL.

Robert J. Quinn

Bibliography

Khazanie, Ramakant. *Elementary Statistics: In a World of Applications.* Glenview, IL: Scott, Foresman and Company, 1979.

binomial distribution in statistics, a function whose values yield the probability of obtaining a certain number of successes in independent trials wherein the probability of a successful outcome is constant from one trial to the next

Gardner, Martin

American Author
1914–

One of the most well-known creators of mathematical puzzles is Martin Gardner. From 1957 to 1982, he wrote a column for *Scientific American* called "Mathematical Recreations." He presented intriguing problems, discussed the mathematics of various games, and demonstrated recreational aspects of mathematical discoveries. He always aimed to entertain and stimulate his readers, which ranged from high school students to college professors.

Early Work

Born in 1914 in Tulsa, Oklahoma, Martin Gardner became fascinated with mathematics in high school when he took Pauline Baker's geometry course. She communicated a love for the subject that he readily absorbed. Gardner also had other academic interests. He graduated from the University of Chicago in 1936, with a major in philosophy, and did graduate work in the philosophy of science.

Most of Gardner's early writing had little to do with philosophy or mathematics. Before World War II, he worked as a reporter for the *Tulsa Tribune*. After serving in the U.S. Navy, he supported himself as a freelance writer, working for eight years as a contributing editor to *Humpty Dumpty's Magazine*. This ended in 1957 when, drawing on his interest in magic, he sold his first article to *Scientific American*.

Fascinated when a magician showed him a paper toy called a hexaflexagon, Gardner contacted the inventor, John Tukey, a mathematician at Princeton, and with Tukey's permission and help, he wrote an article about hexaflexagons and the mathematics behind them. Delighted, the *Scientific American* editors published it and asked for more. Martin Gardner scoured

Martin Gardner is a prolific writer and an expansive, stimulating thinker. Many of his columns and books are about mathematics.

New York City for old books on recreational mathematics and found enough material to get the column going. Shortly thereafter, he began to draw material from recreational mathematics journals.

Gardner had a gift for simplifying ideas and communicating them wittily in a warm, playful spirit. His writing was so well received that mathematicians whose work had recreational aspects—Solomon Golomb, John Conway, Roger Penrose, and Frank Harary, among others—shared their discoveries with him. Through these contacts his columns became more sophisticated, and he enabled mathematicians to present their work to a much larger audience.

Popular Columns

Central to his work was the belief that mathematics, whether formal or recreational, is enormously interesting and of vital importance to humankind. Mathematics is the solving of puzzles. Good puzzles, even if they appear to be of trivial importance, open the door to all sorts of useful interconnections, often leading to "better and better answers to puzzles posed by nature."

One of his most popular columns was on John Conway's Game of Life, a population simulation game. A few counters are placed on a large checkerboard. Counters are born or die according to these rules:

(1) a counter survives to the next round if it has two or three neighboring counters;

(2) a counter dies if it has four or more neighbors or one or zero neighbors; and

(3) each empty cell with exactly three neighbors will give birth to a new counter in the next round.

The game is fascinating because of the great variety of population behaviors that arise from different beginning arrangements of counters.

Another favorite article was on a method of encoding messages called trapdoor functions, which are functions whose inverses—the key to decoding the message—are computationally impossible to discover in thousands of years. Martin Gardner's article was the first to discuss the work of Ron Rivest, who combined trapdoor functions with prime number factorization, creating coding systems that could be used in the electronic transmission of information over the Internet.

The Works of Martin Gardner

Over the years Martin Gardner published challenging problems in his columns, the answers of which can be found in the books listed here:

Aha! Gotcha: Paradoxes to Puzzle and Delight.

Aha! Insight.

Fractal Music, Hypercards, and More: Mathematical Recreations from Scientific American Magazine.

Hexaflexagons & Other Mathematical Diversions: The First Scientific American Book of Puzzles and Games.

The Incredible Dr. Matrix.

Knotted Doughnuts and Other Mathematical Entertainments.

Mathematical Carnival.

Mathematical Circus.

Mathematical Magic Show.

Mathematics, Magic, and Mystery.

My Best Mathematical and Logic Puzzles.

New Mathematical Diversions from Scientific American.

The Numerology of Dr. Matrix.

Penrose Tiles and Trapdoor Ciphers.

Riddles of the Sphinx and Other Mathematical Puzzle Tales.

The 2nd Scientific American Book of Mathematical Puzzles and Diversions.

Sixth Book of Mathematical Diversions from Scientific American.

Time Travel and Other Mathematical Bewilderments.

The Unexpected Hanging and Other Mathematical Diversions.

The Universe in a Handkerchief: Lewis Carroll's Mathematical Recreations, Games, Puzzles, and Word Plays.

Wheels, Life, and Other Mathematical Amusements.

The math puzzles Gardner presented to the public were enjoyed by people of all ages, and offered a variety of problems for readers to solve. Some examples include:

A boy and a girl were talking. "I'm a boy," said the one with black hair. "I'm a girl," said the one with red hair. If at least one of them is lying, who has black hair? [From *Wheels, Life, and Other Mathematical Amusements*, 1983]

A cylindrical hole six inches long is drilled right through the center of a solid sphere as shown below. Determine the volume remaining in the sphere. [From *Hexaflexagons & Other Mathematical Diversions: The First Scientific American Book of Puzzles and Games*, 1988]

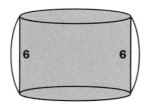

Dissect an isosceles triangle *ABC* with a 120° angle into five triangles similar to *ABC*. [From *Wheels, Life, and Other Mathematical Amusements*, 1983]

A worm is at the end of a 1 kilometer rubber rope. It crawls forward for one second, covering 1 centimeter and then the length of the rope is increased by 1 kilometer. This process is continued indefinitely. When the rope is stretched it is pulled from both

ends. Show that the worm can reach the end of the rope. [From *Time Travel and Other Mathematical Bewilderments*, 1988]

Consider the figure below. As you drink a soda, the center of gravity *C* drops, but when the can is empty, the center of gravity has risen back to its starting point. Assuming that the can is 8 inches high, weighs 1.5 ounces empty and 13.5 ounces full, determine the lowest point reached by the center of gravity *C*. [From *Wheels, Life, and Other Mathematical Amusements*, 1983]

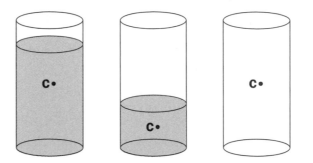

The game of Sim: put six dots on a paper, forming the vertices of a regular hexagon. Each player in turn connects two of the dots; one player uses a blue color, the other a red color. The first player forced to form a triangle of his own color loses. What is the best strategy? [From *Knotted Doughnuts and Other Mathematical Entertainments*, 1987]

A paradox: a man who always keeps his promises tells his wife that "tomorrow for your birthday I will give you an unexpected gift. You have no way of guessing what it is. It is the gold bracelet we saw at the jewelry store." Will his wife be surprised or not? [From *The Unexpected Hanging and Other Mathematical Diversions*, 1991]

Gardner also created the mysterious Dr. Matrix as a foil for playing with numerology. Here, for example, is Dr. Matrix's proof that William Shakespeare helped translate the King James Bible: In Psalm 46, the 46th word from the beginning is SHAKE and the 46th word from the end is SPEAR. Furthermore, the King James Version was completed in 1610 when Shakespeare was 46 years old. SEE ALSO PUZZLES, NUMBER.

Don Barry

Bibliography

Frazier, Kendrick. "A Mind at Play: An Interview with Martin Gardner." *Skeptical Inquirer* 22, no. 2 (1998): 34.

Internet Resources

Notes on Martin Gardner. The Recreational Math Pages. <http://www.citlink.net/citlink/d/dmn1/gardner.htm>.

Genome, Human

The word "genome" means the totality of all the genetic information present in the cells of an organism. Most of this genetic information is contained in chromosomes. A chromosome consists of deoxyribonucleic acid

(DNA) molecules wound up into a compact bundle. Humans have 46 chromosomes in their cells, organized into 23 corresponding pairs.*

The DNA in the chromosomes of an organism consists of a double-stranded molecule formed from four basic units that are repeated many times. The four basic units are called nucleotides. Each nucleotide is made of a sugar, a phosphate group, and a nucleotide base. The sugars in the nucleotides stack up and link together to form a backbone for one strand of the DNA molecule, leaving the nucleotide bases projecting. The four kinds of nucleotide bases found in DNA are adenine, cytosine, guanine, and thymine. A fifth nucleotide base, uracil, is found in ribonucleic acid (RNA) in place of thymine.

The nucleotide bases of DNA are usually designated as A, C, G, and T (or U) respectively. In the double-stranded DNA molecule, each nucleotide base forms a bond with a nucleotide base on the other strand of the molecule, such that A always pairs with T, and C with G. These two strands then wrap around each other, forming a structure known as a double helix. The two strands are antiparallel so that the sequence of bases starting from one end on one strand is repeated, starting from the opposite end on the other strand.

A gene is a unique sequence of bases that occupies a particular position on a chromosome. A single strand of DNA contains hundreds of individual genes. However, there are several different types of genes included in a DNA molecule. Structural genes code for particular amino acid sequences. These are the genes that contain instructions on how to build proteins. Operator genes control the structural genes and regulate their output. Regulatory genes may produce repressor proteins that turn the operator genes on or off or they may act like punctuation marks, signaling the beginning and end of coding sequences. Suppressor genes may suppress the actions of other genes and can reverse the effects of a harmful mutation. Kinetic genes regulate the chromosomes themselves. The 30,000 or so genes in every human cell code for more than one million different proteins including albumin and hemoglobin; brain chemicals like dopamine and serotonin; hormones like insulin, testosterone, and estrogen; and the countless enzymes that keep us alive.

Mathematics of the DNA Code

Structural genes responsible for the production of the amino acid sequences used to build proteins are the best understood of the different kinds of genes. To produce a protein, a section of DNA becomes "unzipped," exposing the nucleotide bases. A molecule of messenger RNA (mRNA) is synthesized by pairing up nucleotide bases. Each group of three nucleotide bases on the RNA molecule, called a codon, codes for a particular amino acid. Since there are four choices (A, C, G, and U) for each of the three-nucleotide bases, each codon can be one of 64 different "words" ($4 \times 4 \times 4 = 64$). However, there are only 20 different amino acids. Several different codons produce the same amino acid. For example, UUU and UUC both produce the amino acid phenylalanine. There are also three codons, UAA, UGA, and UAG, that act as "stop" signals ending the protein chain.

A protein contains around 100 amino acids, so a structural gene must contain at least 300 nucleotide bases. Using this logic, it might then be ex-

*If a single strand of human DNA were unwound and stretched out, it would be over two meters long.

Scanning electron micrograph of a human X chromosome.

THE IMPORTANCE OF MAPPING THE HUMAN GENOME

Many genetic diseases can result from a misspelling in the DNA sequence. Since each DNA codon codes for a particular amino acid, a change in one nucleotide base can result in a different protein being produced. If that protein is essential to health, a genetic disease results. For example, normal hemoglobin differs from the hemoglobin of sickle-cell anemia by only one amino acid out of hundreds.

The genetic maps being developed by the Human Genome Project are available on the Internet and are updated frequently, making accurate genetic information accessible to every researcher and opening up great potential for improving human health through research.

pected that the human genetic code would contain 10 million genes. However, DNA also contains stop and start codons, other regulatory molecules, some sequences (called introns) that are removed before protein synthesis begins, duplicate genes, non-coding sequences, redundant genes, and other non-functioning bits of DNA. As a result, there are probably only around 30,000 individual genes among the 3 billion nucleotide units of human chromosomes.

The Human Genome Project

The U.S. Human Genome Project (HGP) is a joint effort of the Department of Energy (DOE) and National Institute of Health (NIH). The goal of the Human Genome Project is to decipher human heredity through the creation of maps for each of the 23 human chromosomes. The first step in this process is to determine the actual DNA code. In June, 2000, then-U.S. President Clinton, leaders of the Human Genome Project, and officers of Celera Genomics (a private biotechnology firm) jointly announced that the rough draft of the human genetic code was ready for publication. The February 16, 2001 issue of *Science* published articles related to the work of Celera Genomics, and the February 15, 2001 issue of *Nature* published articles relating to the work of the Human Genome Project.

As of July 30, 2001, only the two smallest human chromosomes, 21 and 22, were completely sequenced to the level of accuracy specified by the protocols established by the Human Genome Project. At the time this article was written, 47.1 percent of human DNA had been mapped to final standards and 51.4 percent had been mapped to preliminary standards for a total of 98.5 percent mapped.

The final publication of the human genome map is expected by 2003. However, this final draft will include only the human genome code. Still to be determined are the exact number and locations of genes, how genes are regulated, how the DNA sequence is organized, how chromosomes are organized, which parts of the DNA are redundant or noncoding, how gene expression is coordinated, how genetic information is conserved, and many other concepts essential to understanding the human genetic code. SEE ALSO HUMAN BODY.

Elliot Richmond and Marilyn K. Simon

Bibliography

Bains, William. *Biotechnology from A to Z.* New York: Oxford University Press, 1998.

Davies, Kevin. *Cracking the Genome: Inside the Race to Unlock Human DNA.* New York: Free Press, 2001.

Drlica, Karl. *Understanding DNA and Gene Cloning: A Guide for the Curious,* 3rd ed. New York: John Wiley & Sons, 1997.

Lee, Thomas F. *The Human Genome Project: Cracking the Genetic Code of Life.* New York: Plenum Press, 1991.

Wilson, Edward O. *The Diversity of Life.* Cambridge, MA: Harvard University Press, 1992.

Internet Resources

DOE Human Genome Project. <http://www.ornl.gov/hgmis/>.

Genome Information on the World Wide Web. <http://cib.nig.ac.jp/others/genome-info.html>.

Geography

Geography is the study of the physical and geopolitical aspects of the surface of Earth. Physical geography describes the different surface and climatic conditions around the world. Political geography is concerned with the division of the world into various levels of government, human activity, and production. Geography is not confined to merely describing Earth as it is now, but also understanding how it has evolved and how it may change in the future.

The problems that faced humankind at the dawn of history stimulated both geography and mathematics. In fact, much of early mathematics was concerned with making measurements of the land; so much so that a whole branch of mathematics became known as Earth-measurement, which in Greek is *geometry*. Geometry as a mathematical study is less concerned with its practical roots, but for geographers, geometry and trigonometry are invaluable tools.

Outside of the activities associated with mapmaking, geography was for many years mainly descriptive. The information collected about the physical and social characteristics of the world was reported in a narrative form with little attempt to analyze the data that had been collected. In the late 1940s and early 1950s, a revolution took place in geography when the acceptance of any theory within the science became subject to mathematical analysis. As with other sciences, geography began to use mathematics as the language to describe relationships in the discipline.

The Geographic Matrix

An observation made by a geographer has two main attributes—a location and a physical attribute associated with that location. Each place may have more than one characteristic and each characteristic may be found at more than one location. These data can be recorded in a **matrix** with rows representing characteristics and columns the places where the

matrix a rectangular array of data in rows and columns

City planners and architects must have an understanding of mathematics and physical and political geography in order to optimize their designs. Shown here is a planner using a scale model.

observations have been taken. The organization of data into a matrix greatly aids geographers with the mathematical analysis of the information they gather.

Before geographers collect data, they must select the locations within the region where they will measure the characteristics of interest. This requires an understanding of the **sampling** techniques found in mathematical statistics. From statistical sampling theories the geographer calculates how many locations will be required, which will consequently reveal the number of columns in the matrix. In establishing the appropriate number of locations, it is necessary to ensure that there is sufficient data so that the samples are representative of the whole region.

Three main types of sampling systems are used in selecting locations. The first type is a totally random sample, in which each location in the study is selected at random from all possible points in the region. The second type of sample is a systematic sample, in which an initial point is chosen at random and all other points are determined by fixed intervals from the randomly chosen point. The third type of sample is a stratified sample, in which the region is subdivided into subregions. Within the subregions, points are chosen by either using a totally random sample, or a stratified sample, or by dividing into further subdivisions. This process can continue until the degree of accuracy required matches the number of sampling points. For example, in studying a country, a geographer may first break the country into regions. Then the regions may subdivide by using political divisions such as a state, and this may go further by using counties, and at this level there may be a random selection of sampling points.

Ultimately, the selection of sampling locations should permit a rapid, accurate, and economical amount of calculation in order to analyze the data. The selection process should also be such that final analysis is comparable to data collected in other regions so that regional comparisons may be made. In addition, consideration needs to be given to national and international standards, and to enabling comparisons with data collected over time.

Analysis of the Geographical Matrix

When the collected data have been placed in a geographic matrix, an analysis of a region can proceed in many ways. One common method of analysis is an examination of how a characteristic is distributed over a region by examining the row of the matrix for that characteristic. For example, attention may be focused on the way in which the rural population is distributed over an area such as the Great Plains of the United States.

Secondly, a geographer may try to get an understanding of the complexity of a location by identifying its characteristics. In other words, the column for that location may be analyzed. For instance, interest may be in the rainfall, soil type, or most successful crop production at a location in order to make recommendations for other places with similar characteristics. If the location is an urban area, a geographer might try to connect transportation access data, raw material availability, and expert labor supply, in order to explain why a particular industry is successful at that location.

sampling selecting a subset of a group or population in such a way that valid conclusions can be made about the whole set or population

A third way to make comparisons is between rows. This enables an understanding of which characteristics are found together or separately, or to what degree they might mix. For example, looking at common characteristics for two economically successful locations can show why they contribute to the locations' success.

A fourth option for a method of analysis is to make a comparison of columns. This allows the geographer to describe which locations are similar and which are very different. For instance, by analyzing locations where the weather data are the same, a geographer can classify climates that are similar. All of these analyses require the statistical techniques of correlation and regression (defining and characterizing relationships among data).

Optimization Problems Solved by Geographers

Although mathematics has become an essential tool of modern geography, it was also present in the geography of the nineteenth century. In 1826, Von Thünen collected data on land values in agricultural communities; he also collected data on how farmers used land. His data were centered on a town that was the main market for a region.

Von Thünen found that for each particular type of crop the costs of getting the produce to market was a product of the distance from town, r, the volume of the crop produced in a unit area of land, v, and the cost of transportation per unit of distance, c. If the crop sells at a price of p and the fixed costs of producing the crop are a, then the net profit is expressed as $R = (p - a)v - rcv$.

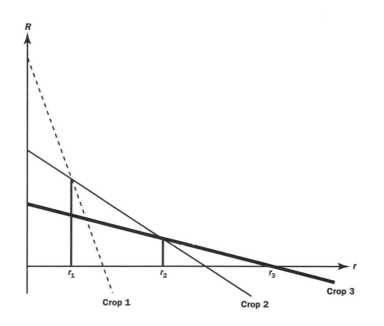

Von Thünen constructed graphs of profit R plotted against the distance from town, r for various crops. The figure above shows the graphs for three crops. Crop 1 produces the highest profit as long as it is inside a distance of r_1 of the market. Between a distance of r_1 and r_2 crop 2 is the most profitable, and between r_2 and r_3 crop 3 is the most profitable. At r_3 all three crops become unprofitable. Von Thünen suggested that the land around a market be used to reflect these rings, and that there should be no cultivation of these crops beyond r_3 at all, as there was no profit in farming at this distance (see below).

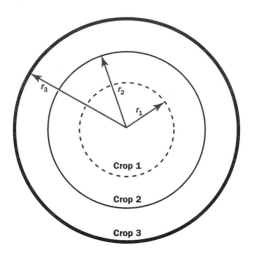

The modern equivalent of this geographical distribution model is the understanding of why the location of a shopping center or a factory affects each one's success or failure. From the geographical matrix the locations of various resources that are required by a manufacturing plant can be established. Given the locations of different raw materials, labor resources, and transportation of raw materials to the factory, the location for the optimum manufacturing plant can be calculated and compared to an existing plant.

A geographer's data can also be used to support or refute the location of a manufacturing plant at a particular location. However, this is only part of the solution, for once the goods have been manufactured they have to be distributed to market centers, and this has an associated cost that can affect the decision concerning a manufacturing plant's location. By weighting distances with regard to cost, an optimum location can be found by finding the equivalent of the center of gravity of the system.

In the location of a factory, one of the problems that has to be tackled is the distribution of the product to market. Here another branch of mathematics aids the analysis. Graphs and trees deal with the analysis of networks, and can be employed in finding solutions to this part of the problem. One of the classic problems of networks, the travelling salesman problem, is concerned with the most efficient route for a travelling salesman to take in order to cover all the customers. This is also the route that the supply trucks will be interested in following. The full understanding of this problem is still the object of mathematical research.

Calculus in Geography

A major problem of geography is the modeling of population change. Change in populations implies that geographers are interested in data that are time dependent. Therefore any data collection has to be repeated at various intervals, the most familiar way being the United States census that is required every 10 years by law.

The census gives data over long periods of time, but annual sampling is necessary in order to monitor more detailed changes. The data can then be matched to a mathematical model. The most common model for population growth results in the construction of a differential equation in which the change in population, with respect to time, varies directly with time and can be solved through calculus.

Calculus also helps model the way in which the profile of a hill develops. Another application of calculus gives a mathematical model of the freezing of water in a lake. If air above a lake maintains temperatures below the freezing point of water for a prolonged period of time, the thickness of the ice will continue to increase. The rate of advance of the ice depends on the rate at which heat can be carried away from the surface by convection currents in the water below the ice surface. The model leads to a **differential equation**.

Fractals and River Watersheds

The way in which rivers begin their life as a collection of small springs or gullies that collect rain and spill into brooks or streams has been better understood in recent times by the analysis offered by mathematics through **fractals**. In river systems, fractal scaling can be seen in the organization of the river network at various levels of observation; that is, they conform to the fractals first described by Benoit B. Mandelbrot. Research around 1990 described the scaling properties of the geometry of several river systems and a calculation was made of their fractal dimension.

Probability and the Layout of Villages

Probability leads to an understanding of the way villages develop over a long period of time, given that there has been no deliberate planning. The model requires the description of two objects, a closed cell with an entrance, and an open cell (see figure below).

differential equation an equation that expresses the relationship between two variables that change in respect to each other, expressed in terms of the rate of change

fractal a type of geometric figure possessing the properties of self-similarity (any part resembles a larger or smaller part at any scale) and a measure that increases without bound as the unit of measure approaches zero

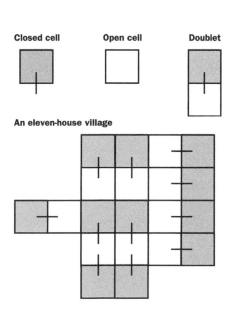

These cells are joined together to form a doublet so that the entrance always faces onto an open cell—corresponding to a house opening out onto the public space. In the modeling process, the doublets are allowed to accumulate with the condition that each new doublet that joins the village does so with its open cell having at least one edge common with another open cell. Which open cell a new doublet joins is chosen at random. This modeling process has been successful in describing a number of old villages in which town planning did not influence the layout. SEE ALSO CARTOGRAPHER; FRACTALS; GLOBAL POSITIONING SYSTEM; MANDELBROT, BENOIT B.; MAPS AND MAPMAKING; PROBABILITY, THEORETICAL.

Phillip Nissen

Bibliography

Haining, Robert. *Spatial Data Analysis in the Social and Environmental Sciences.* Cambridge, U.K.: Cambridge University Press, 1993.

Hillier, B., and J. Hanson. *The Social Logic of Space.* Cambridge, U.K.: Cambridge University Press, 1984

Rodriguez-Iturbe, Ignacio, and Andrea Rinaldo. *Fractal River Basins: Chance and Self-Organization.* Cambridge, U.K.: Cambridge University Press, 1997.

Wilson, A.G., and M. J. Kirby. *Mathematics for Geographers and Planners.* Oxford, U.K.: Clarendon Press, 1975.

Geometry Software, Dynamic

Tucked in with the business news of the day was this headline from the December 9, 1996 issue of *The Wall Street Journal* newspaper: "Teen Math Whizzes Go Euclid One Better." High-schoolers David Goldenheim and Daniel Litchfield had revisited a 2,000-year old challenge from the Greek mathematician Euclid and solved it in a new way. Given an arbitrary segment, the freshmen found a geometric recipe for dividing its length into any number of equal parts. The mathematics community hailed the students' work as "elegant" and "significant."

Goldenheim and Litchfield devised their segment-splitting technique through old-fashioned conjecturing and reasoning. Yet there was nothing traditional about their geometric tools of choice. The duo conducted their experiments without the aid of a compass or even a ruler. Instead, they turned to technology and a new breed of computer software programs known collectively as "dynamic geometry."

At first glance, the word "dynamic" might sound like an odd way to describe geometry. The dictionary defines "dynamic" as "characterized by vigorous activity and producing or undergoing change," but the images in geometry textbooks are immobile, forever frozen in place.

Consider a picture of a triangle. Any illustration represents a particular triangle with specific side lengths and angle measures. Triangles, however, can be small, large, narrow, or wide. No single image captures this generality.

By contrast, a triangle drawn with dynamic geometry software possesses more freedom. With a click and a drag of the mouse, you can tug a corner of the triangle and watch the object adjust before your eyes. The shape remains triangular, but its sides and angles grow and shrink in a smooth, con-

tinuous motion. The effect is similar to an animated movie, only here you are the one controlling the movement.

In science, you devise experiments and then test your theories. Mathematics classes often have fostered a more hands-off approach: textbooks state what to prove. With dynamic geometry software, mathematics regains its rightful place as a laboratory science. Any object constructed on the screen allows you to roll up your sleeves and search for patterns.

Suppose you draw an arbitrary quadrilateral, find the midpoints of its four sides, and then connect these points to their adjacent partners (see the leftmost picture below). By doing so, you form a new quadrilateral (represented by dashed segments) nested inside the original. Measuring its sides and angles with the software reveals a surprise. Opposite sides are equal in length and parallel—the very qualities of a parallelogram. A coincidence?

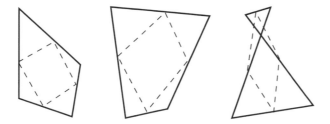

A mouse tug to any corner of the outer quadrilateral reconfigures the construction into new positions. Within seconds, you can view hundreds of quadrilaterals, each with their midpoints connected. In every one, the dashed quadrilateral remains a parallelogram. Even a twisted pretzel shape cannot disturb the parallel sides (see the rightmost picture). Such visual evidence is quite compelling; it is not a watertight proof, and it does not explain why we should expect to see a parallelogram, but it is a useful start.

A Brief History

As director of Swarthmore College's Visual Geometry Project, Eugene Klotz was among the founders of the dynamic geometry movement. His original goals for geometry software were relatively modest. Bothered by the cumbersome nature of ruler-and-compass constructions, Klotz imagined a software package that would make it easier to draw shapes like lines and circles. He comments:

> Basic motor skills were keeping students from being able to draw. I thought we needed to have something that allowed people to make the basic constructions. So to me, our software was a drawing tool. You'd make a geometric drawing that was precise and accurate, and scroll over the page to see what was going on.

This vision of geometry software was a non-interactive one: once drawn, objects on the screen could not be reshaped via mouse dragging. The missing "dynamic" element was to come from a student, Nicholas Jackiw, whom Klotz advised during Jackiw's freshman year at Swarthmore.

Jackiw was perhaps an unlikely choice for a mathematics project. He had steered away from mathematics in high school and college, focusing instead on English and computer science. Still, when Jackiw viewed Klotz's geometry proposal, he sensed something was missing. Jackiw's interest in programming computer games provided an unexpected source of inspiration. If a computer game could immerse players in an interactive world, then why not geometry? Jackiw says:

> It's the video game aspect that gives me my sense of interactivity when dealing with geometry . . . Looking at the input devices of video games is a tremendously educational experience. In the old days, you had games with very interesting controls that were highly specific. . .The video game Tempest had a marvelous input device. . .The types of games they would write to suit this bizarre and unique device were always interesting experiments in what does this hand motion transport you to in your imagination. I wanted to have a good feel in all of my games.

The mouse of a Macintosh computer was not an ideal input device for games, but it was suitable for virtual environments where objects could be dragged. The illustration program MacDraw, in particular, contained the rudimentary features of dynamic geometry, as one could draw and move a segment with the mouse and change its length. When Jackiw took the basic premise of MacDraw and applied it (with considerable reworking) to geometry, Klotz found the results striking:

> I remember how shocked I was when I first saw it. Jackiw had played with a Macintosh long enough to know that you should be able to drag the vertex or a side of a triangle and protrude the figure. I was flabbergasted. I mean, he made the connection, and I didn't.

One of the earliest programs to showcase the graphical capabilities of the computer was Ivan Sutherland's "Sketchpad." A hand-held light pen allowed the user to draw and manipulate points, line segments, and arcs on a cathode ray tube monitor. In honor of Sutherland's work, Klotz named their new program, "The Geometer's Sketchpad." The product received its commercial release in the spring of 1991.

Interestingly, the Swarthmore group was not alone in its thinking. Working in France, Jean-Marie Laborde and his programming team simultaneously developed the software package Cabri Geometry, which also featured dynamic movement. Initially, neither the Sketchpad nor Cabri people knew of the other's existence. When Laborde and Klotz finally met, they marveled at the similarities in their software. Klotz says:

> We had just that Fall got into our dragging bit, and were very proud of what we had. We thought, God, people are going to really love this. But Cabri had scooped us, and we had scooped them. It was one of these, you know, just amazing things where . . . maybe you can sort out the exact moment, maybe there was a passing meteor, or something.

Student Exploration

Dynamic geometry software programs are great for learning geometry, and they can also be fun. The top picture below shows two circles and a segment AB connecting them. As points A and B spin around their respective circles, what path does point M, the midpoint of segment AB, trace? Dynamic geometry makes this investigation simple to perform. The result, shown in the lower picture below, is an attractive spiral.

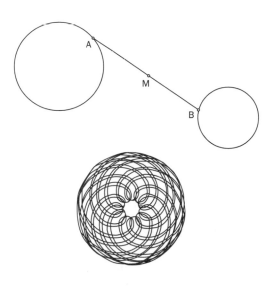

Other applications of the software display its versatility. Students can build a working clock, model planetary motion, create a spinning Ferris Wheel, and investigate algebra in a geometric way.

Since words alone cannot convey the experience of using dynamic geometry software, students can try programs themselves. Free demonstration copies of various software programs are available on the Internet. SEE ALSO COMPUTER-AIDED DESIGN; COMPUTER SIMULATIONS.

Daniel Scher

Internet Resources

Cabri Geometry. <http://www-cabri.imag.fr/index-e.html>.

The Geometer's Sketchpad. Key Curriculum Press. <http://www.keypress.com>.

Geometry, Spherical

Spherical geometry is the three-dimensional study of geometry on the surface of a sphere. It is the spherical equivalent of two-dimensional planar geometry, the study of geometry on the surface of a plane. A real-life approximation of a sphere is the planet Earth—not its interior, but just its surface. (Earth is more accurately called an "oblate spheroid" because it is slightly flattened at the ends of its axis of rotation, the North and South Poles.) The surface of a sphere together with its interior points is usually referred to as the spherical region; however, spherical geometry generally refers only to the surface of a sphere.

As seen in the figure on the next page, a sphere is a set of points in three-dimensional space equidistant from a point O called the center of the sphere. The line segment from point O (at the center of the sphere) to point P (on the surface of the sphere) is called the radius r of the sphere, and the radius r extended straight through the sphere's center with ends on opposite points of the surface is called the diameter d of the sphere (with a value of $2r$;

that is, two times the value of the radius). As an example, the line that connects the North Pole and the South Pole on Earth is considered a diameter*.

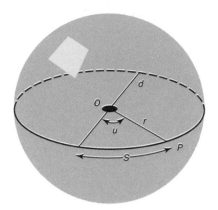

An infinite line that intersects a sphere at one point only is called a tangent line. An infinite plane can also intersect a sphere at a single point on its surface. When this is the case the plane is also considered tangent to the sphere at that point of intersection. For example, if a basketball were lying on the floor, the floor would represent a tangent plane because it intersects the ball's surface (the sphere) at only one point.

Great and Small Circles

The shortest path between two points on a plane is a straight line. However, on the surface of a sphere there are no straight lines. Instead, the shortest distance between any two points on a sphere is a segment of a circle. To see why this is so, consider that a plane can intersect a sphere at more than one point. Whenever this is the case, the intersection results in a circle. A great circle is defined to be the intersection of a sphere with a plane that passes through the center of the sphere. For example, see the circle containing points C and D in the illustration below. Similar to a straight line on a plane, the shortest path between two points on the surface of a sphere is the arc of a great circle passing through the two points.

The size of the circle of intersection will be largest when the plane passes through the center of the sphere, as is the case for a great circle. If the plane does not contain the center of the sphere, its intersection with the sphere is known as a small circle. For example, see the circle containing points A and B in the illustration below.

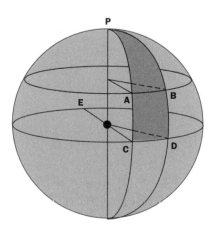

As a real-world example, assume a cabbage is a sphere, and is cut exactly in half. The slice goes through the cabbage's center, forming a great circle. However, if the slice is off-centered, then the cabbage is cut into two unequal pieces, having formed a small circle at the cut.

Spherical Triangles

Consider a circle of radius r. A portion of the circle's circumference is referred to as an arc length, and is denoted by the letter s. The first illustration of this article shows a circle of radius r and arc length s. The angle θ is defined as $\theta = \frac{s}{r}$. Rearranging this equation in terms of s yields $s = \theta r$. So the arc length s of a great circle is equal to the radius r of the sphere times the angle **subtended** by that arc length.

subtend to extend past and mark off a chord or arc

Connecting three nonlinear points on a plane by drawing straight lines using the shortest possible route between the points forms a triangle. By analogy, to connect three points on the surface of a sphere using the shortest possible route, draw three arcs of great circles to create a spherical triangle. A triangle drawn on the surface of a sphere is only a spherical triangle if it has all of the following properties:

(1) the three sides are all arcs of great circles;

(2) any two sides, summed together, is greater than the third side;

(3) the sum of the three interior angles is greater than 180°, and

(4) each spherical angle is less than 180°.

In the second illustration of the article, triangle PAB is not a spherical triangle (because side AB is an arc of a small circle), but triangle PCD is a spherical triangle (because side CD is an arc of a great circle).

The left portion of the figure directly below demonstrates how a spherical triangle can be formed by three intersecting great circles with arcs of length (a,b,c) and vertex angles of (A,B,C).

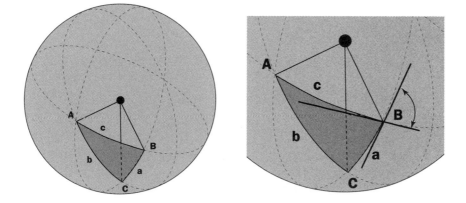

The right portion of the figure directly above demonstrates that the angle between two sides of a spherical triangle is defined as the angle between the tangents to the two great circle arcs for vertex angle B.

The above illustration also shows that the arc lengths (a,b,c) and vertex angles (A,B,C) of the spherical triangle are related by the following rules for spherical triangles.

sine if a unit circle is drawn with its center at the origin and a line segment is drawn from the origin at angle (so that the line segment intersects the circle at (x, y), then y is the sine of θ

cosine if a unit circle is drawn with its center at the origin and a line segment is drawn from the origin at angle θ so that the line segment intersects the circle at (x, y), then x is the cosine of θ

Sine Rule: $\left(\frac{\sin a}{\sin A}\right) = \left(\frac{\sin b}{\sin B}\right) = \left(\frac{\sin c}{\sin C}\right)$

Cosine Rule: $\cos a = (\cos b \cos c) + (\sin b \sin c \cos A)$.

Spherical Geometry in Navigation

Spherical geometry can be used for the practical purpose of navigation by looking at the measurement of position and distance on the surface of Earth. The rotation of Earth defines a coordinate system for the surface of Earth. The two points where the rotational axis meets the surface of Earth are known as the North Pole and the South Pole, and the great circle perpendicular to the rotation axis and lying halfway between the poles is known as the equator. Small circles that lie parallel to the equator are known as parallels. Great circles that pass through the two poles are known as meridians.

Measuring Latitude and Longitude. The two coordinates of latitude and longitude can define any point on the surface of Earth, as is demonstrated within the diagram below. Great circles become very important to navigation because a segment along a great circle provides the shortest distance between two points on a sphere. Therefore, the shortest travel-time can be achieved by traveling along a great circle.

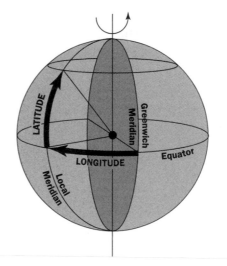

The longitude of a point is measured east or west along the equator, and its value is the angular distance between the local meridian passing through the point and the Greenwich meridian (which passes through the Royal Greenwich Observatory in London, England). Because Earth is rotating, it is possible to express longitude in time units as well as angular units. Earth rotates by 360° in 24 hours. Hence, Earth rotates 15° of longitude in 1 hour, and 1° of longitude in 4 minutes.

The latitude of a point is the angular distance north or south of the equator, measured along the meridian, or line of longitude, passing through the point.

Measuring Nautical Miles.   Distance on the surface of Earth is usually measured in nautical miles, where 1 nautical mile (nmi) is defined as the distance subtending an angle of 1 minute of arc at the center of Earth. Since there are 60 minutes of arc in a degree, there are approximately 60 nautical miles in 1 degree of Earth's surface. A speed of 1 nautical mile per hour (nmph) is known as 1 knot and is the unit in which the speed of a boat or an aircraft is usually measured.

A Case Study in Measurement.   As noted earlier, Earth is not a perfect sphere, so the actual measurement of position and distance on the surface of Earth is more complicated than described here. But Earth is very nearly a true sphere, and for our purposes this demonstration is still valid.

The terms and concepts that have been developed can be applied to a real-world example. Consider a voyage from Washington, D.C. ("W" in diagram below) to Quito, Ecuador ("Q" in diagram below), which is nearly on the equator at 0° latitude, 77° West longitude. The latitude and longitude of Washington, D.C. is about 37° North latitude, 77° West longitude. If the entire voyage from Washington, D.C. to Quito (on the equator) is along the great circle of longitude 77°, we can use the equation $s = \theta r$ to find the distance s that the airplane travels from Washington D.C. to Quito.

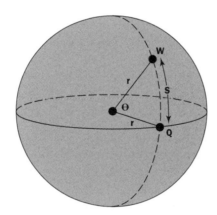

For this example, $\theta = 37°$ (the angle between W and Q). Knowing that 2π **radians** equals 360° (one complete revolution around a great circle), we now convert the angle from degrees to radians: $(37°)(\frac{2\pi \text{ radians}}{360°}) = 0.628$ radians. Denoting the radius of Earth as r, we use the "arc-length" equation developed earlier, that is $s = \theta r$, to compute the arc length between Washington, D.C. and Quito.

Placing the values of $\theta = 0.628$ radians and $r = 3{,}443$ nautical miles (nmi) (the average radius-value for Earth) into the equation yields: $s = \theta r = (0.628 \text{ rad} \times 3{,}443 \text{ nmi}) = 2{,}163$ nmi. Therefore, along the arc of the great circle of longitude 77°, from Washington D.C. to Quito, Ecuador, our trip covers a distance of 2,163 nmi. SEE ALSO TRIANGLES; TRIGONOMETRY.

William Arthur Atkins (with Philip Edward Koth)

radian an angle measure approximately equal to 57.3°, it is the angle that subtends an arc of a circle equal to one radius

Bibliography

Abbott, P. *Geometry (Teach Yourself Series)*. London, U.K.: Hodder and Stoughton, 1982.

Henderson, Kenneth B., Robert E. Pingry, and George A. Robinson. *Modern Geometry: Its Structure and Function.* New York: Webster Division, McGraw-Hill Book Company, 1962.

Ringenberg, Lawrence A., and Richard S. Presser. *Geometry.* New York: Benziger, Inc. with John Wiley & Sons, 1971.

Selby, Peter H. *Geometry & Trigonometry for Calculus.* New York: John Wiley & Sons, 1975.

Ulrich, James F., Fred F. Czarnec, and Dorothy L. Guilbault, *Geometry.* New York: Harcourt Brace, 1978.

Internet Resources

The Geometry of the Sphere. Mathematics Department at Rice University, Houston, Texas. <http://math.rice.edu/~pcmi/sphere/>.

Spherical Geometry. Mathematics Department at the University of North Carolina at Charlotte. <http://www.math.uncc.edu/~droyster/math3181/notes/hyprgeom/node5.html#SECTION00500000000000000000>.

Geometry, Tools of

Plane (or Euclidean) geometry is the branch of mathematics that studies figures (such as points, lines, and angles) constructed only with the use of the straightedge and the compass. It is primarily concerned with such problems as determining the areas and diameters of two-dimensional figures. To determine geometric designs four important tools of geometry—compass, straightedge, protractor, and ruler—are used. Technically a true geometric construction with Euclidian tools, originally used by the ancient Greeks, uses only a compass or a straightedge. The ruler and protractor were later inventions. Today, the study of geometry is an essential part of the training of such professionals as mathematicians, engineers, physicists, architects, and draftspersons.

As early as 2000 B.C.E. geometers were concerned with such problems as measuring the sizes of fields and irrigation systems, and laying out accurate right angles for corners of buildings and monuments. Greek mathematician Euclid (c. 300 B.C.E.) and other geometers formalized the process of building geometrical figures with the use of specific tools. The ancient Greeks introduced construction problems that required a certain line or figure to be constructed by the use of the straightedge and compass alone. Simple examples are the construction of a line that will be twice as long as another line, or of a line that will divide a given angle into two equal angles.

Basic Tools

Straightedge.   A straightedge is a geometric tool used to construct straight lines. It contains no marks. As the name says, it is a "straight edge." A ruler can be used as a straightedge by simply ignoring the measuring marks on it.

Ruler.   A ruler is a geometric tool used to measure the length of a line segment. A ruler is basically a straightedge with marks usually used for measuring either inches or centimeters. To use a ruler, place the zero mark on the point to begin the measurement. To stop measuring, look at the mark on the ruler that lies over the point at which the measurement is to end.

Compass. A compass is a V-shaped tool used to construct circles or arcs of circles. (See sketch below on left.) One side of the "V" holds a pencil and the other side is a point. The point anchors the compass at one location on the paper as the tool is turned so the pencil can trace circles, arcs, and angles. A compass is adjustable: the setting determines how far away from the point the arc would be located. Once the user determines the correct setting the compass is turned around its anchoring point so that the pencil creates a mark, an arc, or a full circle.

Protractor. A protractor is a geometric tool in the shape of a semicircular disk, as shown above on the right. It is used to measure the size of an angle in degrees—usually from 0 to 180 degrees. To use a protractor, lay the protractor on the angle to be measured. There will be a mark on the bottom of the protractor (the straight edge of it) indicating its middle. Place this mark over the origin of the angle, and align the straight edge of the protractor with one side of the angle. Where the other side of the angle intersects the protractor there will be a mark with a number next to it. This measurement is the measure of the angle.

Solving Construction Problems

Construction problems are generally solved by following six steps.

1. Provide a general statement of the problem that describes what is to be constructed.

2. Draw a figure representing the given parts.

3. Provide a statement of what is given in step 2.

4. Provide a specific statement of the result to be obtained.

5. Develop the construction, with a description (reason) for each step.

6. Provide a statement proving that the desired result was obtained.

As an example using a straightedge: Given line segments a and b, construct the line segment $c = a + 2b$.

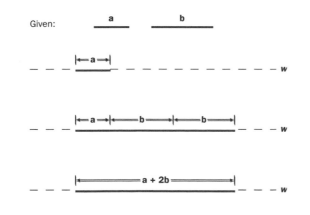

This example is solved as follows. On working line w, draw a line segment equal to the length of line segment a. At the right end of a draw a line segment equal to length of line segment b. At the right end of line segment $a + b$, draw a second line segment equal to length of b. The resulting line segment is the desired line segment $c = a + b + b = a + 2b$.

As an example of using a compass: Construct an angle equal to the given figure $\angle BAC$ with line segments AB and AC.

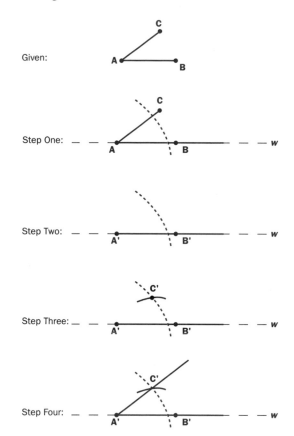

This example is solved as follows. In Step One, place the compass pivot point at A and adjust the compass width to be between A and B, then construct an arc that intercepts both line segments AB and AC. Leaving the compass width unchanged, draw a line **w** and place the pivot point at an arbitrary point A'. Pivot the compass from line **w**, forming an arc like in Step One (as shown in Step Two). The arc's intersection with line **w** is denoted B'.

Referring to Step One, now adjust the compass width to equal the distance between the arc's intersection with AB and AC. With this width, move the compass down to Step Two, place the pivot point at B'; and make an arc that intersects with the first arc, as in Step Three. The line segments $A'C'$ and and $A'B'$, as shown in Step Four, complete the new angle $\angle B'A'C'$ that is equal to the original angle $\angle BAC$.

William Arthur Atkins (with Philip Edward Koth)

Bibliography

Boyer, Carl B. *A History of Mathematics*, 2nd ed. New York: John Wiley & Sons, 1991.

Henderson, Kenneth B., Robert E. Pingry, and George A. Robinson. *Modern Geometry: Its Structure and Function*. New York: Webster Division, McGraw-Hill, 1962.

Ulrich, James F., Fred F. Czarnec, and Dorothy L. Guilbault. *Geometry*. New York: Harcourt Brace, 1978.

Germain, Sophie

French Mathematician
1776–1831

Sophie Germain is remembered for her work in the theory of numbers and in mathematical physics. Germain was born in Paris to a father who was a wealthy silk merchant. She educated herself by studying books in her father's library, including the works of Sir Isaac Newton and the writings of mathematician Leonhard Euler.

When the École Polytechnique opened in 1794, even though women were not allowed to attend as regular students, Germain obtained lecture notes for courses and submitted papers using the pseudonym M. LeBlanc. One of the instructors, noted scientist Joseph-Louis Lagrange, became her mentor.

Sophie Germain's foundational work on Fermat's Last Theorem stood unmatched for more than 100 years.

In 1804 Germain began to correspond with German mathematician Carl Friedrich Gauss, sending him discoveries she made in number theory. Among these was a limited proof of Fermat's Last Theorem, her best known contribution to mathematics. This theorem was finally proved in 1994 using her approach. Germain also corresponded with mathematician Adrien Marie Legendre, who used her suggestions in one of his publications.

In mathematical physics, Germain is known for her work in acoustics and elasticity. She won a prize from the French Academy of Sciences in 1816 for the development of mathematical models for the vibration of elastic surfaces. Subsequently, she was invited to attend sessions of the Academy of Sciences and the Institut de France, but because she was a woman, she could never join either group. SEE ALSO EULER, LEONHARD; FERMAT'S LAST THEOREM; NEWTON, SIR ISAAC.

J. William Moncrief

Bibliography

Gray, Mary W. "Sophie Germain (1776–1831)," in *Women of Mathematics*. Edited by Louise S. Grinstein and Paul J. Campbell. New York: Greenwood Press, 1987.

Ogilvie, Marilyn Bailey. *Women in Science*. Cambridge, MA: MIT Press, 1986.

Global Positioning System

Most people have been lost at one time or another, but what if it were possible to know where you are, anywhere on Earth, 24 hours a day? The Global Positioning System (GPS) can give that information, and it is free to anyone with the proper equipment and a basic knowledge of mathematics.

In the 1980s, the U. S. Department of Defense designed GPS to provide the military with accurate, round-the-clock positional information. Twenty-seven satellites orbiting over 10,000 miles above Earth regularly send information back to Earth. A small piece of equipment, called a GPS receiver, uses this information to compute its position to within a few yards. GPS receivers used for surveying can find positions to within less than one centimeter.

The "constellation" of satellites above the Earth is constantly changing; each orbits Earth twice a day. At any given time there are enough satellite

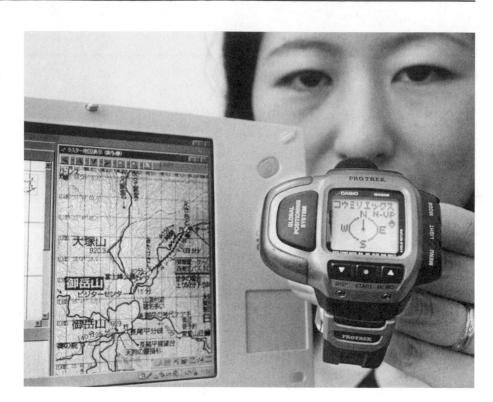

This 84-gram wristwatch receives transmissions from twenty-seven Earth-orbiting Global Positioning System (GPS) satellites. The wearer's location can be precisely determined and portrayed on the digital map of a computer screen.

signals to accurately locate oneself in three dimensions: latitude, longitude, and elevation.

GPS is rapidly becoming a common technology, but it is still a mathematical wonder. Ancient sailors looked to the heavens to estimate their position in the vast oceans. Modern sailors also look to the sky for information, but the modern positioning information they receive is so accurate that any errors are less than the width of the pencil they use to mark their map.

Triangulation

The basic concept of GPS is triangulation. Suppose a person is standing in a valley surrounded by several towering mountain peaks. By using a compass to measure the direction to each peak, this person could locate his or her exact location on a map by using triangulation. After writing down the three measurements (remembering that there are 360 degrees in a circle), a line should be drawn from each peak in the opposite direction just measured.

Then 180 degrees is added or subtracted so that the direction the lines are drawn from each peak will fall between 0 and 360 degrees. For example, if one of the measurements is 270 degrees to peak A, the line from peak A back to the person's position would be 90 degrees. The point at which the three lines intersect is the point at which the person is standing.

The GPS satellites are like mountain peaks; they are known points in space from which lines can be drawn in order to specify a location. Each satellite transmits a radio signal that can be received on Earth and recognized by a GPS receiver. Rather than measure direction, however, a GPS receiver uses the time it takes for each satellite's beacon to reach it and calculates a distance.

Because radio waves travel at the speed of light, the receiver divides the time the signal takes to reach the receiver by the speed of light (186,000 miles per second) and determines the distance. These distances can be used to form spheres around the satellites that will intersect at a specific position just as the lines drawn from the mountain peaks will intersect at a specific position.

Understanding GPS Measurements

Assume a GPS receiver is sitting in Nebraska. Once activated it begins to collect signals from GPS satellites 1, 2, 3, 4, 5, and 6. The distance to each satellite can be determined using the distance formula $d = rt$ (distance, d, equals rate, r, multiplied by time, t, or distance equals velocity multiplied by time). Although all the satellites are 10,900 miles from the surface of the Earth, the distances to each one will vary according to its position in orbit. For example, all the street lights in a city may be 15 feet in the air but they are not all 15 feet from a specific point in the city.

The formula for determining these distances may be simple, but the calculations themselves are anything but simple. The satellites must be precisely timed so that each is synchronized with the other satellites in the constellation and with base stations on Earth. Although each satellite will be at a different distance from a particular point, the time it takes to cover those distances at the speed of light does not seem significant. In order to calculate distance, however, this time is significant to the GPS receiver.

Consider that a signal 10,900 miles from a receiver reaches that receiver in 0.058602 seconds. A signal 10,926 miles away, however, reaches the receiver in 0.0587419 seconds. A 26-mile difference translates into less than fourteen one hundred-thousandths (0.00014) of a second. Clearly, the GPS receiver has some very precise mathematics to work with, further complicated by the fact that the satellites are always moving.

After making these complex measurements, the distance to each satellite will be the hypotenuse of a right triangle created by the receiver's position, the satellite's position, and the position on Earth directly under the satellite. Once these distances are known, spheres can be created surrounding each satellite. Each sphere has a radius equal to the computed distance between the satellite and the receiver. The first sphere, around satellite 1, will have an infinite number of points along its surface so the receiver's position could fall anywhere on that sphere, including points in outer space.

Next, the sphere around satellite 2 is introduced, and the two spheres create an intersection that forms a circle. Now the GPS receiver could be anywhere on that circle, even points in space that, of course, it is not occupying. The third sphere, around satellite 3, intersects the first two spheres and limits the receiver's possible position to two points. The receiver is located at one of the two points. The other point is either in the air above the receiver or in the ground directly below the receiver. If the altitude of the receiver is known, then it is possible to determine which one of the two points is correct. The sphere around satellite number 4 will also reduce the two points to only one. It is amazing, yet basically simple, how one receiver and four satellites can reduce an infinite number of possible locations to only one.

APPLICATIONS OF GPS

Vehicle tracking is one of the fastest-growing GPS applications. GPS-equipped fleet vehicles, public transportation systems, delivery trucks, and courier services use receivers to monitor their locations. Many public service units are using GPS to determine the police car, fire truck, or ambulance nearest to an emergency.

Mapping and surveying companies use GPS extensively. GPS-equipped balloons are monitoring holes in the ozone layer. Buoys tracking major oil spills transmit data using GPS.

These are just a few examples. New applications will continue to be created as GPS technology continues to evolve.

Simulating GPS. To simulate the process of the Global Positioning System all that is needed is some string, scissors, tape, several coins, and four stationary points (the corners of a room will work). At any three-dimensional point in the room (on a desk, for example) a coin should be placed. The end of the string should then be taped into the corner of the room, with the other end pulled to the coin, cut, and then placed back in the corner. This process is repeated for the remaining three corners, and the extra coins are placed elsewhere in the room.

During this preparation, a volunteer waits outside the room. The volunteer should then enter the room and be alerted to the availability of the strings. The volunteer can then start pulling the cut ends of the string outward from the corners beginning with any two. By adding the third and fourth strings and finding where they all intersect, the volunteer should be able to eliminate all the extra coins and find the original coin. This is how GPS works in its most basic form.

Advantages and Disadvantages of GPS

Atmospheric inconsistencies can create inaccuracies in the positions computed by a GPS. Additionally, GPS is a "line of sight" system. Although a user cannot actually see the satellites in space, he or she does need an unobstructed view of the sky in order to utilize GPS. This poses serious challenges to those who choose to use GPS in canyons, cities, or other situations where large, solid objects mask out portions of the sky. When working where obstructions exist, careful planning must be done to ensure enough satellites are in "in view" for proper positioning.

Fortunately, GPS has a built-in feature, the almanac, to aid in identifying the location of satellites. Each satellite "knows" the location and direction of every other satellite. Along with the signal used to provide positions, satellites also transmit the almanac to a GPS receiver. Common GPS planning software can use the almanac to plot the entire constellation of satellites so users can plan ahead for their needs.

For example, if one needed to work in a canyon, planning software may indicate the only feasible time would be from noon until 2:00 P.M. Only during that time will the receiver have an unobstructed path to a sufficient number of satellites, all very high above the horizon, from within the canyon. SEE ALSO FLIGHT, MEASUREMENTS OF; MAPS AND MAPMAKING; NAVIGATION.

Elizabeth Sweeney

Internet Resources

GPS Primer. The Aerospace Corporation. <http://www.aero.org/publications/GPSPRIMER>.

Golden Section

To understand what constitutes a golden section, consider the top line segment shown on the next page. The line segment has three of its points marked. Point *P* partitions the line segment *AB* into two smaller segments:

from left endpoint *A* to point *P* (*AP*), and from *P* to right endpoint *B* (*PB*). The line segments *AP* and *PB* are also shown individually.

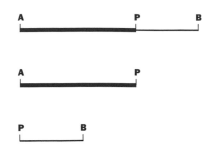

A "golden ratio" can now be formed as the ratio of one line segment to another line segment. Point *P* divides the entire line segment *AB* into a golden section if the following equation is valid:

$$AP/AB = PB/AP.$$

In other words, the length of line segment *AP* divided by the length of the entire line segment *AB* is a ratio, or number, and that number is the same as the ratio of the shortest line segment *PB* and the segment *AP*. It turns out that these ratios are equal to the **irrational number** 0.61803. . .; that is:

$$AP/AB = PB/AP = 0.61803 \ldots$$

Note that the decimal places continue indefinitely. The number 0.61803. . .is called the golden ratio or golden number, whereas the term "golden section" refers to the line segments formed by a point, such as *P*, whose resulting ratio is the golden number.

irrational number a real number that cannot be written as a fraction of the form *a*/*b*, where *a* and *b* are both integers and *b* is not 0

Significance of the Golden Ratio

The golden section and the golden ratio are important to mathematics, art, and architecture. The construction of the golden section goes back at least as far as the ancient Greeks, to the Pythagoreans (ca. 550 B.C.E.–300 B.C.E.). The Pythagoreans believed that numbers were the basis of nature and man, and therefore number relationships like the golden ratio were of utmost importance.

Besides line segments, the golden ratio also appears in many geometric figures. For example, a rectangle is said to be in golden section if its width and length are in the golden ratio (that is, if the width divided by the length equals 0.61803. . .).

Some scholars believe that various temples of the ancient Greeks, like the Parthenon in Athens, were purposefully produced with various dimensions in the golden ratio. Many of the artists and architects of the Renaissance period are believed to have incorporated the golden ratio into their paintings, sculptures, and monuments. A prime example is Leonardo da Vinci (1452–1519), who extensively used golden ratios (or their approximations) in his paintings. In Leonardo's famous drawing "Vitruvian Man," the distance ratio from the top of the head to navel, and from the navel to the soles of his feet approximates the golden ratio.

Many people feel that geometric forms and figures incorporating the golden ratio are more beautiful than other forms. Psychological studies pur-

ALTERNATIVE DEFINITION OF GOLDEN SECTION

Some dictionaries and textbooks define golden section (and number) as the inverse of the definition shown in this article. The formula then becomes (again referring to line segment *AB*) *AB*/*AP* = *AP*/*PB* = 1.61803 . . . .

Sometimes the larger value is denoted by the Greek letter "Phi" (i.e., Phi = 1.61803. . .) while the smaller value of the golden number is denoted by a "small" phi (i.e., phi = 0.61803. . .). Note that Phi = 1 + phi.

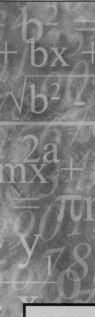

portedly show that people find golden-ratio rectangles more appealing than rectangles of other proportions. SEE ALSO ARCHITECTURE; LEONARDO DA VINCI; NUMBERS, FORBIDDEN AND SUPERSTITIOUS; PYTHAGORAS.

Philip Edward Koth (with William Arthur Atkins)

Bibliography

Eves, Howard. *An Introduction to the History of Mathematics*, 4th ed. New York: Holt, Rinehart and Winston, 1976.

Internet Resources

The Golden Section Ratio: Phi. Department of Computing, University of Surrey, United Kingdom. <http://www.mcs.surrey.ac.uk/Personal/R.Knott/Fibonacci/phi.html>.

Grades, Highway

The term "grade" is used in several different ways with respect to roads and highways. The "sub-grade" lies beneath a roadway and is used as a supporting base. "Grading" a road means to smooth out the roadbed with earth-moving equipment during the construction phase. In this article, the grade of a road is defined as a measure of the road's steepness as it rises and falls along its route. In other words, it is the magnitude of its incline or slope.

The grade of a highway is a measure of its incline or slope. The amount of grade indicates how much the highway is inclined from the horizontal. For example, if a section of road is perfectly flat and level, then its grade along that section is zero. However, if the section is very steep, then the grade along that section will be expressed as a number, usually a percentage, such as 10 percent.

The illustration below shows a highway in profile (from the side). Notice that a right triangle has been constructed in the diagram. The elevation, or height, of the highway increases in the sketch when moving from left to right. The bottom of the triangle is the horizontal distance this section of highway covers. This horizontal distance, sometimes called the "run" of the highway, indicates how far a vehicle would travel on the road if it were level. However, it is apparent that the road is not level but rises from left to right. This "rise" is a measure of how much higher a vehicle is after driving from left to right along the road.

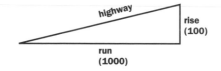

To calculate the grade of a section of highway, divide the rise (height increase) by the run (horizontal distance). This equation, used to calculate the ratio of rise-to-run for highway grades, is the same ratio as the slope "y/x" encountered in a **Cartesian coordinate system**. In the example above, the rise of the highway section is 100 feet, while the run is 1,000 feet. The resulting grade is thus 100 feet divided by 1,000 feet, or 0.1.

Highway grades are usually expressed as a percentage. Any number represented in decimal form can be converted to a percentage by multiplying

---

WHAT DEFINES A HIGHWAY?

A highway is a road with a hard surface, such as asphalt or concrete, that is open for the general public to drive upon. Highways connect towns, cities and industrial areas to one another. Most highways follow the "lay of the land." In other words, highways must rise and fall as hills and valleys are encountered.

Cartesian coordinate system a way of measuring the positions of points in a plane using two perpendicular lines as axes

that number by 100. Consequently, a highway grade of 0.1 is referred to as a "10 percent grade" because 0.1 times 100 equals 10 percent. The highway grade for a section of highway that has a rise of 1 kilometer and a run of 8 kilometers is $\frac{1}{8}$, or 0.125. To convert the highway grade into a percentage, multiply 0.125 by 100, which results in a grade of 12.5 percent.

Applications of Grade

When a new highway or road is being planned, its grade over its various sections is one of the key aspects that must be determined in advance. The grade of the road is very important for the safety of the motorists who will be using it. Most of us have experienced how a rolling bicycle has a tendency to pick up speed as it goes downhill, and how when going uphill the bicycle will slow down unless the cyclist pedals harder. The same situation must be considered when constructing modern highways.

If a grade is too steep, vehicle operators must use excessive braking when going downhill. In contrast, vehicle operators going uphill will have to slow down severely, possibly affecting traffic flow adversely. Grades are of great concern for vehicles carrying or pulling heavy loads, like semi-tractor trailers, or a family car pulling a camper or boat. To avoid these problems the highway engineers who plan and design highways pay close attention to road grades, and design into the highway's construction smaller grades rather than larger ones.

The concept of highway grades can also be applied to other types of pathways that are used by people or vehicles. For instance, residential roads are constructed to have a slight grade from the curb to the center of the road. A grade of 1 percent is considered the minimum required for proper drainage during a rainstorm. For a run of 10 feet, a 1 percent grade means one-tenth of a foot rise from the curb to the middle of the road.

Another situation where grade is an important consideration is in the construction of ramps for the disabled. Wheelchair ramps must have a fairly low grade, because if a ramp is too steep, people may be unable to use it. Nationwide, a generally accepted maximum grade for wheelchair ramps is 8.3 percent, or a ratio of 1:12. SEE ALSO FRACTION; PERCENT; SLOPE.

Philip Edward Koth (with William Arthur Atkins)

Highway engineers plan carefully for the grade to be used in road construction.

Bibliography

Kelly, James, E., and William R. Park. *The Roadbuilders*. Reading, MA: Addison-Wesley, 1973.

Internet Resources

Grade or Super Elevation Calculations. Raleigh, North Carolina: Departments of Math and Physics, Wake Technical Community College. <http://www.wake.tec.nc.us/math/Projects/HighwayPatrol/grade.htm>.

Gradient *See Circles, Measurement of.*

Graphs

A graph is a pictorial representation of the relationship between two quantities. A graph can be anything from a simple bar graph that displays the

measurements of various objects to a more complicated graph of functions in two or three dimensions. The former shows the relationship between the kind of object and its quantity; the latter shows the relationship between input and output. Graphing is a way to make information easier for a viewer to absorb.

Types of Graphs

The simplest graphs show the number of many objects. For example, a bar graph might name the months of the year along a horizontal axis and show numbers (for the number of days in each month) along a vertical axis. Then a rectangle (or bar) is drawn above each month. The height of the bar might indicate the number of days in that month on which it rained, or on which a person exercised, or on which the temperature rose above 90 degrees. See the generic example of a bar graph below (top right).

Another simple kind of graph is a circle graph or pie graph, which shows fractions or percentages. In this kind of graph, a circle is divided into pie-shaped sectors. Each sector is given a label and indicates the fraction of the total area that goes with that label. See the generic example of a pie graph below (top middle).

A pie chart might be used to display the percentages of a budget that are allotted to various expenditures. If the sector labeled "medical bills" takes up two-tenths of the area of the circle, that means that two-tenths, or 20 percent, of the budget is devoted to medical expenses. Usually the percentages are written on the sectors along with their labels to make the graph easier to read. In both bar graphs and pie graphs, the reader can immediately pick out the largest and smallest categories without having to search through a chart or list, making it easy to compare the relative sizes of many objects simultaneously.

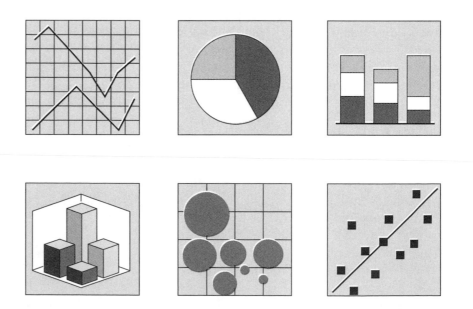

Often the two quantities being graphed can both be represented numerically. For example, student scores on examinations are often plotted on a graph, especially if there are many students taking the exam. In such a graph, the numbers on the horizontal axis represent the possible scores on the exam, and the numbers on the vertical axis represent numbers of students who earned that score. The information could be plotted as a simple bar graph. If only the top point of each bar is plotted and a curve is drawn to connect these points, the result is a line graph. See the generic example of a line graph on the pevious page (top left). Although the points on the line between the plotted points do not correspond to any pieces of information, a smooth line can be easier to understand than a large collection of bars or dots.

Graphs for Continuous Data

Graphs become slightly more complicated when one (or both) of the quantities in the graph can have continuous values rather than a **discrete** set. A common example of this is a quantity that changes over time. For example, a scientist might be observing the rate of growth of bacteria. The rates could be plotted so that the horizontal axis displays units of time and the vertical axis displays numbers (how many bacteria exist).

Then, for instance, the point (3,1000) would mean that at "time 3" (which could mean three o'clock, or three seconds after starting, or various other times, depending on the units being used and the starting point of the experiment) there were one thousand bacteria in the sample. The rise and fall of the graph show the increases and decreases in the number of bacteria.

In this case, even though only a finite set of points represent actual data, the remaining points do have a natural interpretation. For instance, suppose that in addition to the point (3,1000), the graph also contains the point (4,1500) and that both of these points correspond to actual measurements. If the scientist joins all of the points on the graph by a line, then the point (3.5,1200) might lie on the graph, or perhaps the point (3.5,1350).

There are many different lines that can be drawn through a collection of points. Looking at the overall shape of the data points helps the scientist decide which line is the most reasonable fit. In the previous example, the scientist could estimate that at time 3.5, there were 1200 (or 1350) bacteria in the sample. Thus graphing can be helpful in making estimates and predictions.

Graphs for Predictions

Sometimes the purpose for drawing a graph may not be to view the data already known but to construct a mathematical model that will allow one to analyze data and make predictions. One of the simplest models that can be constructed from a set of data is called a best-fit line. Such a line is useful in situations in which the data are roughly linear—that is, they are increasing or decreasing at a roughly constant rate but do not fall precisely on a line. (See graph on the previous page, bottom right.)

A best-fit line can be a very useful tool for analyzing data because lines have very simple formulas describing their behavior. If, for instance, one has collected data up to time 5 and wishes to predict what the value will be at time 15, the value 15 can be inserted into the formula for the line to derive an estimation. One can also determine how good an estimate is likely to be by computing the **correlation** factor for the data. The correlation

discrete composed of distinct elements

correlation the process of establishing a mutual or reciprocal relation between two things or sets of things

111

factor is a quantity that measures how close the set of data is to being linear; that is, how good a "fit" the best-fit line actually is.

Graphs for Functions

One of the most common uses of graphs is to display the information encoded in a function. A function, informally speaking, is an operation or rule that can be applied to numbers. Functions are usually graphed in the cartesian plane (that is, the x,y-plane) with the horizontal or x-axis representing the input variable and the vertical or y-axis representing the output variable. The graph of a function differs from the other types of graphs described so far in that all the points on the graph represent actual information. A concrete relationship, usually given by a mathematical formula, connects the two objects being analyzed.

For example, the "squaring" function takes numbers and squares them. Thus an input of the number 1 corresponds to an output of 1; an input of 2 corresponds to an output of 4; an input of -7 corresponds to an output of 49; and so on. Therefore, the graph of this function contains the points $(1, 1)$, $(2, 4)$, $(-7, 49)$, and infinitely many others.

Does the point $(10, 78)$ lie on this graph? To determine the answer, examine which characteristics all the points on the graph have in common. Any point on the graph of a function represents an input-output pair, with the x-coordinate representing input and the y-coordinate representing output. With the squaring function, each output value is the square of the corresponding input value, so on the graph of the squaring function, each y-coordinate must be the square of the corresponding x-coordinate. Because 78 is not the square of 10, the point $(10, 78)$ does not lie on the graph of the squaring function.

Graphing Notation

It is traditional to name graphs with an equation rather than with words. The equation of any graph, regardless of whether it is the graph of a function, is meant to be a perfect description of the graph—it should tell the viewer the relationship between the x- and y-coordinates of the numbers being graphed.

For example, the equation of the graph of the squaring function is $y = x^2$ because the y-coordinate of any point on the graph is the square of the x-coordinate. The line that passes through the point $(0, 3)$ and slants upwards with slope 4 (that is, at a rate of four units up for every one unit to the right) has equation $y = 4x + 3$. This indicates that for every point on the graph, the y-coordinate is 3 more than 4 times the x-coordinate.

An equation of a graph has many uses: it is not only a description of the graph but also a mechanism for finding points on the graph and a test for determining whether a given point lies on the graph. For example, to find out whether the point $(278, 3254)$ lies on the line $y = 4x + 3$, simply insert $(278, 3254)$, resulting in the inequality $3254 \neq 4(278) + 3$. Because these numbers are not equal, the point does not lie on the line. However, the equation shows that the point $(278, 1115)$ does lie on the line. SEE ALSO DATA COLLECTION AND INTERPRETATION; GRAPHS AND EFFECTS OF PARAMETER CHANGES; STATISTICAL ANALYSIS.

Naomi Klarreich

Bibliography

Larson, Roland E., and Robert P. Hostetler. *Precalculus*, 3rd ed. Lexington, MA: D. C. Heath and Company, 1993.

Warner, Jack. *Graph Attack! Understanding Charts and Graphs*. New Jersey: Regents/Prentice Hall, 1993.

Graphs and Effects of Parameter Changes

The two-dimensional **Cartesian coordinate system** may be used to graph a variety of equations in the form of straight and curved lines. One way to graph an equation is to determine a number of different values for the variables and plot them on the graph. It can be helpful, however, to understand how a change in the **parameters** of an equation affects the resulting line.

Graphs of Straight Lines

The graph of the simple equation $y = 1x$, or $y = x$, is graphed in (a) below. The line passes through every coordinate point where $x = y$, such as $(2, 2)$ or $(-3, -3)$.

Notice what happens to the graph of the equation when the parameters of the equation are changed by using a different coefficient for x, such as $y = 3x$. As part (a) shows, the new line has a steeper slope. If the coefficient is further increased, the slope will become even steeper, and the line will become closer to vertical.

Cartesian coordinate system a way of measuring the positions of points in a plane using two perpendicular lines as axes

parameters independent variables which can be used to rewrite an expression as two separate functions

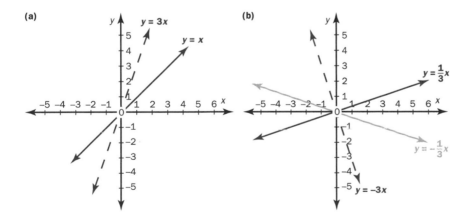

Conversely, if the coefficient for x is decreased, a different change in the line occurs. As part (b) above shows, the line for $y = \frac{1}{3x}$ has a more gradual slope than the line for $y = x$. If the coefficient were to be further decreased, the line would become flatter, and it would appear more like a horizontal line.

If the coefficient is a negative number, an interesting line results. For instance, the graph of the equation $y = -3x$ is shown in part (b) above. Comparing this line with the graph for $y = 3x$ shows that the graph of $y = -3x$ moves down from the left to right (a negative direction) and the graph of $y = 3x$ moves up from left to right (a positive direction). These two lines therefore are described as having a negative and a positive slope, respectively. From this example, it can be seen that the coefficient of x in the equation of a line indicates the slope of the line.

Lines Not Passing through the Origin. All of the lines described above pass through the origin (0, 0), but many lines do not. The line for the equation $y = 3x + 2$ will pass *above* the origin, as shown in part (a) below. The line has the same slope as $y = 3x$, but has been shifted two units *up* the y-axis. The two lines are thus parallel because they have the same slope.

The equation $y = 3x - 2$, also graphed in (a), passes through the y-axis at -2. The slope of the line is 3, which is the same the slope for $y = 3x$. But compared to $y = 3x$, the line for $y = 3x - 2$ has been shifted two units *down* the y-axis.

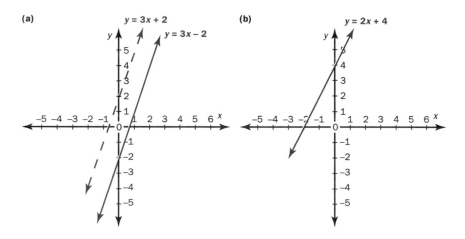

Understanding the role of the coefficient of x in indicating the slope, and the role of the constant in indicating the point where the line will intersect the y-axis, can make it easier to graph an equation. The equation $y = 2x + 4$ will pass through the y-axis at 4 and has a slope of 2, as shown in part (b) above.

The equation $y = 2x + 4$ may be expressed in different forms. For example, $x = \frac{1}{2}y - 2$. The form $y = 2x + 4$, written in general terms as $y = mx + b$, is called the slope intercept form. In this form, the coefficient m is the slope, and the constant b indicates where the line intersects the y-axis. The intersection point is called the y-intercept. The graph of the equation $y = 3x - 4$ has a slope of 3 and intersects the y-axis at -4.

Graphs of Curved Lines

Changes in the parameters of higher-degree equations (that is, higher than first-degree) will result in patterns of changes in their graphs similar to those for straight lines. For example, the graph of $y = x^2$, as shown in part (a) below, is a curve known as a parabola. The coefficient indicates whether the parabola opens facing up or facing down, and whether it is narrow or broad.

Changing the coefficient of x^2 to a negative value results in a parabola that is a mirror-image of the parabola for $y = x^2$. The parabola for $y = x^2$ opens upward, and the parabola for $y = -x^2$ opens downward.

If the coefficient of x^2 is changed so the equation is $y = 3x^2$, notice the changes to the graph of the equation, as depicted in part (b) below. The parabola still passes through the origin, but it is narrower than $y = x^2$. If the coefficient of the graph were increased even more, then the parabola would become even narrower. Conversely, if the coefficient of the original equation were decreased, the resulting parabola would still pass through the origin, but would become broader, as depicted in (b) below as $y = \frac{1}{2} x^2$.

Compare the parabola in (b) below for $y = 3x^2$ to the parabola for $y = -3x^2$. As with the equations $y = x^2$ and $y = -x^2$, one parabola is the mirror image of the other. The two parabolas open in opposite directions.

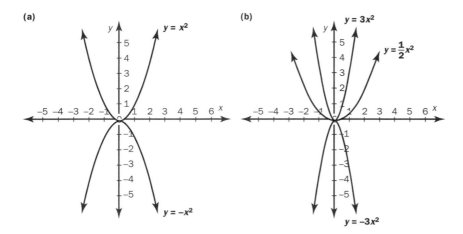

(a)

(b)

Curves Not Passing through the Origin. Changing a parameter of the equation $y = x^2$ to $y = x^2 + 2$ will change the point at which the parabola crosses the y-axis. In this case, the parabola does not pass through the origin, but passes through the y-axis at 2, as shown below. The parabola has been shifted two units *up* the y-axis. Similarly, the parabola of $y = x^2 - 5$ is shifted 5 units *down* the y-axis, and passes through the y-axis at -5.

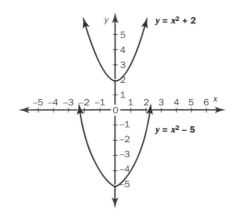

In the general equation for a parabola, $y = ax^2 + b$, the coefficient a indicates the shape of the parabola and in which direction the parabola opens, upward or downward. The value of b indicates where the parabola intersects the y-axis.

More complex equations and their graphs will also show patterns that result from changes in the parameters of the equations. Knowing how changes in the various parameters of an equation affect the graph of the equation is helpful for drawing, interpreting, and applying equations and their graphs. SEE ALSO GRAPHS.

Arthur V. Johnson II

Bibliography

Bellman, Allan, Sadie Bragg, Suzanne Chapin, Theodore Gardella, Bettye Hall, William Handlin, and Edward Marfune. *Advanced Algebra: Tools for a Changing World*. Needham, MA: Prentice Hall, 1998.

Heating and Air Conditioning

In the late nineteenth and early twentieth centuries, heating a home was a matter of tossing another log or more coal into the fireplace or stove. "Air conditioning" was the shade of a backyard tree. Twenty-first century homes use far more sophisticated technological tools—tools that a homeowner is likely to take for granted.

A heating and air conditioning contractor has to be as much of a scientist as a builder or technician. The course requirements of typical heating and air conditioning programs at community or junior colleges place a heavy emphasis on chemistry, physics, engineering, and mathematics, including **geometry** and **algebra**. Good heating and air conditioning contractors are able to compute formulas and equations in order to arrive at volumes, pressures, and degrees. They must be able to accurately measure distances, angles, circles, arcs, temperatures, weights, and volumes. They also must identify and interpret geometric figures, graphs, scales, and gauge indications. Further, they must know the scientific principles that are central to their work, including heat transfer, **combustion**, temperature, pressure, electricity, and magnetism. They should also know the physical and chemical properties of commonly used substances such as **refrigerants** and **hydrocarbons**.

The Science of Cooling

The science of cooling is rooted in the Second Law of Thermodynamics, which states that heat only flows from higher to lower temperature levels, and never the other way around. Using this law, physicists can explain exactly how an air conditioner (or a refrigerator, which uses the same process) works. They can also use related principles, such as those of **exergy** and **anergy**, to design better, more efficient cooling systems.

How does a typical air conditioner work? It lowers the temperature by continuous extraction of heat energy using a thermodynamic cycle. The most common of these cycles is called the vapor-compression refrigeration cycle, sometimes called the Rankine cycle. In this cycle, a substance known as the "working fluid," or refrigerant, goes through cyclical changes of state in a closed loop. This loop is made up of four parts: an evaporator, a compressor, a condenser, and a throttle valve. The evaporator is installed in the space to be cooled while the other parts are installed outside of the space.

geometry the branch of mathematics that deals with the properties and relationships of points, lines, angles, surfaces, planes, and solids

algebra the branch of mathematics that deals with variables or unknowns representing the arithmetic numbers

combustion chemical reaction combining fuel with oxygen accompanied by the release of light and heat

refrigerant fluid circulating in a refrigerator that is successively compressed, cooled, allowed to expand, and warmed in the refrigeration cycle

hydrocarbon a compound of carbon and hydrogen

exergy the measure of the ability of a system to produce work; the maximum potential work output of a system

anergy spent energy transferred to the environment

Before it enters the evaporator, the working fluid is a liquid or liquid-vapor mixture. Its pressure is low, and its temperature is below that of the space to be cooled, also called the "cold room." In the evaporator, the fluid takes up heat from the cold room because of the temperature difference. The fluid-vapor is then brought from low to high pressure in the compressor, which increases its temperature. In a well-designed system, the temperature of the fluid-vapor leaving the compressor should be above that of the surroundings, providing the temperature difference necessary for removing heat from the fluid to the surroundings. This occurs in the condenser, where the fluid undergoes a phase change from vapor to liquid because heat has been removed. The loop is closed by the throttle valve, where the fluid is expanded from the high condenser pressure to the low evaporator pressure.

One issue that scientists struggle with is finding a good working fluid. Water would be, at first glance, the ideal fluid because it is inexpensive and safe. Its thermodynamic properties, though, prevent it from being the best choice. Water vapor has a very low density, so using it would require huge piping volumes and a lot of work on the part of the compressor. **Chlorofluorocarbons** (CFCs) work better, but unfortunately they contribute to ozone depletion in the stratosphere. In large industrial refrigeration plants, ammonia (NH_3) is the most common choice.

Contractors who install air-conditioning systems are probably not thinking about the vapor-compression refrigeration cycle. They are, however, thinking about what size air conditioner is needed to keep you comfortable on hot summer days. Factors that must be measured and taken into account in deciding on the size of an air-conditioning system are:

- the geographical location, and therefore average temperatures during the cooling season;
- the length of walls in the rooms, including walls not exposed to direct sunlight, those that are exposed to direct sunlight, and interior walls;
- the type of wall frame construction (framing, masonry, etc.);
- the ceiling height;
- the ceiling area, and the presence and amount of insulation above the ceiling;
- the space's floor area;
- the width of doors and arches;
- the window area, the orientation of the windows (north, south, etc.), and the type of glass (single-pane, double-pane, block);
- the number of people who normally occupy the room (giving off body heat);
- the amount of heat given off by lights and appliances; and
- the hours of operation.

Taken together, these factors determine the cooling capacity that is needed, usually measured in British thermal units (BTUs); one BTU is the amount of energy needed to raise the temperature of a pound of water one degree Fahrenheit.

chlorofluorocarbons
compounds similar to hydrocarbons in which one or more of the hydrogen atoms has been replaced by a chlorine or fluorine atom

The Science of Heating

In many respects the science of heating a home is much simpler than cooling: Unless you have solar heat or a windmill, something somewhere gets burned, and the heat is transferred into your living space either directly (as is in the case of natural gas, propane, or heating oil) or indirectly (as in the case of electricity). When a furnace runs, it ignites the fuel with burners that heat up the heat exchanger. A blower moves air across the heat exchanger, and the warm air is then circulated through the living area by a duct system. Fumes from the burned fuel are expelled through a flue (a pipe designed to remove exhaust gases from a fireplace, stove, or burner).

To determine how big a furnace needs to be, the same information listed for air conditioning is necessary. The result of these calculations is what a heating contractor calls a "heat load," which is measured in BTUs. For example, a contractor might determine that a house's heat load is 61,000 BTUs and that an 80,000 BTU furnace running at 80 percent efficiency, providing 64,000 BTUs, is a good approximate fit. A problem with a higher efficiency furnace is that it can often "short cycle," meaning that it will turn off before all the cold air in the home has cycled through the furnace.

The simplest type of furnace is called a "single-stage" furnace. This means that the furnace is either on or off and the fan blower is adjusted to a single setting that provides the optimum amount of heat based on the home's heat load. Most furnaces, however, are "two-stage" furnaces, and these provide more comfort and typically a higher efficiency.

When a two-stage thermostat senses that a room is cold and sends an electrical signal to the furnace to run, the furnace operates at two-thirds strength. If after a set amount of time the thermostat is still calling for heat, the furnace switches to 100 percent capacity. This gives the furnace's blowers time to circulate warm air throughout the house. If the furnace operated at 100 percent right away, it might circulate enough hot air to satisfy the thermostat but not enough to warm colder pockets in other areas of the house.

Michael J. O'Neal

Bibliography

Bell, Arthur A., Jr. *HVAC: Equations, Data, Rules of Thumb.* New York: McGraw-Hill, 2000.

Haines, Roger W., and C. Lewis Wilson. *HVAC Systems Design Handbook.* New York: McGraw-Hill, 1998.

Mull, Thomas E. *HVAC Principles and Applications Manual.* New York: McGraw-Hill, 1997.

Hollerith, Herman

American Mathematician and Inventor
1860–1929

The presidential race between Texas Governor George W. Bush and U.S. Vice-President Al Gore in November 2000 illustrated the importance of accurately counting every vote. The hand recounts also revealed how collecting and interpreting vast amounts of data by hand can pose many difficulties,

---

FUZZY LOGIC AND THERMOSTATS

Early generations of electronic controls, including the thermostats on furnaces and air conditioners, were always either on or off. Today's controls are computerized, thereby enabling them to use "fuzzy logic," or a computer's ability to "learn" and "think" in shades of gray rather than black-and-white.

Thus, instead of turning on a furnace all the way when the temperature in a building falls to a certain point, a fuzzy logic thermostat turns the heat on just a little as the temperature approaches a specific setting. This feature helps maintain the temperature at a steady, constant value and avoids cycles of chilliness followed by blasts of hot air.

Herman Hollerith invented the tabulating machine, and his company, through mergers, eventually became IBM.

binary existing in only two states, such as "off" or "on," "one" or "zero"

digital describes information technology that uses discrete values of a physical quantity to transmit information

including, but not limited to, error and bias. Herman Hollerith's invention of a tabulating machine was the first attempt to solve these problems.

During the 1880 U.S. census, the logistical problems of gathering and tabulating great amounts of data quickly enough for the data to remain useful was first recognized. In fact, the data from the 1880 census took nearly seven years to tabulate, far too long for the results to accurately reflect statistics that were needed for determining seats in the U.S. House of Representatives. The U.S. Census Bureau devised a competition in which a prize would be awarded for the best method of tabulating census data.

Herman Hollerith, a former statistician for the U.S. Census Bureau and professor of mechanical engineering at the Massachusetts Institute of Technology, won the competition. His work had led him to an interest in the mechanical manipulation of data. It seemed to lend itself perfectly to being automated. He edged out two competitors who invented "chip" and "slip" systems with his "card" system. His tabulating machine was put to use in the very next census in 1890.

Hollerith's "integrating machine" punched holes into stiff paper cards similar to the ones he had seen conductors using on trains. By punching holes next to the appropriate descriptors on the card, such as "large nose" or "dark hair," the conductor could create a profile of each passenger. Hollerith designed his cards to be the same size as dollar bills so that storage cabinets for currency could also be used for the "Hollerith cards."

Hollerith's system was essentially a **binary** system. "Punched" and "not punched" corresponded to the 1s and 0s we are familiar with in the twenty-first century's **digital** data storage systems. The cards were run under a group of brushes that completed electrical circuits when a "punch" was encountered. A corresponding mechanical counter then advanced for each punch, and in this way counted the total.

The Hollerith tabulating device allowed the 1890 census to be completed in only six weeks and at a savings of $5 million, an almost unbelievable improvement. In addition, data could be sorted and organized based on selected characteristics with little additional effort. More data than ever before could be collected and analyzed.

Fueled by the success of his machine, Herman formed the Herman Hollerith Tabulating Machine Company in 1896. However, his machine was so expensive the Census Bureau developed their own system for the 1910 census. Competition forced Hollerith to merge with another company, and the Computing-Tabulating-Recording Company was created in 1911. Thomas J. Watson later reorganized it into International Business Machines (IBM) Corporation. The success of Hollerith's machine was the basis of IBM's success and has led him to be remembered as a founder of information processing. SEE ALSO MATHEMATICAL DEVICES, MECHANICAL; CENSUS.

Laura Snyder

Bibliography

Maxfield, Clive "Max," and Alvin Brown. *Bebop Bytes Back: An Unconventional Guide to Computers.* Madison, AL: Doone Publications, 1998.

Parkinson, Claire L. *Breakthroughs: A Chronology of Great Achievements in Science and Mathematics.* Boston: G. K. Hall & Co., 1985.

Internet Resources

O'Connor, J. J., and E. F. Robertson. "Herman Hollerith." School of Mathematics and Statistics, University of St. Andrews, Scotland. July 1999. <http://www-history.mcs.St-andrews.ac.uk/history/Mathematicians/Hollerith.html>.

Russo, Mark. "Herman Hollerith: The World's First Statistical Engineer." <http://www.History.rochester.edu/steam/hollerith/>.

Hopper, Grace

American Mathematician and Computer Programming Pioneer
1906–1992

American mathematician and computer pioneer Grace Murray Hopper was called "Amazing Grace" by coworkers because of her determined ways. Born to parents who believed in quality education, Hopper was fascinated with gadgets, and she disassembled clocks and built vehicles with her "Struct-iron" kit. She was strongly influenced by her parents, and described her mother as having a "very great interest in mathematics" and her father as having "a house full of books, constant interest in reading, and insatiable curiosity."

Hopper entered Vassar in 1924 to study mathematics and physics and graduated with a bachelor's degree. She performed mathematics research at Yale and earned her master's degree in 1930 and her doctorate degree in 1934. During this era, these were rare achievements, especially for a woman.

Grace Hopper is best known for her contribution to the design and development of the COBOL programming language for business applications. She is shown here working on an early form of computer.

digital describes information technology that uses discrete values of a physical quantity to transmit information

compiler a computer program that translates symbolic instructions into machine code

machine language electronic code the computer can utilize

Hopper taught mathematics at Vassar and continued her tenure there as a professor until 1943. Her unusual methods applied mathematics to real life. She required her probability students to play dice and instructed students to plan a city by managing expenses.

Hopper's great-grandfather, a Navy rear-admiral, was her personal hero. When the United States entered World War II in 1941, she was crestfallen when the U.S. Navy would not accept women. By 1943 a shortage of men allowed women to enter the ranks. Hopper eagerly joined, but was rejected because she was too old, did not weigh enough, and was considered essential to the war effort as a civilian professor of mathematics. Undaunted, Hopper convinced the Navy to accept her, and in 1943, she started officer training, graduating at the top of her class. Assigned to Harvard's Computation Project, she worked with Howard Aiken on the Mark-I, which is considered one of the first programmable **digital** computers.

Post-War Years

In 1946 Hopper ended her Navy duty but remained a reservist and was appointed a Harvard research fellow and continued work on the Mark-II and Mark-III computers. Even though colleagues said only scientists had enough knowledge to use computers, Hopper was undaunted and continued to write programs that made computers easily accessible.

In 1949 Hopper joined the Eckert-Mauchly Corporation as a senior mathematician where she worked on UNIVAC (UNIVersal Automatic Computer), the first computer to handle both numeric and textual information. Her original staff was comprised of four men and four women. Hopper liked hiring women, she said, because "Women turn out to be very good programmers for one very good reason. They tend to finish up things, and men don't very often finish."

During this time, Hopper designed an improved **compiler** that translated instructions from English commands to **machine language**. This reduced the need for writing tedious machine code. She finished the A-O compiler in 1952 using easy terms like SUB (for subtraction) and MPY (for multiplication).

In 1957 Hopper developed FLOW-MATIC, the first commercial, data-processing compiler that allowed computers to be used for automated billing and payroll calculation. FLOW-MATIC became the foundation for Hopper's next development in 1959, the computer language COmmon Business Oriented Language, or COBOL. Whereas IBM's FORTRAN programming language used a highly condensed, mathematical code, COBOL used common English language words. COBOL was written for use on different computers and was intended to be independent of any one computer company. For her wide-reaching influence on COBOL's development, Hopper was deemed the "grandmother of COBOL."

Later Honors

Hopper retired from the Navy in 1966 but was recalled to help standardize computer languages. In 1969 she was named the first computer science "Man of the Year" by the Data Processing Management Association and was known among coworkers as "the little old lady who talks to computers."

Her office contained a skull-and-crossbones flag and a clock that ran backward to remind people to use flexible thinking.

Grace Hopper retired in 1986 as the oldest Naval officer on active duty. In 1991 President George Bush awarded Rear-Admiral Hopper the National Medal of Technology, saying she was the first woman to receive America's highest technology award as an individual, and recognizing her "as a computer pioneer, who spent a half century helping keep America on the leading edge of high technology." Throughout her life, Hopper held to her belief that "Most problems have more than one solution." SEE ALSO COMPUTERS, EVOLUTION OF ELECTRONIC.

William Arthur Atkins (with Philip Edward Koth)

Bibliography

Billings, Charlene W. *Grace Hopper: Navy Admiral and Computer Scientist Pioneer*. Hillside, NJ: Enslow Publishers, 1989.

"Unforgettable Grace Hopper." *Reader's Digest*, October 1994.

Whitelaw, Nancy. *Grace Hopper: Programming Pioneer*. New York: Scientific American Books for Young Readers, 1995.

Internet Resources

"The Wit and Wisdom of Grace Hopper," *Yale University Department of Computer Science*, <http://www.cs.yale.edu/homes/tap/Files/hopper-wit.html>. (From The OCLC Newsletter, March/April, 1987, no. 167).

Human Body

Humans come in different shapes and sizes. There is no shape or size that is considered "right." Medical professionals have created healthy guidelines for people. When a baby is born, doctors track many variables to make sure it is developing correctly. These charts and guidelines are not perfect, but they form a framework from which to assess a person's health.

Tracking Growth

Over the years, physicians have developed various methods for tracking growth. Keeping a record of a child's growth patterns helps doctors determine if the child is developing properly. As a person ages, doctors continue to monitor growth, helping patients maintain a healthy weight. Physicians also review height to check for problems of the spine, bone, and other medical conditions.

Growth Charts. Pediatric growth charts have been used by medical professionals since 1977. The charts are used for many measurements of growth in a child. For example, when a child's height is measured, she is then placed into a percentile. If a child is in the seventy-fifth percentile in height, it means that she would be taller than 75 percent of all other children in her age group.

Originally, the sampling for growth charts was taken from a small portion of the population. These children were primarily Caucasian, formula-fed, and middle-class. This sample was problematic because it did not reflect the diversity of the United States. To help make charts that were representative of the whole, and in turn were more accurate, samples were taken

scaling the process of reducing or increasing a drawing or some physical process so that proper proportions are retained between the parts

sampling selecting a subset of a group or population in such a way that valid conclusions can be made about the whole set or population

outliers extreme values in a data set

✱The tallest man in documented medical history was Robert Wadlow, who at 22 years old stood 8 feet, 11.1 inches tall, weighed 440 pounds, and wore a size 37AA shoe.

from a much larger portion of the population and from people with varying backgrounds.

There are various mathematical concepts behind growth charts. **Scaling** is one important factor in charting growth in an infant. Though often associated with architecture, humans also undergo scaling. While an infant is much smaller than an adult, the support material remains the same: bone. Bone is a type of tissue that can only support a limited degree of force due to strain. This is evident in the number of broken bones humans can experience when faced with too much strain—for instance, as a result of activities such as sports. As humans grow, their bones also grow but only with a narrow tolerance for strain.

"Average" Height. The determination of "average" human dimensions is based on statistics and illustrates the statistical concepts of **sampling**, central tendency, and **outliers**. For example, rare genetic or medical conditions can cause a small percentage of the human population to be very tall or very short. Persons diagnosed with gigantism✱ may reach adult heights of more than 8 feet, whereas persons with dwarfism are commonly less than 4 feet, 10 inches tall.

Because the heights of "average" people are statistically determined by *excluding* individuals with these rare conditions, the physical dimensions of tall or short people are therefore deemed "disproportionate" or "outside the average." Yet if the sampling set included *only* individuals with these special conditions, and excluded everyone else, then their statures would be considered well within average. Hence, what is considered average depends on the sampling and calculation methods by which it is derived.

Many consumer products are built for "average" people—they are constructed for persons within an average height and weight range and who are not physically challenged. Such construction can cause difficulties for those who are not "average." As a result, some manufacturers offer products to help people make the necessary adjustments. For example, some people could not drive automobiles comfortably without enhancements like adjustable foot pedals, which bring the brake and accelerator pedals closer or farther away from drivers. This allows shorter and taller people to drive more easily, keeping a safe distance from the car's steering wheel airbag. Gadgets also exist to help disabled drivers, including hand controls that can be used to brake or accelerate.

Allometry. Another mathematical principle known as allometry (from the Greek word *alloios*, which means different) is especially important in the study of how humans grow. Biological allometry and human anatomy are concerned with the different growth rates that an organism experiences throughout its lifetime. A human infant does not have the same proportions of limb-to-head-to-body ratios as a human adult. The head of an infant compared to its body size is much different from an adult's. As a human grows, limbs and body size increase considerably while the head does not. This change in ratio occurs in all kinds of animals. A baby horse is born with extraordinarily long legs compared to its body. As it grows, the body catches up with the legs.

An entire branch of science deals with the allometric changes of organisms. One of the modern methods of observing allometric change is to place imaginary points on the organism, in this case, a human infant's head. A computer scans for the imaginary points and constructs a grid system. As the infant grows, these points are continually tracked, and the points shift in position relative to one another. When the infant reaches adulthood, it is possible to see how the skull grew, where it grew the fastest and the slowest, and how the proportions have changed. The initial square grid looks wavy and distorted. Changes in body shape and physiology, such as in bone structure, breathing rate, and muscle strength can be expressed as variables and tracked. The basic allometric equations used to monitor these changes are as follows:

$$y = a \times x^b \text{ and } \log y = \log a + b \log x.$$

This equation is used by biologists to plot two **variables** on logarithmic co-ordinates (using logarithmic scales on the x and y axes of a Cartesian coordinate system). The result is a straight line. Many biological measurements that relate to change in body size use this general equation. The exponent b represents the **slope** of the line. This equation can help biologists track the changes in variables (the arbitrary points used to make an initial grid). Computers can track the three-dimensional (3-D) changes that occur with growth and produce allometric 3-D scaling grids.

How Much Should a Person Weigh?

The new indicator used for weight measurements is the Body Mass Index (BMI). Formerly, weight-for-stature charts had been used when assessing weight. With this type of chart, a person's weight was evaluated only in relation to one variable, his or her height. When looking at a person's BMI, other factors, such as age, are considered.

A BMI is the fraction of a person's weight divided by his height squared. If a person is between the range of 20–25, then he is said to fall within a healthy weight range. Once a person goes above a BMI of 25, he may suffer from weight-related health problems. Additionally, people with a BMI of less than 20 may also suffer health problems from being underweight. The BMI is the preferred way to chart weight because it looks at more variables than how much a person weighs and what his height is. The body mass index can also help doctors be aware of people who may be more predisposed to being either overweight or underweight.

While all growth charts are helpful in determining development, they really serve only as guidelines. There is no one correct height or weight for a person, only a range of what is healthy. Growth charts do not serve the purpose of locating an "ideal." Instead, they help to indicate whether someone is healthy. SEE ALSO DÜRER, ALBRECHT; LEONARDO DA VINCI; LOGARITHMS; RATIO, RATE, AND PROPORTION; SCALE DRAWINGS AND MODELS.

Brook E. Hall

There is no such thing as an ideal weight. Instead, every person has a range of what is healthy for her based on a number of variables, including age, height, sex, and muscle mass.

variable a quantity that may assume any one of a set of values known as the domain

slope the ratio of the vertical change to the corresponding horizontal change

Bibliography

Hildebrand, Milton. *Analysis of Vertebrate Structure*, 3rd ed. New York: John Wiley & Sons, 1988.

Kardong, Kenneth. *Vertebrates: Comparative Anatomy, Function, and Evolution*. Dubuque, IA: William C. Brown Publishers, 1995.

Schmidt-Nielsen, Knut. *Scaling: Why Is Animal Size So Important?* New York: Cambridge University Press, 1984.

Serway, Raymond, and Jerry Faughn. *College Physics*. Philadelphia: Saunders College Publishing, 1985.

Internet Resources

CDC Growth Charts: United States. Texas Medical Association. <http://www.texmed.org/has/prs/cdcbackground.asp>.

Human Genome Project *See Genome, Human.*

Hypatia

Greek Philosopher and Mathematician
370–415 C.E.

Hypatia of Alexandria was a leading mathematician and philosopher of the ancient era. Her father, Theon, was the last known head of the Museum at Alexandria, Egypt, an ancient center of classical learning. He tutored Hypatia and passed on to her his love of mathematics. Eventually her reputation as a mathematician exceeded and outlasted his.

Only fragments of Hypatia's work and a list of several titles of her treatises on mathematics remain. She translated and popularized the works of Greek mathematicians, including Diophantus's (third century) *Arithmetica*, a book noted for **integral solutions** to **linear equations**, and Apollonius's *Conic Sections*. Hypatia also edited the *Almagest*, an important work by the Greek astronomer and mathematician Claudius Ptolemy. She taught and wrote about a number of math topics on which further progress was not made until centuries later.

One of Hypatia's most eminent students, Synesius, wrote her letters asking her advice on scientific matters, and these letters are one of the key sources about her work. He credits her with detailed knowledge of the **astrolabe** and the **hydroscope**, as well as other devices used for studies in astronomy and physics. Historians living in her time praised her learning, as well as her beauty and character.

Hypatia's ties to a politician who disagreed with Alexandria's Christian bishop led to Hypatia's death in 415 C.E., when she was murdered by a mob of religious fanatics. Following Hypatia's murder, many of her students migrated to Athens, which by 420 C.E. acquired a considerable reputation in mathematics.

All of Hypatia's works are believed to have been lost in the seventh century, when the books of the library at Alexandria were burned by Arab invaders. SEE ALSO APOLLONIUS OF PERGA.

Shirley B. Gray

Bibliography

Deakin, Michael. "Hypatia and Her Mathematics." *American Mathematical Monthly* 101 (1994): 234–243.

Narins, Brigham, ed. *World of Mathematics*. Detroit: Gale Group, 2001.

Olsen, Lynn M. *Women in Mathematics*. Cambridge, MA: MIT Press, 1974.

A Byzantine church historian wrote that Hypatia was so learned in literature and science that she exceeded all philosophers of her time.

integral solutions solutions to an equation or set of equations that are all integers

linear equation an equation in which all variables are raised to the first power

astrolabe a device used to measure the angle between an astronomical object and the horizon

hydroscope a device designed to allow a person to see below the surface of water

IMAX Technology

Ask anyone who has seen an IMAX film in an IMAX theater to describe their experience, and they will probably use words like "huge," "giant," and "awesome." This reaction is exactly what the designers of the IMAX film technology had in mind—a motion picture experience like no other. What exactly is it that makes IMAX films so different?

IMAX's History

In the late 1960s, filmmakers experimented with multiple-screen films. They used up to three cameras to film movies in a very wide format, which could then be played back to an audience using three projectors at three times the normal width. However, these systems had many problems. First, three cameras had to be used simultaneously to film the movie. Then the three projectors that were used to show the film had to be perfectly aligned and synchronized. Another problem was that the edges of each projector's image tended to vary in brightness.

Knowing that multiple-screen films were very popular with audiences, a group of Canadian filmmakers and business people decided to design a system that had the same large-scale effect as a multiple-screen film, but with a single camera and projector. After several years of work, the first IMAX film premiered at the 1970 World Expo in Osaka, Japan. The whole system was a hit, and since that time IMAX theaters have been built and are in use all over the world.

The Characteristics of IMAX

The magic of IMAX motion pictures stems from the combination of specialized equipment that is used to film and project IMAX movies. Every part of the system has been developed especially for IMAX films.

Screen Size. The first thing an IMAX theater patron is likely to notice is the screen size. The typical IMAX screen is about 50 feet tall and 70 feet wide. With this large screen, and the positioning of the seats in the theater, the screen fills even the **peripheral vision** of the audience. So when the camera moves, the audience experiences the sensation of movement. The sensation of motion can be made more spectacular when the film has been shot at high speeds, like from the cockpit of a jet fighter or from the front car on a roller coaster.

peripheral vision the outer area of the visual field

A typical 45-minute large-format IMAX movie uses 3 miles or 15,840 feet of film. Here a projectionist loads the film onto the large-scale reel.

Some IMAX flat screens are as large as 100 feet high. Even more spectacular are IMAX dome screens. IMAX dome screens can be almost 90 feet in diameter. In the dome, the audience sits at a reclined angle so that spectators look up at an angle toward the center of the domed screen. Even in flat-screened IMAX theaters, the audience area is designed so that every seat has a full, unobstructed view of the screen. In an IMAX theater, patrons feel like they are *in* the movie, rather than just watching it.

Sound System. Nearly everyone has experienced some sort of surround sound system in regular movie theaters, but IMAX theaters have sound systems that are loud enough and spectacular enough to complement their unique visual experience. IMAX theaters have six-channel wrap-around sound systems. That means up to six different audio tracks can be channeled anywhere in the theater to give the audience the perception that not only are the images in motion, but so are the sounds. With up to 13,000 watts of power driving dozens of speakers, the sound systems are loud enough to recreate the concussion that is felt during a space shuttle launch.

Film Size. Motion picture film is divided into frames. In the camera, the film is moved behind the lens and shutter and each frame is exposed for just a moment. When the film is developed and played back in a projector, the moving frames recreate the motion that was captured by the camera.

The size of the film frame affects the quality of the image that is produced. Standard motion picture film is 35 mm (millimeters) wide, and has a height of 4 perforations. The perforations are tiny holes on the edges of the film that the camera and projector use to move the film. High-quality motion picture film is 70 mm wide and has a height of 5 perforations. IMAX film is even larger. It is 70 mm wide and has a height of 15 perforations. Additionally, IMAX film is run through cameras and projectors horizontally, so the perforations are at the top and bottom of the frame. Regular film is run through the cameras and projectors vertically, so the perforations are on the sides of the frame. Because of its size, IMAX film is often referred to as 15/70 film.

Special Cameras. IMAX movies are not just regular movies that have been printed on 15/70 film. The making of an IMAX movie begins with filming, during which special IMAX cameras use 15/70 film. The cameras weigh over 50 pounds apiece, and the film is loaded in cartridges that weigh about 5 pounds. Because of the speed of the IMAX film in the cameras, each film cartridge will provide only 5 to 7 minutes of footage. This makes for quite a bit of film reloading, or the use of multiple cameras.

Mega Projectors. The projectors used to produce the unparalleled IMAX movie experience have been compared in size to a compact car. To begin, the film is loaded into the projector on reels that are the size of truck wheels. The reels are mounted horizontally on either side of the projector because IMAX film moves horizontally instead of vertically. The film itself moves through the projector in a unique way that is called a "rolling loop." Air is used to hold each frame momentarily on the rear of the lens, producing a picture that is far more steady and clear than a normal motion picture projector.

To produce an image bright enough to light up the giant IMAX screens, the projectors use special xenon bulbs that consume up to 15,000 watts of power. This is equivalent to 150 100-watt light bulbs. With a bulb so bright, special measures must be taken to cool the projector. Both air, flowing at 800 cubic feet per minute, and water, flowing at 5 gallons per minute, cool the bulb, which can have a surface temperature of 1,300° F.

IMAX Movies

Because of the expense and technical difficulties of filming IMAX movies, most of the 110 or so films that exist are short films, 40 minutes or less in length. Due to the spectacular visual quality of the IMAX format, many films are documentaries that are intended to show the audience images that are normally inaccessible. Consequently, the impact of the films about space exploration, wildlife, wilderness areas, or extreme environments is unforgettable.

The IMAX film system is a remarkable experience for audiences all over the world. Since everything about the system is like a regular movie multiplied by several factors, perhaps the adage "bigger is better" really applies to the IMAX system. SEE ALSO RATIO, RATE, AND PROPORTION.

Max Brandenberger

Internet Resources

IMAX Motion Picture Systems. <http://www.1570films.com/imax.htm>.

IMAX Corporation. <http://www.imax.com>.

"IMAX—Above the World and Below the Sea." *The Tech Museum of Innovation.* <http://www.thetech.org/ops/imax/imax_overview.html>.

DOES FILM SIZE MATTER?

The area of an IMAX film frame—the area that is exposed—is over ten times larger than 35 mm (millimeter) film, and over three times larger than standard 70 mm film. This extra area makes the images sharper and more vibrant than other film formats.

Induction

In mathematics, induction is a technique for proving certain types of mathematical statements. The induction principle can be illustrated by arranging a series of dominoes in a line. Suppose two facts are known about this line of dominoes.

1. The first domino is knocked over.

2. If one domino is knocked over, then the next domino is always knocked over.

What can be concluded from these statements? If the first domino is knocked over, then the second domino is knocked over, which knocks over the third, fourth, fifth, and so on, until eventually all of the dominoes fall.

Induction is a simple but powerful idea when applied to mathematical statements about positive integers. For example, consider the following statement: $n^2 \geq n$ for all positive integers, n. To prove that this statement is true using induction, it is necessary to prove two parts: first, that the statement is true for $n = 1$; and second, that if the statement is true for a positive integer $n = k$, then it must be true for $n = k + 1$. Demonstrating both of these parts proves that the mathematical statement has to be true for all positive integers.

Suppose using the induction principle it has been shown that $n^2 \geq n$. It is then instructive to see how the statement is true for all positive integers, n. The first part says that $n^2 \geq n$ is true for $n = 1$, which is, in effect, knocking over the first domino. According to the second part, $n^2 \geq n$ is also true for $n = k + 1$ when it is true for $n = k$, so it is true for $1 + 1 = 2$. This proves that the next domino is always knocked over. Now apply the second part again and take $k = 2$. Continuing this process proves that $n^2 \geq n$ is true for all positive integers.

Using the induction principle, it can also be shown that $2n$ is always an even number for all positive integers, n. Substitute 1, 2, 3, and 4 for n, and the results are 2, 4, 6, and 8, which are all even numbers. But how can it be certain that, without fail, every positive integer n will result in an even number for $2n$? It looks obvious, but often what looks obvious is not necessarily a valid proof. The induction principle, however, provides a valid proof.

The mathematical statement we want to prove is that $2n$ is an even number when n is a positive integer. To test the first part, we know that for $n = 1$, $2n$ is 2×1, or 2. The first even number is 2. So the statement is true for $n = 1$. To test the second part, suppose that $2n$ is an even number for some positive integer $n = k$. Therefore, $2k$ is even. Remember, adding 2 to any even number always produces an even number. So $2k + 2$ is also an even number, but $2k + 2 = 2(k + 1)$. Hence, $2(k + 1)$ is an even number. Assuming that the statement is true for $n = k$ leads to the fact that the statement is true for $n = k + 1$. Therefore, the induction principle proves that $2n$ is an even number for all positive integers, n. SEE ALSO Proof.

Rafiq Ladhani

Bibliography

Amdahl, Kenn, and Jim Loats. *Algebra Unplugged.* Broomfield, CO: Clearwater Publishing Co., 1995.

Miller, Charles D., Vern E. Heeren, and E. John Hornsby, Jr. *Mathematical Ideas*, 9th ed. Boston: Addison-Wesley, 2001.

Inequalities

An inequality is a mathematical statement that looks exactly like an equation except that the equals sign is replaced with one of the five inequality symbols.

$\neq$	not equal to
$<$	less than
$\leq$	less than or equal to
$>$	greater than
$\geq$	greater than or equal to

Imagine two friends of ages 9 and 12. Each of the five inequality symbols can be used to write a statement about their ages, depending on which aspect about their ages is to be emphasized.

$9 \neq 12$ says that 9 is not equal to 12

$9 < 12$ says that 9 is less than 12

$9 \leq 12$ says that 9 is less than or equal to 12

$12 > 9$ says that 12 is greater than 9

$12 \geq 9$ says that 12 is greater than or equal to 9

Notice that $9 < 12$ and $12 > 9$ are two ways to represent the same relationship; when the 9 and 12 are reversed, the inequality is also reversed.

The difference in meaning of "greater than" and "greater than or equal to" is subtle. For example, let a represent the age of a person. How would an equality be written to show that the age limit for voting is 18?

The expression $a > 18$ means that the age has to be greater than 18. The expression $a \geq 18$ means that the age either can be greater than 18 or it can be equal to 18. Since a person who is exactly 18 years old is allowed to vote, the inequality $a \geq 18$ is the correct one to use for this situation.

Various limits in society can be expressed using inequalities. Just a few examples are speed limits, minimum and maximum bank withdrawals, minimum and maximum fluid levels, grade requirements for college admittance, and minimum sales to make a fundraising goal. Some common phrases that indicate inequality within word problems are "minimum," "maximum," "at most," "at least," and superlatives like "oldest" and "smallest."

Solving Inequalities

Every possible equation can be made into an inequality. Furthermore, inequalities are solved the same way as equations, with one exception; namely, when an inequality is multiplied or divided by a negative number on both sides of the inequality sign.

For example, start with the true statement $5 < 6$. When both sides are multiplied by -2, the statement becomes $-10 < -12$. This resulting

---

SUMMARIZING INEQUALITIES

Two points must be remembered when dealing with inequalities.

- If each side of an inequality is multiplied or divided by a positive number, then no changes are made to the inequality symbol.

- If each side of an inequality is multiplied or divided by a negative number, then the equality symbol must be reversed.

statement is false because -10 is greater than -12. Since multiplying (or dividing) an inequality by a negative number results in a false statement, the inequality symbol must be reversed to maintain a true statement. In this example, the correct answer is $-10 > -12$. As another example, to solve $-4x > 12$, divide both sides by -4, and then reverse the inequality to yield $x < -3$.

A Practical Example. Consider the following problem. A student has saved \$40, and wants to save a total of at least \$300 to buy a new bicycle and bicycle gear. His job pays \$7.25 an hour. Find the number of hours he needs to work in order to save at least \$300.

To solve this problem, let h be the number of hours he needs to work. The words "at least" indicate that the combination of savings and pay must be greater than or equal to \$300. The solution below shows that the student must work 36 or more hours to meet his goal of saving \$300.

$$\$40 + 7.25h \geq \$300$$

$$7.25h \geq 260 \qquad \textit{Subtract 40 from each side.}$$

$$h \geq 35.9 \qquad \textit{Divide each side by 7.25.}$$

Graphing Inequalities

The number lines in the top five rows of the boxed figure illustrate each case that may arise in graphing inequalities in one variable, x. A closed circle on a number indicates that it is included in the solution set, and an open circle indicates that it is not included in the solution set. Shading to the left with a darkened arrow on the end indicates all numbers of lesser value are included in the solution set; shading to the right with a darkened arrow on the end indicates all numbers of greater value are included in the solution set.

Graphing Compound Inequalities. Compound inequalities are two inequalities separated by the words "and" or "or." The solution set to a compound inequality that is separated by the word "and" is the region where the two graphs overlap. This is known as an intersection.

Consider how to write a compound inequality that represents the possible ages of a teenager, and then how to graph the solution set. To write this inequality, let a represent age. So $a \geq 13$ and $a < 20$. The graph of the intersection is shown in the sixth number line in the boxed figure.

Compound inequalities that represent solutions that fall between two numbers are frequently written in an abbreviated notation with the variable in the middle. Hence, the inequality described above can also be written as $13 \leq a < 20$.

The solution set to a compound inequality that is separated by the word "or" is the combination of all points on both graphs. This is known as a union.

Consider how to write a compound inequality to represent the possible ages of a sibling who is not a teenager, and then how to graph the solution set.

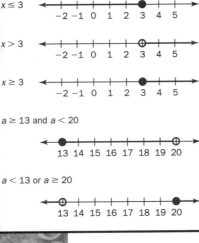

Examples of graphs of inequalities in one variable.

To write this inequality, let a represent age. So $a < 13$ or $a \geq 20$. The graph of the union is shown in the seventh number line in the boxed figure.

The corollary to compound inequalities in one variable is a system of inequalities in two variables. The solution to a system of inequalities is the intersection of the two graphs, just like the solution to a system of equations. However, the intersection of a system of inequalities usually consists of a whole region of points. This is especially useful since real-world problems often involve choosing from several possible solutions.

Inequalities in Two Variables

The graph below shows how to graph a linear inequality in two variables. Graphs in two variables are drawn using either a solid or dashed line. A solid line indicates that the points on the line are included in the solution set, and a dashed line indicates that the points on the line are not included in the solution set. For a linear graph, the solid or dashed line divides the plane into two regions, only one of which will be the solution set.

Consider how to solve and graph $y + 7 > 3x + 8$. First, subtract 7 from both sides to obtain $y > 3x + 1$. Graph the equation $y = 3x + 1$ using a dashed line. The dashed line divides the plane into two regions. Choose one point from each region that will be easy to substitute into the inequality. The points chosen below are (0, 0) and (0, 2). Only one of the two points will be a solution to the inequality, indicating which region includes the set of solutions.

First, substitute (0, 0).

$y > 3x + 1$

$0 > (3 \times 0) + 1$

$0 > 1$ (FALSE)

Next, substitute (0, 2).

$y > 3x + 1$

$2 > (3 \times 0) + 1$

$2 > 1$ (TRUE)

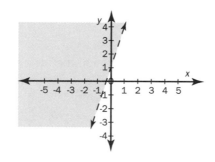

Hence, the point (0, 2) is a solution to the inequality. If more points in the same region are tested, they will also be solutions. Hence, the graph of the solution set includes points to the left of, but not including, the line $y = 3x + 1$, as shown above. SEE ALSO FUNCTIONS AND EQUATIONS.

Michelle R. Michael

Bibliography

Dantzig, George B. *Linear Programming and Extensions.* Princeton, NJ: Princeton University Press, 1998.

Infinity

Few concepts in mathematics are more fascinating or confounding than infinity. While mathematicians have a longstanding disagreement over its very definition, one can start with the notion that infinity (denoted by the symbol ∞) is an unbounded number greater than all real numbers.

Writing about infinity dates back to at least the Greek philosopher Aristotle (384 B.C.E.–322 B.C.E.). He stated that infinities come in two varieties; actual infinities (of which he could find no examples) and potential infinities, which he taught were legitimate only as thought. Indeed, the German Karl Gauss (1777–1855) once scolded a fellow mathematician for using the concept, stating that use of infinity "is never permitted in mathematics."

The French mathematician and philosopher René Descartes (1595–1650) proposed that because "finite humans" are incapable of producing the concept of infinity, it must come to us by way of an infinite being; that is, Descartes saw the existence of the idea of infinity as an argument for the existence of God. English mathematician John Wallis (1616–1703) suggested the use of ∞ as the symbol for infinity in 1655. Before that time, ∞ had sometimes been used in place of M (1000) in Roman numerals.

Defining Infinity

Although students are typically taught that "one cannot divide by 0," it can be argued that $\frac{1}{\infty} = 0$ (read as "one divided by infinity"). How is this possible? Observe the following progression.

$$\frac{1}{1} = 1.0$$

$$\frac{1}{2} = 0.5$$

$$\frac{1}{4} = 0.25$$

$$\frac{1}{8} = 0.125$$

$$\frac{1}{16} = 0.0625$$

$$\frac{1}{32} = 0.03125$$

Note that as the denominator, or the divisor, becomes larger, the value of the fraction (or the "quotient") becomes smaller. What happens if the denominators become very large?

$$\frac{1}{512} = 0.00195$$

$$\frac{1}{4,096} = 0.00024$$

$$\frac{1}{10,000,000} = 0.0000001$$

One can see that as the denominator becomes extremely large, the fraction values approach 0. Indeed, if one thinks of infinity as "ultimately large," one can see that the value of the fraction will likewise be "ultimately small," or 0. Hence, one informal (but useful) way to define infinity is "the number that 1 can be divided by to get 0." Actually, there is no need to use the number 1 as the numerator here; any number divided by infinity will produce 0.

Using algebra, one can come up with another definition of infinity. By transforming the following equation we see that infinity is what results if 1 is divided by 0.

If $\frac{1}{\infty} = 0$

Then $1 = \infty \times 0$

And $\infty = \frac{1}{0}$.

Notice that this approach to informally defining infinity produces an equation (the middle equation of the three above) in which something times 0 does not give 0! Because of this difficulty, and because the rules of algebra used to write and transform the equations apply to numbers, some mathematicians claim that division by 0 should not be allowed because ∞ may not be a defined number. They argue that dividing by 0 does *not* give infinity, but rather that infinity is undefined.

Another method of attempting to define infinity is to examine sets and their elements. If in counting the elements of a set one-by-one the counting never ends, the set can be said to be infinite.

Infinity as a Slope. Infinity is also sometimes defined as "the slope of a vertical line on the coordinate plane." In **coordinate geometry**, it is accepted that the slope of any straight line is defined as the change in vertical height divided by the change in horizontal distance between any two points on the line. The slope is often shown as a fraction in lowest terms, and sometimes called "rise over run."

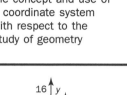

coordinate geometry
the concept and use of a coordinate system with respect to the study of geometry

In the figure, the slope of line (a) is $\frac{1}{2}$. If a line is very steep, the rise will be very large compared to the run, giving a very large numerical slope. The slope of line (b) is $\frac{13}{1}$. A much steeper line will result in a fraction such as $\frac{1,000,000,000}{1}$. Such a line would appear to be vertical, even though it would not be quite vertical if viewed in greater detail. Thus, the slope of extremely steep lines approaches infinity, and the slope of a "completely steep" line, that is, a vertical line, can be thought of as equal to infinity.

Yet on a "completely steep" or vertical line, any two points give a run of 0. This means that one could define the slope of the line as any number over 0. This again allows the conclusion that division by 0 results in infinity, unless one maintains that the slope of a vertical line is undefined.

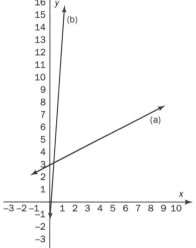

The Nature of Infinity

Although several definitions of infinity were provided, note that none of them state that infinity is the highest possible number. Consider this: On a number line, how many points are between points 4 and 5? An infinite number, of course, because actual points have no dimension, even though their two-dimensional representations have a very small dimension on the paper, blackboard, or computer screen. But consider further: How many points are between points 4 and 6? Also an infinite number, certainly, but this set appears to be twice as large as the one between points 4 and 5. This use of **set theory** as an approach to understanding infinity forces one to look at several curious possibilities.

As a line becomes steeper (b), its slope will approach infinity. Yet the slope of a vertical line may be considered undefined rather than infinite because the calculation requires division by 0.

1. There are different sizes of infinity.

2. A set with an infinite number of elements is the same size as one of its "smaller" subsets.

3. Elements can be added to a set that already has an infinite number of elements.

set theory the branch of mathematics that deals with the well-defined collections of objects known as sets

Which of these possibly contradictory statements is true? It may be impossible to answer the question. Galileo (1564–1642) felt that the second statement was true. The great German mathematician and founder of set theory Georg Cantor (1845–1918) added to our understanding of infinity by choosing not to see the statements as contradictions at all, but to accept them as simultaneous truths. Cantor defined orders of infinity. An infinite

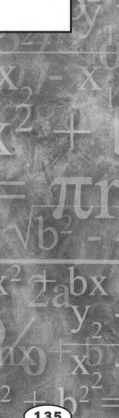

DEVELOPMENT OF SET THEORY

German mathematician Georg Cantor (1845–1918) was an active contributor to the development of set theory. He also became known for his definition of irrational numbers.

set that can be put into one-to-one correspondence with the counting numbers is the smallest infinite set, called aleph null. Other larger infinite sets are called aleph one, aleph two, and so on. One can see that working with infinity produces various counterintuitive and even paradoxical results; this is why it is such an interesting concept.

There are numerous examples of infinity in pre-college mathematics. One case: it is accepted that 0.999. . . is exactly equal to 1.0. Yet how can a number which has a 0 in the units place be exactly equal to a number with a one in that place? The idea that there are an infinite number of nines in the first number allows us to make sense of the proposition. The number 0.999. . . is said to "converge on 1," meaning that 0.999. . . becomes 1 when the infinite number of nines is considered.

Another example of how infinity comes into play in common mathematics is in the decimal representation of π (pi), or 3.14159. . . . The digits making up π go on forever without any pattern, even though the size of π never gets even as large as 3.15.

No one has ever come across an infinite number of real things. Infinity remains a concept, brought to life only by the imagination. SEE ALSO DESCARTES, AND HIS COORDINATE SYSTEM; DIVISION BY ZERO; LIMIT.

Nelson Maylone

Bibliography

Gamow, George. *One Two Three. . .Infinity: Facts and Speculations of Science.* Mineola, NY: Dover Publications, 1998.

Hofstadter, Douglas. *Godel, Escher, Bach: An Eternal Braid.* New York: Basic Books, 1999.

Morris, Richard. *Achilles in the Quantum Universe: The Definitive History of Infinity.* New York: Henry Holt and Company, 1997.

Rucker, Rudy. *Infinity and the Mind.* Princeton, NJ: Princeton University Press. 1995.

Vilenkin, N. *In Search of Infinity.* New York: Springer Verlag, 1995.

Wilson, Alistair. *The Infinite in the Finite.* New York: Oxford University Press. 1996.

statistics the branch of mathematics that analyzes and interprets sets of numerical data

probability the likelihood an event will occur when compared to other possible outcomes

Insurance agents use computers and mathematics to assess risk, determine premiums, and calculate the amount of claims.

Insurance Agent

Insurance agents help people buy insurance plans to protect against illness, accidents, or emergencies. The three major categories of insurance are life, health, and property. Insurance agents may be self-employed or they may work for a particular insurance company. Insurance agents work for individuals or for companies to select an insurance provider, fill out complex application forms, and maintain records. In the event of a loss, agents help their clients settle insurance claims.

Most companies prefer to hire insurance agents who have college degrees. Insurance agents often have bachelor's degrees in business or economics. However, some companies will hire a person without a college degree if that person has proven sales ability or success in other types of work.

The mathematics of insurance can be very complicated. Computers help insurance companies use **statistics** to estimate the **probability** of an

event occurring. For example, the odds of an individual being involved in an automobile accident vary depending upon the driver's age, sex, driving history, location, and type or style of car. These statistics are used to determine appropriate rates for insurance plans. The riskier a person appears, based on the statistics, the higher the rate he or she will have to pay for insurance. Computers make it easier and faster to process insurance application forms and service requests.

Mathematics is used in the insurance business in other ways. For group coverage, insurance agents have to calculate the total cost, based on the number of persons being covered. Also, discounts may apply to the policy, thereby yielding some percentage off the normal cost. Most importantly to an insurance agent, the agent's pay, or commission, is often a percentage of the dollar amount of the policy sold. SEE ALSO PROBABILITY, THEORETICAL; STATISTICAL ANALYSIS.

Denise Prendergast

Bibliography

Farr, J. Michael. *America's Top White-Collar Jobs—Detailed Information on 112 Major Office, Management, Sales, and Professional Jobs,* 4th ed. Indianapolis: JIST Works, Inc., 1999.

Internet Resources

Occupational Outlook Handbook, 2000–2001 Edition. <http://stats.bls.gov/ocohome.htm>.

Integers

Integers are the set of numbers {. . . , −4, −3, −2, −1, 0, 1, 2, 3, 4, . . .} that encompass the counting numbers, {1, 2, 3, . . .}, the negative of the counting numbers, {. . . −3, −2, −1} and zero. Integers can be shown on a simple number line.

The integers on the left side of zero (0) are called negative numbers, and are represented by a negative sign (−) placed before them, as in −5, −10, and −15.✳ The integers on the right side of 0 are called positive numbers. Examples include 5, 10, and 15. The positive integers are known as counting numbers or natural numbers. The positive integers and 0 are called whole numbers. Zero is an integer but it is neither positive nor negative.

Integers are used in everyday life. A debt or a loss is often expressed with a negative integer. A gain is usually expressed with a positive integer. When the temperature is warmer than the zero point of the temperature scale, it is represented with a positive sign; when it is colder than the zero point, it is represented with a negative sign. SEE ALSO NUMBERS, REAL; NUMBERS, WHOLE; ZERO.

Marzieh Thomasian

✳**Some historians believe the first evidence of the use of negative numbers was around 300 B.C.E. in China.**

Bibliography

Aufmann, Richard N., and Vernon C. Baker. *Basic College Mathematics,* 4th ed. Boston: Houghton Mifflin Company, 1991.

Integral *See Calculus.*

Interest

When you borrow money to buy a car or a house you are not only expected to pay back that money, but to pay interest on it, too. Interest is a fee paid by a borrower to the lender for the use of money. It is calculated as a percentage of the loan amount. When you deposit money into a savings account or certificate of deposit or buy a savings bond, you are loaning money and so you are paid interest. Interest plays an important role in economics because it serves as an incentive for those with available money to lend it to those needing it. There are many different ways that this fee is expressed and calculated.

Types of Interest

The term "simple interest" refers to a percentage of the loan that must be paid back in addition to the original loan. For example, if you borrow $1,000 at 10 percent simple interest and pay it back five years later, you will pay back the $1,000 plus 10 percent or $100 additional dollars for each year, a total of $500 in interest.

Few loans, however, are actually based on simple interest. Loans are usually based on "compound interest," where the total of the outstanding original money and the accumulated interest are calculated on a regular basis to compute the interest owed. In the preceding example, if interest were to be compounded annually (i.e., once each year), the interest for the first year would still be $100. But in the second year the borrower would owe interest not just on the original $1,000, but on the additional $100 of interest that was owed to the lender for the first year. The total interest for the second year would be $110. Similarly in the third year the interest would grow to $121. By the end of 5 years the total interest, compounded annually, would be $610.51, in contrast to the $500 in simple interest. This is illustrated in part (a) of the table.

"Discount interest" is interest that is subtracted from the loan when it is first made. Following the above examples, if you borrowed $1,000 at a discount interest rate of 10 percent, you would only receive $900, but would be expected to pay back $1,000. Since in this case you have really only borrowed $900, which you end up paying $100 interest on, you are paying a higher rate of interest than with simple or compound interest. In this example, a 10 percent discount rate would be the same as an 11.11 percent compound rate.

Compound interest is not necessarily compounded on an annual basis. By compounding interest more often the lender is able to get interest on interest. This can have a significant affect on the total earnings made on a savings deposit or other loan. One thousand dollars in a savings account paying 6 percent interest compounded annually would earn $60 in interest in one year. What if that same account were compounded monthly, as shown in part (b) of the table? Six percent is not earned each month. Instead, the annual rate of 6 is divided by the number of months, 12, giving a half percent per month. So, using the table, you will note that after the first month, the account earns $5. But during second month there is now $1,005 in the account. The extra $5 also earns interest.

Examples of Interest

(a) Compounded Annually

Year	Beginning value	Interest at 10%	Total at end of year
1	1,000.00	100	1,100.00
2	1,100.00	110	1,210.00
3	1,210.00	121	1,331.00
4	1,331.00	133.1	1,464.10
5	1,464.10	146.41	1,610.51

(b) Compounded Monthly

Month	Beginning value	Interest at 6%	Total at end of month
1	1,000.00	5.00	1,005.00
2	1,005.00	5.03	1,010.03
3	1,010.03	5.05	1,015.08
4	1,015.08	5.08	1,020.15
5	1,020.15	5.10	1,025.25
6	1,025.25	5.13	1,030.38
7	1,030.38	5.15	1,035.53
8	1,035.53	5.18	1,040.71
9	1,040.71	5.20	1,045.91
10	1,045.91	5.23	1,051.14
11	1,051.14	5.26	1,056.40
12	1,056.40	5.28	1,061.68

You can see from part (b) of the table that you earn an extra $1.68 by compounding the same savings monthly. In this case the **rate** is still 6 percent, but the yield is 6.168 percent. The rate is sometimes called APR and the yield APY, for annual percentage rate and annual percentage yield, respectively. Note that if a bank offers you a yield of 6 percent they are actually offering you a rate of less than 6 percent. When comparing interest rates, it is important that you do not confuse rates with yields.

So if you get a little more for computing interest monthly, what would happen if you computed it daily? The 6 percent rate would be divided by the number of days in the year (365) and the result would be the interest for one day. While this is only about $0.16, that extra $0.16 starts to earn interest too. By the end of the year, this results in $61.83 in interest being earned in the account or the yield for a 6 percent APR savings account compounded daily, day in to day out, which is 6.183 percent. Although the interest could be computed over smaller intervals, the interest calculation is a function that approaches a **limit**. The limit is so closely approached at the daily compounded value that there is little to be gained by compounding the interest more than daily.

Interest and Loans

Loans such as automobile, credit cards, and home mortgage loans work in a similar fashion, with the bank serving as the lender. Automobile and mortgage loans are generally **fixed term**, meaning that they are expected to be paid off completely at a set time in the future. Automobile loans are usually a 3- to 5-year term, while home mortgage loans can be for terms as long as 30 years. These loans allow the consumer to buy these expensive items before they have all of the money for them, and pay for them while they use them. The cost of this convenience, however, is the interest. Home mortgage loans can also be either at a fixed rate, agreed to at the start of the loan, or can be variable-rate loans, where the interest rate can change. Although variable rate loans are generally offered at a lower percentage than fixed-rate loans, the borrower must face the risk that the interest rate could be adjusted and become higher than the rate that was offered for the fixed-rate loan.

Credit card loans generally have a significantly higher interest rate and require a minimum payment each month. Borrowers frequently find that they make no progress in lowering their credit card debt because more credit is incurred as the outstanding balance is paid off.

Credit cards are an extremely convenient but expensive financial tool, and many borrowers get into serious financial trouble when they let their credit card debt grow. For example, if you have a credit bard balance of $1,000, the interest on this balance will be $15 per month if the annual interest rate of the card is 18 percent. The minimum payment that the card issuer charges will be somewhat higher than the monthly interest charge, but not by much. For this example, assume a minimum payment of $50. By paying only the minimum required payment each month, and adding interest, your balance is not significantly reduced from month to month. At this rate it could take years to pay off your balance.

rate the portion of the principal, usually expressed as a percentage, paid on a loan or investment during each time interval

limit a mathematical concept in which numerical values get closer and closer to a given value or approach that value

fixed term for a definite length of time determined in advance

When a borrower pays off a loan such as a house mortgage or a car loan, they make a payment at regular intervals, usually monthly. Some of the payment pays the interest on the loan for that month. The rest is applied to the current outstanding value of the loan and reduces it, so that the loan will be completely paid off at the agreed upon time. In the case of a 30-year home loan, a borrower will find that the largest part of the monthly payment is applied to interest payments at first and a small amount is applied to the balance of the loan, called the principal. The result is that after a few years you still owe nearly the full loan amount. Slowly the borrower makes progress against the principal, until finally after 30 years the loan is paid off.

For example, if a borrower borrows $100,000 on a 30-year mortgage at 8 percent fixed rate, after one year the borrower will have paid $8,805.17, not including taxes or insurance, but will have only reduced the principal by $835.36 (the remaining $7,969.81 goes towards interest). It is valuable to realize that if the loan has no per-payment penalty, you can significantly reduce the total cost of the loan by making additional payments in the early years, as these additional payments apply completely to the loan principal. For example, if after the first year the borrower was able to pay back an additional $904, the loan would be paid off a full year earlier, avoiding the last year of payments totaling $8,805.17. In this way a few extra payments each year or a slightly higher monthly payment can significantly reduce the term on the loan and result in significant savings.

By building a savings account that benefits from compound interest, a small investment will grow well over time. If a person who is 20 years old deposits $100 monthly into a savings account that pays 7 percent interest, they would have deposited $48,000 by age 60. But thanks to compound interest, there would be over $265,000 in the savings account. SEE ALSO PERCENT.

Harry J. Kuhman

Bibliography

McNaughton, Deborah J. *Destroy Your Debt! Your Guide to Total Financial Freedom.* Winter Park, FL: Archer-Ellison Publishing Company, 2001.

Interior Decorator

Although the terms "interior decorator" and "interior designer" refer to different professions, they are often used interchangeably. Technically, an interior decorator focuses on a room's surface—its color and decor and the artistic arrangement of the objects within it. An interior designer is more of an architect, concerned with the design and structure of the room. Nevertheless, the two fields have merged, and anyone interested in a career in interior decorating needs the same kind of training and experience. In the United States, this begins with a 4- or 5-year degree program from a school accredited by the Foundation for Interior Design Education and Research. These programs typically include course work in interior design, art, architecture, and technology. After graduation and 2 years of work experience, the aspiring interior decorator is qualified for the state licensing examination administered by the National Council for Interior Design Qualification.

Interior decorators and designers must use mathematics to achieve accurate measurements and make drawings to scale.

As one prominent practitioner comments, being an interior decorator is "more than lingering over fabric swatches or doodling out designs." An interior decorator must know as much about business (including budgeting), engineering principles, materials science, drafting, and building safety codes as about color and arrangement. The interior designer has to be able to take accurate measurements of room areas, angles, elevations, and the like. A critical skill is the ability to envision and make drawings to scale to ensure that furnishings and other objects fit in the space being decorated. It is also a good idea for designers to develop strong computer skills, especially the ability to use CAD (computer-aided design) programs. SEE ALSO ARCHITECT.

Michael J. O'Neal

Bibliography

Ball, Victoria Ross. *Opportunities in Interior Design and Decorating Careers.* Lincolnwood, IL: VGM Career Horizons, 1995.

Gibbs, Jenny. *A Handbook for Interior Designers.* New York: Sterling Publishing, 1997.

Internet

For many people, a good deal of the day is spent online. The ability to send e-mail messages and "surf" the World Wide Web has already become matter-of-fact. But an amazing amount of technology and mathematics must occur for e-mail and Internet access to be successful.

A Brief History of the Internet

The general consensus is that the conception of the Internet occurred in the early 1960s as part of the Department of Defense's Advanced Research Projects Agency (ARPA), which was conceived and headed by J. C. R. Licklider from the Massachusetts Institute of Technology. The intent was to share supercomputers among researchers in the United States.

Because computers in the 1960s were so large and expensive, it was important to find a way for many people, often at different locations, to be able to use the same computer. By the end of the decade, ARPANET was developed to solve this problem, and in 1969 four universities—Stanford, University of California–Los Angeles, University of California–Santa Barbara, and the University of Utah—were the first to be successfully connected.

The ARPANET was not available for commercial use until the late 1970s. By 1981 there were 213 different hosts (central computers) available on the ARPANET, although many were completely incompatible with one another because each "spoke" a different language. Things were somewhat disjointed until Bob Kahn and Vint Cerf created TCP/IP (Transfer Control Protocol/Internet Protocol), which became the common language for all Internet communication. This transformed the disparate collection known as ARPANET into one cohesive group, the Internet.

Even though the intent of the ARPANET and Internet was to allow researchers to share data and access remote computers, e-mail soon became the most popular application to communicate information. In the 30-plus

Vinton Cerf is the co-developer of the computer networking protocol, TCP/IP, which has become the common language for Internet communications.

years since then, not much has changed. In an average week, approximately 110 million people are online in the United States. If, on average, each of those people sends ten e-mails per week (a conservative estimate), then there are more than a billion e-mails sent every week.

Traveling on the Internet

Although e-mail is something that is often taken for granted, a great deal must happen for an e-mail message to go from one device to another. Depending on its destination, an e-mail message's travel path can be either very short or very long.

Sending e-mail is similar in some ways to sending a letter through regular mail: there is a message, an address, and a system of carriers that determines the best way to deliver the mail. The biggest differences between sending e-mail and regular mail are the first and last steps.

When an e-mail message is sent, it is first broken down into tiny chunks of data called "IP packets." This is accomplished by a mailing program (such as Outlook Express or Eudora) using the TCP Internet language. These packets are each "wrapped" in an electronic envelope containing web addresses for both the sender and recipient.

Next, the packets are sent independently through the Internet. It is possible that every single packet (and there can easily be hundreds of them) is sent on a different path. They may go through many levels of networks, computers, and communications lines before they reach their final destination.

The packets' journey begins within the Internet Service Provider (ISP) or network (AOL or MSN, for example), where the address on the envelopes is examined. Addresses are broken into two parts: the recipient name and the domain name. For example, in an e-mail message sent to

John_Doe@msn.com, "John_Doe" is the recipient name and "msn.com" is the domain name.

Based on the domain name, the router (a piece of equipment that determines the best path for the packets to take) will determine whether the packets remain on the network or need to be sent to a different router. If the former is the case, the packets are sent directly to the recipient's e-mail program and reassembled using TCP.

If the recipient is on a different network, things get more complex. The packets are sent through the Internet, where an Internet router determines both where they need to go and the best path to get there. Decisions like these are made by problem-solving programs called **algorithms**, which find the optimal path for sending the packets.

algorithm a rule or procedure used to solve a mathematical problem

Each packet is sent from one network to another until it reaches its final destination. Because they determine where the packets should go, routers can be likened to different transportation stations within a huge transportation system containing buses, trains, and airplanes. To get from one part of the world to another, a message may have to go through several stations and use multiple types of transportation.

For example, assume that two travelers are both starting in New York City and heading for Los Angeles. They get separated and end up taking different modes of transport yet still end up at the same point. This is what happens to the packets when they make the trip from the originating computer to their eventual destination; that is, they can get separated and sent on different paths to their final destination. Routers determine the optimal path for each packet, depending on data traffic and other factors.

The packets often arrive at the final destination at different times and in the wrong order. The recipient will not see an e-mail message until all of the packets arrive. They are then recombined in the correct order by the recipient's mail program, using TCP, into a message that the recipient can read.

Connection Speed

How quickly all of this occurs can be influenced by many factors, some within the control of the e-mail user and others beyond it. One factor that can be controlled is the way information is received and sent to and from the originating computer. Popular types of connections available in 2001 are telephone modems, DSL (Digital Subscriber Line), Cable, T1 and T3.

Telephone modems are the earliest and slowest of the possible types of connections. In relation to the transportation metaphor used previously, they would be the buses. Under optimal conditions, one can download or upload information at rates of between 14 and 56 kbps (kilobits per second) with a modem. (One kilobit equals one thousand bits.) A *bit* is what makes up the data that are sent.✶

✶**Eight bits equals one byte, and one byte equals a single character (a letter or numeral).**

Actual transmission speeds for modems tend to be much slower than the optimal speeds because there is a vast, constant stream of data being transferred back and forth. Compare this to driving on a highway. Even though the speed limit may be 65 miles per hour (mph), because of traffic and road conditions, one may need to drive less than 65 mph. On the Internet, it is almost always rush hour.

bandwidth a range within a band of wavelengths or frequencies

Under perfect conditions, the 56,000 characters of data per second—which comes out to over 3 million characters per minute—that can downloaded may sound like a lot of information, but it really is not. Most text messages (such as e-mail messages) are relatively small and will download quickly using a modem. Audio, video, or other multimedia files, however, cause more of a problem. These files can easily be upwards of 5 or 10 million bytes each, and thus use a much greater **bandwidth**.

Faster alternatives to modems are now widely available. The most common alternatives for home use are DSL and cable modems. DSL works through the phone line. Speeds for DSL tend to be in the range of 1.5 mbps (megabits per second). One megabit is equal to 1,000 kilobits.

Cable modems, unlike DSL, have nothing to do with phone lines. Cable modems transmit data using the cable that carries cable television signals. They offer fast speeds of up to 6 mbps. Even though this is a very good speed, an ISP may limit the available bandwidth, which restricts the size of files that can be uploaded or downloaded.

For large companies, universities, and the Internet Service Providers, speeds need to be high and bandwidths need to be enormous. T1 and T3 lines, which are dedicated digital communication links provided by the telephone company, are used for this purpose. They typically carry traffic to and from private business networks and ISPs, and are not used in homes.

Both T3 and T1 lines have their advantages in certain areas. With T3 connections one can potentially access speeds of nearly 45 mbps, or somewhere around one thousand times that of a modem. Transmission speeds for T1 lines are considerably slower, running at 1.5 mbps. The advantage of T1 is privacy. T1 connection lines are not shared with other users. In contrast, T3 connection lines (as well as modems, cable, and DSL) are shared.

Consider the highway metaphor once again. Having a T1 line is like maintaining a private two-lane highway on which only certain people are allowed to drive. Having a T3 line is more like driving on a 4-lane autobahn (the highway system in Germany, where there is no speed limit), with three of the lanes clogged up with slow-moving trucks. On the autobahn the potential exists to go very fast, but the traffic often prevents drivers from reaching high speeds. So whether the T1 or T3 is more desirable depends on which is more valued—speed or privacy.

When an e-mail message is sent, there is a very good possibility that the packets will encounter nearly all of these types of connections on their journeys—just like people can use planes, trains, and automobiles. The next time you hit the "send" button, think about all of the logical and mathematical operations that are about to happen. SEE ALSO COMPUTERS AND THE BINARY SYSTEM; INTERNET DATA, RELIABILITY OF; NUMBERS, MASSIVE.

Philip M. Goldfeder

Bibliography

Abbate, Janet. *Inventing the Internet*. Cambridge, MA: MIT Press, 1999.

Gralla, Preston. *How the Internet Works: Millennium Edition*. Indianapolis: QUE, 1999.

Lubka, Willie, and Nancy Holden. *K·I·S·S Guide to the Internet*. New York: Dorling Kindersley, 2000.

Internet Resources

Average Weekly Web Usage: United States. <http://www.nielsen-netratings.com>.

Brain, Marshall. *How E-mail Works.* <http://www.howstuffworks.com/email1.htm>.

Finnie, Scot. *20 Questions: How the Net Works.* <http://coverage.cnet.com/Content/Features/Techno/Networks/index.html>.

Frequently Asked Questions About T1. <http://www.everythingt1.com/faq.html>.

Timeline: PBS Life on the Internet. <http://www.pbs.org/internet/timeline/index.html>.

Internet Data, Reliability of

The Internet can be a wonderful resource for all types of information including **quantitative** data. The Internet is accessible, both for those who want to obtain information and for those who want to make data available. Since there is so much readily accessible information, Internet users must learn to filter the data they find on the **World Wide Web**, because the providers of information may misuse numbers and mathematics in order to appear convincing. Therefore, Internet users should learn to evaluate data carefully, critically, and even skeptically.

To start, your local librarian could be of invaluable assistance in helping you discriminate between useful Internet sources of information and those web sites that would be a waste of time to visit. Remember that anyone can publish a web page on the Internet, and many web sites may be of little value in a search for specific quantitative information. Many librarians, particularly reference librarians, are specialists trained to effectively and efficiently search and obtain information for library patrons. The information specialist at your local library can save you significant time in your search for valid and reliable Internet data.

Filtering Information through the URL

Because the Internet is such a vast source of information of varying quality, web resources must be evaluated for authority, reliability, objectivity, accu-

quantitative of, relating to, or expressible in terms of quantity

World Wide Web the part of the Internet allowing users to examine graphic "web" pages

Users of the Internet and its World Wide Web must think critically about the information they find. Statistics may appear authoritative, but their reliability can vary widely depending on their source.

racy, and currency. More traditional sources of information, such as an article in an encyclopedia, are screened with all those criteria in mind by authors, reviewers, editors, and publishers. That is not the case for most of the information on the Internet. No one has to approve the content of web sites, so it is your job to assess the appropriateness of the data you find on the Internet.

The domain name of the web page can reveal a great deal about the authority of the information on the web page. The domain name is the first part of the uniform resource locator (URL), and is the code that identifies the source of the web page. For example, of the address abc.com, the "abc" is the domain name.

Agencies of the U.S. government are assigned the .gov suffix, so you can trust that most of the information on those web sites has been screened for accuracy. The .edu suffix is usually assigned to 4-year degree-granting institutions. Much of the information posted on these sites has been prepared by scholars. Remember, however, that students also can post information on academic web pages, and sometimes faculty members post controversial and biased information to support their position. Thus, information on university web pages should still be treated with skepticism.

The .org domain suffix was originally meant for charities and non-profit organizations, a .com ending meant the site was for commercial businesses, and the .net suffix indicated the site is concerned with network issues. There are many sites with .com, .org, or .net suffixes that contain invaluable, reliable, and accurate information, but remember that the people creating those sites have particular economic, social, or political purposes in establishing a web presence. There is great potential that the data presented on their web pages may not be as complete, accurate, and unbiased as you require.

Web Pages with Authors

Beyond the domain name, the authority of the web page can be ascertained from the page itself. The name of the author(s) should be clearly visible in the header or footer of the web page, with contact information (e-mail, phone number, and address) provided. If the author is affiliated with an organization, this information should be clearly evident on the web page. You should scrutinize the author's education, experience, and reputation in the field you are investigating. That is easily accomplished by finding biographical information, often linked to the web page, and by looking for evidence of peer-reviewed, scholarly work by the author.

Closely connected to the authority of the web page is the reliability of the data found at that Internet site. Evidence that the information is reliable can be determined by observing if the information presented on the web site is of a reputable author or organization, if the data are taken from books or sources subject to quality control processes, or if the site itself is an online journal that is refereed by editors or other experts in the field.

Related to the reliability of the quantitative information obtained from a web page is the objectivity of the author. One of the purposes of a web site is for the author or organization to persuade viewers to adopt a particular point of view, and sometimes this is done in a subtle and surreptitious manner. The bias manifests itself in the presentation of incomplete or, worse, inaccurate quantitative information slanted toward the perspective of the author. If the data look too good to be true, they probably are. Be wary of a hidden agenda, which can often be detected from the explicit or implicit purpose of the page. That purpose can only determined by careful and critical viewing of the site.

Looking at Information with a Skeptical Eye

Finally, you can assess the accuracy and currency of information found at an Internet site by observing if the information is timely and comprehensive. The document should be dated, particularly if the subject information is known to change rapidly. Sites that have many outdated links are not well-maintained and probably are not current. Web pages that acknowledge opposing points of view or are sponsored by non-commercial enterprises have a tendency to be more reliable.

While looking for data on the Internet, be aware that **search engines** do not evaluate web sites for the reliability or relevance of the information they contain. The various search engines have different **algorithms** for selecting sites, and those algorithms are generally not matched to your needs. For example, some search engines give priority to sites that are associated with sponsors of the search engine, and some give priority to the most popular web pages. Although search engines do not evaluate the quality of web pages, "evaluative" web sites examine other sites based on quality of content, authority, currency, and other useful criteria.

Additionally, the lack of professionalism exhibited on the web page tells a great deal about the data contained on the page. The presence of spelling errors is an important indicator, as is the illogical organization of the site. Source documentation is extremely important, especially when it comes to the presentation of statistics and other quantitative information. The authors providing the Internet data should clearly identify the sources of the information they post, so that you can corroborate and confirm the validity of the data. If the source of the data is not clearly explained or specified, the information should be suspect. If there are links to the source data, this is a very good sign that the information may be accurate and reliable. Another positive indicator is the inclusion of a bibliography displaying related sources with proper attribution.

As a general rule, you should challenge all of the information you find on the Internet. Information coming from reliable sources, such as those sites containing a .gov domain name or a respected author, does not require as stiff a scrutiny as information posted on a personal web page. Validate the information by finding other Internet sources or printed sources that support the information found on an Internet site. You should never use Internet information you cannot verify. Information is power, and in learning to become skeptical and critical readers and viewers of Internet data, you will obtain the power that comes with having accurate information. SEE ALSO INTERNET.

Dick Jardine

search engine software designed to search the Internet for occurrences of a word, phrase, or picture, usually provided at no cost to the user as an advertising vehicle

algorithm a rule or procedure used to solve a mathematical problem

Internet Resources

Cohen, Laura, and Trudy Jacobson. "Evaluating Internet Resources." <http://library.albany.edu/internet/evaluate.html>.

Grassian, Esther. "Thinking Critically about Discipline-based WWW Resources." <http://www.library.ucla.edu/libraries/college/help/critical/discipline.htm>.

Harris, Robert. "Evaluating Internet Research Sources" <http://www.media-awareness.ca/eng/med/class/teamed2/harris.htm>.

Kirk, Elizabeth. "Evaluating Information Found on the Internet."<http://milton.mse.jhu:8001/research/education/net.html>.

"Evaluating Web Sites." <http://www.lib.lfc.edu/internetsearch/evalWeb.html>.

Inverses

The additive inverse of a number undoes the effect of adding that number. This means that, for example, the effect of adding a number by subtracting the same number can be undone. So, if 7 is added to 4, the result is 11. If 7 is subtracted from 11, the addition is undone, and the result is 4.

$$4 + 7 = 11 \text{ and } 11 - 7 = 4$$

Multiplication and division are related in the same way: They are inverse operations that undo each other. If 6 is multiplied by 3, the result is 18. Then 18 can be divided by 3 to undo the multiplication, and the result is 6.

$$6 \times 3 = 18 \text{ and } 18 \div 3 = 6$$

Most mathematical operations have an inverse operation that undoes or reverses its effect. The squaring of a number, for example, as in $7^2 = 49$, can be undone by taking the square root. The square root of 49 is 7. Thus, squaring and taking the square root are also inverse operations.

Inverse operations can also be used to find the additive inverse of a specific number. For example, -9 is the additive inverse of 9 since the sum of -9 and 9 is 0. Additive inverses come in pairs; 9 is the additive inverse of -9, just as -9 is the additive inverse of 9. Any two numbers are additive inverses if they add up to 0.

Visualize a pair of additive inverses on the number line. The number 9 and its additive inverse -9 are both nine units away from 0 but on opposite sides of 0. For this reason, -9 is called the opposite of 9, and 9 is the opposite of -9. The opposite of a number may be positive or negative. The opposite of -4 is 4, a positive number. The opposite of 8 is -8, a negative number. The number -2 can be read as "the opposite of 2" or as "negative 2."

A negative number is always to the left of 0 on a number line. Every number on the number line has an additive inverse. The additive inverse of 0 is 0 because $0 + 0 = 0$.

Multiplicative inverses come in pairs also. Any two numbers are multiplicative inverses if they multiply to 1. For example, because the product of 3 and $\frac{1}{3}$ is 1, 3 and $\frac{1}{3}$ are multiplicative inverses. In the same way, $\frac{2}{3}$ and $\frac{3}{2}$ are multiplicative inverses because their product is 1.

Decimal numbers also have inverses, of course. The decimal number 0.04 can be written as the fraction $\frac{4}{100}$, so the multiplicative inverse of 0.04 is $\frac{100}{4}$, which equals 25. This can be checked by multiplying 0.04 and 25 to

SUMMARIZING INVERSES

Inverses can be summarized in a few sentences.

Additive inverses add to 0. The additive inverse of a number is the opposite of the number. The additive inverse of a positive number is a negative number.

Multiplicative inverses multiply to 1. A number and its multiplicative inverse are called reciprocals. The reciprocal of a number is 1 divided by that number. The reciprocal of a fraction is the same as the fraction flipped.

verify that the product is indeed 1. The additive inverse of 0.04 is -0.04 because these two numbers add to 0.

A pair of numbers that multiply to 1, such as $\frac{1}{3}$ and 3 or 0.04 and 25, are also called reciprocals. To find the reciprocal of any number, write 1 over that number. Thus $\frac{1}{3}$ is the reciprocal of 3. One shortcut for finding the reciprocal of a fraction is to "flip" the fraction. The reciprocal of $\frac{2}{3}$ is $\frac{3}{2}$; the reciprocal of $\frac{7}{10}$ is $\frac{10}{7}$. Pairs of reciprocals always multiply to give a product of 1.

Every number on the number line, except 0, has a multiplicative inverse. The multiplicative inverse of 0, or the reciprocal of 0, is undefined because division by 0 is undefined. SEE ALSO INTEGERS; MATHEMATICS, DEFINITION OF; NUMBERS, REAL.

Lucia McKay

Bibliography

Anderson, Raymond. *Romping Through Mathematics*. New York: Alfred A. Knopf, 1961.

Klein Bottle *See Mathematics, Impossible.*

Knuth, Donald

American Computer Scientist and Mathematician
1938–

Donald Ervin Knuth is considered one of the world's leading computer scientists and mathematicians. Yet in high school, Knuth found mathematics uninspiring. Although he achieved the highest grade-point average in the history of his high school, Knuth doubted his ability to succeed in college mathematics; and so did his advisor. So when Knuth graduated from high school in 1956, he entered the Case Institute of Technology (now Case Western Reserve) in Cleveland, Ohio, on a physics scholarship.

In his freshman year, Knuth encountered Paul Guenther, a mathematics professor who persuaded him to switch majors from physics to mathematics. Fearing he would fail, Knuth spent hours working out extra calculus problems, only to discover that his abilities far exceeded those of his classmates. One particularly difficult professor assigned a special problem and offered an immediate "A" in the course to any student who could solve it. Although Knuth initially considered the problem unsolvable, he did not give up. Making another attempt one day, Knuth solved the problem, earned his "A," and skipped class for the rest of the semester. The following year, Knuth earned an "A" in abstract mathematics and was given the job of grading papers for the very course he had skipped.

Knuth graduated *summa cum laude* from Case in 1960 with a Bachelor of Science (B.S.) and Master of Science (M.S.) in mathematics. He went on to earn his Doctor of Philosophy (Ph.D.) in mathematics from the California Institute of Technology in 1963, and joined the faculty as an assistant professor of mathematics. In 1968 Knuth joined the faculty at Stanford University, and served until his retirement in 1993, after which he was designated Professor Emeritus of the Art of Computer Programming.

Knuth's awards and honors include 17 books, more than 150 papers, 18 honorary doctorates, the 1974 Turing Award, Stanford University's first chair in computer science, the 1979 National Medal of Science (which was presented by then-President Jimmy Carter), and the 1996 Kyoto Prize for

Donald Knuth, (seated), shown here in 1980 with Herman Zaph at Stanford University, pioneered the TeX and METAFONT systems for digital typography. Knuth is perhaps most famous for his pioneering multivolume works, *The Art of Computer Programming* and *Computers and Typesetting*.

lifetime achievement in the arts and sciences (awarded by the Inawori Foundation).

Randy Lattimore

Bibliography

Albers, Donald J., and Gerald. L. Alexanderson, eds. *Mathematical People: Profiles and Interviews*. Boston: Birkhäuser, 1985.

Knuth, Donald E. *The Art of Computer Programming*. 3 vols. Reading, MA: Addison-Wesley, 1968.

Shasha, Dennis, and Cathy Lazere. *Out of Their Mind: The Lives and Discoveries of 15 Great Computer Scientists*. New York: Springer-Verlag, 1995.

Internet Resources

"Donald Knuth's Home Page." 2001. <http://www-cs-faculty.stanford.edu/~knuth>.

Kovalevsky, Sofya

Russian Mathematician and Educator
1850–1891

Russian mathematician Sofya Kovalevsky was born in Moscow, Russia, the daughter of a minor nobleman. She became interested in mathematics at a very young age, when an uncle discussed mathematical concepts with her. Because of a wallpaper shortage, her nursery was papered with her father's lecture notes from a course in calculus, and at age 11 she studied the notes, recognizing principles her uncle had discussed. Under a tutor, she became so enamored with mathematics that she neglected her other studies.

When her father stopped her mathematics lessons, Kovalevsky borrowed an algebra book and read it while the family slept. At age 14 she read a physics textbook written by a neighbor and taught herself **trigonometry** so that she could understand the optics section. The neighbor recognized her ability and persuaded her father to send her to St. Petersburg, Russia, to continue her education.

trigonometry the branch of mathematics that studies triangles and trigonometric functions

Long, Hard Road to Success

The story of Kovalevsky's adult life was one of doors closing in her face because she was a woman. After finishing her secondary education, she arrived in Heidelberg, Germany, in 1869 to study mathematics and natural sciences, only to discover that the university did not admit women. Instead, she attended classes unofficially for three semesters. In 1870 she decided to try her fortunes at the University of Berlin. Again, the university did not admit women, but an eminent professor agreed to tutor her privately. By 1874 she had written papers on Abelian integrals and Saturn's rings. A third paper, on partial differential equations, was published in an influential mathematics journal. On the recommendation of Kovalevsky's tutor, Germany's University of Göttingen granted her a Ph.D. in 1874.

Unable to get a job teaching mathematics, Kovalevsky returned home, where shortly after her arrival, her father died. In her grief she neglected mathematics for the next 6 years. Instead, she wrote fiction, theater reviews, and science articles for a newspaper. Later in her life, Kovalevsky would go on to write plays.

In 1880 Kovalevsky resumed her study of mathematics. In 1882 she began work on the **refraction** of light and published three papers on the subject. Finally, in 1883 a door opened—she was granted a temporary appointment at the University of Stockholm in Sweden, where she taught courses in the latest mathematical topics. There she published a paper on crystals in 1885. She was appointed editor of a new journal, *Acta Mathematica*, and organized conferences with leading mathematicians.

In 1888 Kovalevsky entered a paper titled "On the Rotation of a Solid Body about a Fixed Point" in a competition sponsored by the French Academy of Science. The committee thought so highly of the paper that it increased the prize money. In 1889 she won a prize from the Swedish Academy of Sciences for further work on the same topic and was elected as a corresponding member to the Imperial Academy of Sciences in Russia. Later that year the university granted her status as a professor.

Unfortunately, Kovalevsky's triumph did not last long. In 1891, at the summit of her career, she died of pneumonia in Stockholm. She was just 41 years of age.

Michael J. O'Neal

Internet Resources

Sofia Kovalevsky. Biographies of Women Mathematicians.
    <http://www.agnesscott.edu/1riddle/women/kova.htm>.

Sofya Kovalevsky was able to use her strength in mathematics to achieve positions that were highly uncommon for women of her time. She became the first female mathematician to hold a chair at a European university.

refraction the change in direction of a wave as it passes from one medium to another

Landscape Architect

According to the American Society of Landscape Architects, a landscape architect plans and designs the use, allocation, and arrangement of land and water resources through the creative application of biological, physical, mathematical, and social processes. While architects design buildings and structures, landscape architects are "architects of the land," designing parks, housing developments, zoos, waterfronts, and so on, as well as stormwater drainage systems, wetlands, and species habitats. Some of the specializations they pursue include regional landscape planning, urban planning, ecological planning and design, and historic preservation and reclamation. Forty-six states require landscape architects to be licensed by completing a bachelor's degree in the field and passing the Landscape Architect Registration Examination.

Among other skills, landscape architects must be sound mathematicians and be able to integrate mathematical models and planning methods into a technical design. To do this, it is necessary to take accurate measurements and compute areas, volumes, and the quantity of materials needed for each component of the job, all while staying within a budget. It is important for landscape architects to be competent with CAD (computer-aided design) software to help plan projects. Additionally, they need to understand the underlying mathematics principles in construction processes and support systems, as well as in methods of construction. For example, problems of drainage would require the landscape architect to manipulate contours and spot elevations, to calculate slopes, grades, and volumes of material, and to understand hydraulics. SEE ALSO ARCHITECT.

Michael J. O'Neal

The work of a landscape architect is cross-disciplinary because it spans tasks ranging from urban planning to designing species habitats.

Bibliography

Dines, Nicholas T. *Landscape Architect's Portable Handbook.* New York: McGraw-Hill Higher Education, 2001.

Internet Resources

American Society of Landscape Architects. <http://www. asla.org>.

Leonardo da Vinci

Italian Painter, Scientist, and Mathematician
1452–1519

Leonardo da Vinci was born in the Italian town of Vinci. As a young boy, he showed a talent for painting. When he was 20 years old, he joined the painters' guild in Florence. Within a few years, Leonardo's talent was known all across Europe. Although he completed only thirty paintings, two of them—the *Mona Lisa* and *The Last Supper*—are among the most easily recognized paintings of all time.

Leonardo was more than a painter: He was a scientist and mathematician who explored botany, mechanics, astronomy, physics, biology, and optics. Leonardo developed prototypes of the modern helicopter, submarine, and parachute, and he attributed his scientific discoveries to mathematics. He wrote, "There is no certainty in science where mathematics cannot be applied."

Although Leonardo dabbled in different areas of mathematics, geometry was his chief focus. He discovered a proof of the Pythagorean theorem, dissected various geometric figures, and illustrated a book about geometry and art. At one point in Leonardo's life, a friend of his noted that "his mathematics experiments have distracted him so much from his painting that he can no longer stand his paint brush."

During the last three years of his life, Leonardo was a guest of Francois I, King of France. The king hoped Leonardo would produce some masterpieces for the royal court. He never did. Leonardo finished a few paintings he had already started and spent the rest of his time making scientific explorations. He died in Amboise, France.

Arthur V. Johnson II

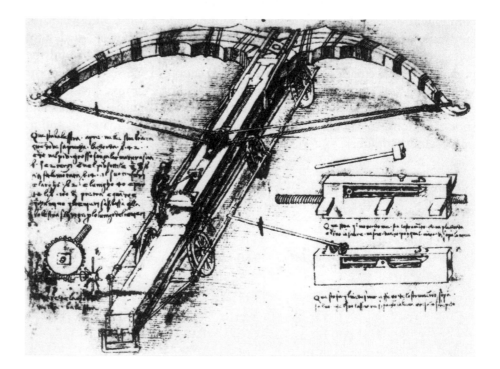

Although known for his paintings, Leonardo da Vinci developed improvements to war implements, such as this mechanical crossbow.

Bibliography

Boyer, Carl B. *History of Mathematics*. New York: John Wiley & Sons, Inc., 1968.

Johnson, Art. *Classic Math: History Topics for the Classroom*. Palo Alto, CA: Dale Seymour Publications, 1994.

Internet Resources

MacTutor History of Mathematics Archive. University of St Andrews. <http://www-groups.dcs.st-and.ac.uk/~history/Mathematicians.html>.

Light

Light is a form of electromagnetic radiation. Other types of electromagnetic radiation include radio waves, microwaves, infrared, ultraviolet, x-rays, and gamma rays. All electromagnetic waves possess energy. Moreover, electromagnetic waves (including light) are produced by accelerated electric charges (such as electrons). Light moves through space in a wave that has an electric part and a magnetic part. That is why it is called an electromagnetic wave.

Speed of Light

Light travels through empty space at a high speed, very close to 300,000 kilometers per second (km/s). This number is a universal constant: it never changes. Since all measurements of the speed of light in a vacuum always produce exactly the same answer, the distance light travels in a certain amount of time is now defined as the standard unit of length. For convenience, the speed of light is usually written as the symbol, c.

Characteristics of Waves

All waves, including light waves, share certain characteristics: They travel through space at a certain speed, they have frequency, and they have wavelength. The frequency of a wave is the number of waves that pass a point in one second. The wavelength of a wave is the distance between any two corresponding points on the wave. There is a simple mathematical relationship between these three quantities called the wave equation. If the frequency is denoted by the symbol f and the wavelength is denoted by the symbol λ, then the wave equation for electromagnetic waves is:

$$c = f\lambda.$$

Since c is a constant, this equation requires that a light wave with a shorter wavelength have a higher frequency.

Waves also have amplitude. Amplitude is the "height" of the wave, or how "big" the wave is. The amplitude of a light wave determines how bright the light is.

Wavelength and Color

There is a simple way to remember the order of wavelengths of light from longest to shortest: ROY G. BIV. The letters stand for red, orange, yellow, green, blue, indigo, and violet. (This violet is not the same as the crayon color called violet, which is a shade of purple.) The human eye perceives different wavelengths of light as different colors. Red is the color of the longest wavelength the human eye can detect; violet is the shortest. Red light has a wavelength of around 700 nanometers (nm). (A nanometer is one-billionth of a meter.) Light with a wavelength longer than 700 nm is called infrared. ("Infra" means "below.") Violet light is around 400 nm. Electromagnetic radiation with a shorter wavelength is called ultraviolet. ("Ultra" means "beyond.") It is best not to use the terms "ultraviolet light" or "infrared light," for instance, because the word "light" should be applied only to wavelengths that the human eye can detect.

Refraction and Lenses

What happens when light encounters matter depends on the type of material. Glass, water, quartz, and other similar materials are transparent. Light passes through them. However, light slows down as it passes through a transparent material. This happens because the light is absorbed and reemitted by the atoms of the material. It takes a small amount of time for the atom to reemit the light, so the light slows down. In water, light travels around $0.75c$ or 225,000 km/s. In glass, the speed is even slower, $0.67c$. In diamond, light travels at less than half its speed in vacuum, $0.41c$.

When a beam of light passes from vacuum (or air) into glass, it slows down, but if the beam hits the glass at an angle, it does not all slow down at the same time. The edge of the beam that hits the glass first slows down first. This causes the beam to bend as it enters the glass. The change in direction of any wave as it passes from one material to another and speeds up or slows down is called **refraction**. Refraction causes water to appear to be shallower than it is in reality. Refraction causes a diamond to sparkle.

Refraction is also what creates a mirage. Sometimes the air a few centimeters above the ground is much warmer than air a few meters farther up. As light from the sky passes into this warmer air, it speeds up and bends away from the ground. An observer may see light from the sky and be fooled into thinking that it is a lake. Sometimes, even trees and houses can be seen in the mirage, but they will appear upside down.

Refraction of light allows a lens to perform its function. In a converging lens, the center of the beam reaches the lens first and slows down first. This causes the beam to be bent toward the center of the lens. A parallel beam of light passing through a good-quality lens will be bent so that all the light arrives at a single point called the focal point. The distance from the lens to the focal point is called the focal length, f. A diverging lens spreads the beam out so that it appears to be coming from the focal point.

In a slide projector, the lens projects an image of an object (the slide) onto a screen. The distance from the lens to the image and the distance of the lens to the object are related to the focal length by this strange-looking formula (d_i is the image distance and d_o is the object distance):

$$\frac{1}{f} = \frac{1}{d_i} + \frac{1}{d_o}.$$

Interpreting this formula is a little difficult. Remember that the focal length of the lens does not change, so $\frac{1}{f}$ is a constant. If the image distance (d_i) gets larger, the object distance (d_o) must get smaller to make the fractions add to the same constant value.

The refraction of light passing through water causes the spoon to look "disjointed" when viewed from the side.

refraction the change in direction of a wave as it passes from one medium to another

Reflection and Mirrors

When light hits a surface, it can also be **reflected**. Sometimes light is both refracted and reflected. If the object is opaque, however, the light will just be reflected. When light is reflected from a surface, it bounces off at the same angle to the surface. The angle of incidence is equal to the angle of reflection. SEE ALSO VISION, MEASUREMENT OF.

Elliot Richmond

reflected light or sound waves returned from a surface

Bibliography

Epstein, Lewis Carroll. *Thinking Physics*. San Francisco: Insight Press, 1990.

Giancoli, Douglas C. *Physics*, 3rd ed. Englewood Cliffs, NJ: Prentice Hall, 1991.

Haber-Schaim, Uri, John A. Dodge, and James A. Walter. *PSSC Physics*, 7th ed. Dubuque, IA: Kendall/Hunt, 1990.

Hewitt, Paul G. *Conceptual Physics*. Menlo Park, CA: Addison Wesley, 1992.

Light Speed

Many science fiction writers feel that humans will only be able to feasibly explore the Milky Way galaxy (and beyond) when it is possible to travel at, or above, the speed of light. Unmanned probes have already been sent to explore the solar system and beyond. NASA's *Voyager I* and *Voyager II* blasted off from Earth in the late 1970s to explore the outer planets and are now far beyond them.

The Light-Year

The dimensions of the universe are so enormous that they overwhelm conventional units of distance (such as the meter, kilometer, or mile). Therefore, a much larger unit distance is needed—the light-year. A light-year is the amount of distance that light travels in vacuum in one Earth year. Astronomers have found light-years to be a convenient distance when measuring the distance between stars and other celestial bodies.

In one second, light travels approximately 186,000 miles. To extend this out one year, multiply 186,000 miles times the number of seconds in a minute (60), times the number of minutes in an hour (60), times the number of hours in a day (24), and times the number of days in a year (365). As a result, light travels approximately 5,865,696,000,000 (more than 5.8 trillion) miles in one year—the distance in one light-year.

To better grasp the distance involved in traveling in outer space, imagine flying NASA's space shuttle from Los Angeles to New York City. This journey would take approximately 20 minutes at a speed of about 17,000 mph (miles per hour). At that speed, a journey to the Sun would take about 228 days. Beyond the Sun, the next closest stars to Earth are those of the triple star system of Alpha Centauri A, Alpha Centauri B, and Proxima Centauri at 4.3 light-years away, more than 25 trillion miles distant. This flight on the shuttle would take about 170,000 years!

A voyage from Earth to the center of the galaxy, a distance of about 30,000 light-years, would take about 1.2 billion years. Even the two *Voyager* spacecraft, the fastest machines ever launched from Earth, are now traveling at only 10 miles per second, not even one ten-thousandth the speed of light. These spacecraft would take 78,000 years to reach the Alpha Centauri star cluster.

As one can see, it would take extremely long periods of time to travel from Earth to other stars at conventional speeds, which is why the prospect of faster-than-light space travel has become so popular. It seems to be the only way to travel throughout the universe.

Is Traveling at the Speed of Light Possible?

Albert Einstein (1879–1955) developed his special theory of relativity in 1905. It declared that any material object can approach the speed of light, but it is impossible to go at or above this cosmic speed limit. The speed of light (denoted as c) in a vacuum—an approximation of what actually is found in interstellar space—is a fundamental constant of physics and nature. The speed of light is as basic as gravity, which Einstein tackled in his 1915 general theory of relativity.

According to Einstein, if one could travel at the speed of light, then time would stretch to infinity and distances would be abolished altogether. Yet one obstacle to traveling at the speed of light is that matter attempting to attain light speed requires more and more energy but with very little resulting additional speed. At a speed above the speed of light, an object theoretically would be going "backwards in time," an occurrence viewed by many scientists as impossible.

Interstellar space travel appears to be extremely, if not prohibitively, expensive, even if future technologies could make it possible. All the propulsion systems proposed so far for faster-than-light voyages, such as warp drives, would require huge amounts of energy—more energy that is even conceivable to produce. On the one hand, there are many trivial ways in which things, in a sense, can be going faster than light, and there may be other more genuine possibilities. On the other hand, there are also good reasons to believe that real faster-than-light travel and communication will always be unachievable.

Ways of Traveling Faster than the Speed of Light

One way to (apparently) travel faster than light is to make light travel slower. Light in a vacuum travels at a speed c, which is a universal constant, but in a dense medium such as water or glass, light slows down to $\frac{c}{n}$, where n is the refractive index of the medium (for instance, $n = 1.0003$ for air and $n = 1.4$ for water). It is possible for particles to travel through air or water at faster than the speed of light in the medium. Therefore, going faster than the speed of light really means exceeding the speed of light in vacuum c, not in a medium such as air or water.

Another way to (apparently) travel faster than light is to misrepresent speeds. If spaceship A is traveling away from a point at $0.7c$ in one direction, and another spaceship B is traveling away from the same point at $0.8c$ in the opposite direction, then the total distance between A and B may be thought to be increasing at $1.5c$ (derived from $0.7c + 0.8c$). However, this is not what is normally meant by relativistic speeds.

The true speed of spaceship A relative to spaceship B is the speed at which an observer in B observes the distance from A to be increasing. The

two speeds must be added using the relativistic formula for addition of velocities:

$$w = \frac{(u + v)}{(1 + uv/c^2)}$$

where

$v = 0.7c$ is the speed of spacecraft A,

$u = 0.8c$ is the speed of spacecraft B, and

c is the speed of light.

After inserting the appropriate values into the equation, the relative speed w is actually about $0.96c$ (that is, 0.96 times the speed of light) and, therefore, not faster than the speed of light.

Another way to (apparently) travel faster than light is to observe how fast a shadow can move. If you project a shadow of your finger using a nearby lamp onto a far away wall and then move your finger, the shadow will move much faster than your finger. It can actually move much faster than this if the wall is at some oblique angle. If the wall is very far away, the movement of the shadow will be delayed because of the time it takes light to get there, but its speed is still amplified by the same ratio. The speed of a shadow is therefore not restricted to being less than the speed of light.

These are all examples of things that can go faster than light, but they are not physical (material) objects. It is not possible to send information on a shadow, so faster-than-light communication is not possible in this way. Faster-than-light travel cannot logically be deduced just because some "things" go faster-than-light or appear to do so. This is not what is meant by faster-than-light travel, although it shows how difficult it is to define what is really meant by traveling faster than the speed of light.

Proposals for Faster-than-Light Travel

One proposal for traveling faster than the speed of light is to use *wormholes*. A wormhole is a four-dimensional shortcut through space-time in which two regions of the universe are connected by a narrow passageway. The wormhole would permit matter/energy to proceed from one spot in the universe to another in a shorter time than it would take light otherwise. Wormholes are a feature of general relativity, but to create them it is necessary to change the **topology** (or the physical features) of space-time.

topology the study of those properties of geometric figures that do not change under such nonlinear transformations as stretching or bending

The complete wormhole geometry consists of a black hole, a white hole, and two universe-regions connected at their horizons by a wormhole. According to Einstein's theory of gravitation, empty space is actually a tightly woven fabric of space and time. Massive objects warp the space-time fabric, just as a bedsheet would be pushed down into a deep valley if a whale were to lie on it. Anything that comes near the valley naturally rolls in, and that "falling" is the force perceived as gravity. If the whale twists around on the bed, its motion carries the bedsheet along.

If Einstein's theory is correct, space-time should likewise be dragged around massive objects. Black holes (like whales on a bedsheet) are objects that are so massive and dense that immense gravity warps space around the core, not allowing light or anything else to escape. A white hole, however, is a black hole running backward in time. Just as black holes (supposedly) pull things in, white holes (supposedly) push things out. This so-called

naturally made warping of space in the form of wormholes could provide a means of quickly traveling to distant regions of space.

A warp drive, sometimes called hyperspace drive, is a (theorized) mechanism for warping space-time in such a way that an object could move faster than light. The most famous spaceship to use warp drive (at least in science fiction) is Star Trek's *U.S.S. Enterprise*. Its concept expands space-time behind the spaceship and contracts space-time in front of the spaceship. The warp in space-time makes it possible for an object to go faster than light speed.

But the problem with developing a warp drive is the same problem with formulating large wormholes. To construct it, one would need a ring of exotic negative energy wrapped around the spaceship. Even if such exotic matter can exist, it is unclear how it could be deployed to make the warp drive work.

A more likely scenario for deep-space travel makes use of Einstein's special theory of relativity. For objects moving at relativistic speeds (speeds near but below the speed of light), there is an observable stretching out of time relative to an observer in a stationary reference frame. For example, say a spacecraft travels at a constant speed of nine-tenths the speed of light (0.9c) from Earth to Alpha Centauri, a distance of 4.3 light-years. According to **time dilation**, the time observed on Earth would be faster than the time onboard the spacecraft according to the equation

$$t^* = t\{(1 - (\tfrac{v^2}{c^2}))\}^{1/2}$$

where

t^* is the time indicated by the spacecraft clock,

t is the time indicated by Earth's clock, and

c is the speed of light.

Therefore, according to Earth's clock, the spacecraft took 4.8 years to complete the trip (4.3 light-years divided by 0.9c). However, onboard the spacecraft, the journey takes only $t^* = 4.8\{(1 - (\tfrac{(0.9c)^2}{c^2}))\}^{1/2}$, or 2.1 years.

A Future Reality

With present technology, it is possible to (theoretically) produce spaceships that could slowly accelerate to near the speed of light so that a trip to the nearer stars would (in Earth time) take perhaps a few hundred years. However, in the spaceship, the entire trip, due to time dilation, would perhaps take a few dozen years, depending on the time it took to accelerate up (and then accelerate down) to and from light speed and how closely to light speed the spacecraft traveled.

It is rather difficult to define exactly what is really meant by faster-than-light travel and communication. Many things such as shadows can go faster than light speed but not in a useful way that can carry information. There are several serious possibilities for real faster-than-light mechanisms that have been proposed in the scientific literature, but technical difficulties still exist.

The **Heisenberg uncertainty principle** tends to stop the use of apparent faster-than-light quantum effects for sending information or matter. In general relativity there are potential means of faster-than-light travel, but they may be impossible to actually construct. It is highly unlikely that en-

time dilation the principle of general relativity which predicts that to an outside observer, clocks would appear to run more slowly in a powerful gravitational field

Heisenberg uncertainty principle the principle in physics that asserts it is impossible to know simultaneously and with complete accuracy the values of certain pairs of physical quantities such as position and momentum

gineers will be building spaceships with faster-than-light drives in the foreseeable future. It is curious, however, that theoretical physics, as presently understood, seems to leave the door open to the possibility.

Just because today something seems impossible, that does not mean that it will never become feasible. SEE ALSO COSMOS; EINSTEIN, ALBERT; SPACE EXPLORATION; UNIVERSE.

William Arthur Atkins (with Philip Edward Koth)

Bibliography

Calder, Nigel. *Einstein's Universe.* New York: Greenwich House, 1979.

Hawking, Stephen W. *A Brief History of Time: From the Big Bang to Black Holes.* Toronto: Bantam Books, 1988.

Sagan, Carl. *Cosmos.* New York: Random House, 1980.

Shu, Frank H. *The Physical Universe: An Introduction to Astronomy.* Mill Valley, CA: University Science Books, 1982.

Smith, Elske V. P., and Kenneth C. Jacobs. *Introductory Astronomy and Astrophysics.* Philadelphia: Saunders College Publishing, 1973.

Internet Resources

Millis, Marc G. *Warp Drive When?* NASA Glenn Research Center. <http://www.grc.nasa.gov/WWW/PAO/warp.htm>.

Limit

The concept of limit is an essential component of **calculus**. Limits are typically the first idea of calculus that students study. Two fundamental concepts in calculus—the **derivative** and the **integral**—are based on the limit concept. Limits can be examined using three intuitive approaches: number sequences, functions, and geometric shapes.

Number Sequences

One way to examine limits is through a sequence of numbers. The following example shows a sequence of numbers in which the limit is 0.

$$1, \frac{1}{2}, \frac{1}{4}, \frac{1}{8}, \frac{1}{16}, \frac{1}{32}, \frac{1}{64}, \cdots$$

The second number in the sequence, $\frac{1}{2}$, is the result of dividing the first number in the sequence, 1, by 2. The third number in the sequence, $\frac{1}{4}$, is the result of dividing the second number in the sequence, $\frac{1}{2}$, by 2.

This process of dividing each number by 2 to acquire the next number in the sequence is continued in order to acquire each of the remaining values. The three dots indicate that the sequence does not end with the last number that appears in the list, but rather that the sequence continues infinitely.

If the sequence continues infinitely, the values in the sequence will get closer and closer to 0. The numbers in the sequence, however, will never actually take on the value of zero. The mathematical concept of approaching a value without reaching that value is referred to as the "limit concept." The value that is being approached is called the limit of the sequence. The limit of the sequence $1, \frac{1}{2}, \frac{1}{4}, \frac{1}{8}, \frac{1}{16}, \frac{1}{32}, \frac{1}{64}, \cdots$ is 0.

calculus a method of dealing mathematically with variables that may be changing continuously with respect to each other

derivative the derivative of a function is the limit of the ratio of the change in the function; the change is produced by a small variation in the variable as the change in the variable is allowed to approach zero; an inverse operation to calculating an integral

integral a mathematical operation similar to summation; the area between the curve of a function, the x-axis, and two bounds such as $x = a$ and $x = b$; an inverse operation to finding the derivative

The example below displays several sequences and their limits. In each case, the values in the sequence are getting closer to their limit.

Example 1: 0.9, 0.99, 0.999, 0.9999, 0.99999,   Limit: 1
0.999999, 0.9999999, . . .

Example 2: 5.841, 5.8401, 5.84001, 5.840001,   Limit: 5.84
5.8400001, 5.84000001, . . .

Example 3: $-1, -\frac{1}{2}, -\frac{1}{3}, -\frac{1}{4}, -\frac{1}{5}, -\frac{1}{6}, -\frac{1}{7}, -\frac{1}{8}, -\frac{1}{9}, -\frac{1}{10}, \ldots$ Limit: 0

Not all sequences, however, have limits. The sequence 1, 2, 3, 4. . . increases and does not approach a single value. Another example of a sequence that has no limit is $-1.1, 2.2, -3.3, 4.4, -5.5, 6.6, \ldots$. Because there is no specific number that this sequence approaches, the sequence has no limit.

Functions

Limits can also be examined using functions. An example of a function is $f(x) = \frac{1}{x}$. One way to examine the limit of a function is to list a sample of the values that comprise the function. The left-hand portion of the table can be used to examine the limit of the function $f(x) = \frac{1}{x}$ as x increases.

As the values in the x column increase, the values in the $f(x)$ column get closer to 0. The limit of a function is equal to the value that the $f(x)$ column approaches. The limit of the function $f(x) = \frac{1}{x}$ as x approaches infinity is 0.

TABLE OF SAMPLE VALUES FOR THE FUNCTION $f(x) = \frac{1}{x}$

As x increases		As x approaches 0			
x	f(x)	x	f(x)	x	f(x)
1	1	1	1	−1	−1
2	$\frac{1}{2}$	$\frac{1}{2}$	2	$-\frac{1}{2}$	−2
3	$\frac{1}{3}$	$\frac{1}{4}$	4	$-\frac{1}{3}$	−3
4	$\frac{1}{4}$	$\frac{1}{5}$	5	$-\frac{1}{4}$	−4
5	$\frac{1}{5}$	$\frac{1}{6}$	6	$-\frac{1}{5}$	−5
6	$\frac{1}{6}$	$\frac{1}{7}$	7	$-\frac{1}{6}$	−6
7	$\frac{1}{7}$	$\frac{1}{8}$	8	$-\frac{1}{7}$	−7
.		.		.	
.		.		.	
.		.		.	
100	$\frac{1}{100}$	$\frac{1}{100}$	100	$-\frac{1}{100}$	−100
.		.		.	
.		.		.	
.		.		.	

Functions can also be plotted on a **Cartesian plane**. A graph of the function $f(x) = \frac{1}{x}$ is shown in the figure. The color curve represents the function. As the x values increase, the color curve or the $f(x)$ values get closer and closer to 0. Once again, the limit of the function $f(x) = \frac{1}{x}$ as x goes to infinity is 0.

It is important to consider what value x is approaching when determining the limit of $f(x)$. If x were approaching 0 in the preceding example, $f(x)$ would not have a limit. The reason for this can be understood using the middle and right-hand portions of the table.

The table suggests that the values for $f(x)$ continue to increase as x approaches 0 from values that are greater than 0. The table also suggests that the values for $f(x)$ continue to decrease as x approaches 0 from values that are less than 0. Because the $f(x)$ values do not approach a specific value, the function $f(x) = \frac{1}{x}$ does not have a limit as x approaches 0.

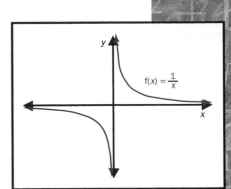

The limit of this function as x goes to infinity is 0. The function does not have a limit as x approaches 0.

Cartesian plane a mathematical plane defined by the x and y axes or the ordinate and abscissa in a Cartesian coordinate system

Geometric Shapes

A typical application of the limit concept is in finding area. For example, one method for estimating the area of a circle is to divide the circle into small triangles, as shown below, and summing the area of these triangles. The circle in (a) is divided into six triangles. If a better estimate of area is desired, the circle can be divided into smaller triangles as shown in (b).

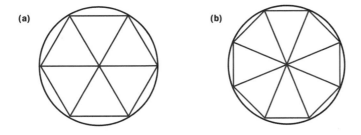

(a) (b)

If the exact area of the circle is needed, the number of triangles that divide the circle can be increased. The limit of sum of the area of these triangles, as the number of triangles approaches infinity, is equal to the standard formula for finding the area of a circle, $A = \pi r^2$, where A is the area of the circle and r is its radius.

In summary, limit refers to a mathematical concept in which numerical values get closer and closer to a given value or approaches that value. The value that is being approached is called the "limit." Limits can be used to understand the behavior of number sequences and functions. They can also be used to determine the area of geometric shapes. By extending the process that is used for finding the area of a geometric shape, the volume of geometric solids can also be found using the limit concept. SEE ALSO CALCULUS; INFINITY.

Barbara M. Moskal

Bibliography

Jockusch, Elizabeth A., and Patrick J. McLoughlin. "Implementing the Standards: Building Key Concepts for Calculus in Grades 7–12." *Mathematics Teacher* 83, no. 7 (1990): 532–540.

Internet Resources

"Limits" Coolmath.com. <http://www.coolmath.com/limit1.htm>.

Lines, Parallel and Perpendicular

In mathematics, the term "straight line" is one of the few terms that is left undefined. However, most people are comfortable with this undefined concept, which can be modeled by a pencil, a stiff wire, the edge of a ruler, or even an uncooked piece of spaghetti. Mathematicians sometimes think of a line as a point moving forever through space. Lines can be curved or straight, but in this entry, only straight lines are considered.

A line, in the language of mathematics, has only one dimension—length—and has no end. It stretches on forever in both directions, so that its length cannot be measured. When a line is modeled with a piece of spaghetti, a line segment is actually being represented. The model of a line segment has thickness (or width), while the idea that it models—a mathematical line—does not. So a mathematical line is a notion in one's mind, rather than a real object one can touch and feel, just as the notion of "two" is an idea in one's mind—that quality and meaning that is shared by two apples, two trucks, and the symbols //, 2, ☺☺, and ii.

Think of two straight lines in a **plane** (another undefined term in **geometry**). Someone can model this idea, imperfectly, by two pencils or two pieces of spaghetti lying on a desktop. Now, mentally or on a desktop, push these lines around, still keeping them on the plane, and see the different ways two lines can be arranged. If these two lines meet or cross, they have one point in common. In the language of mathematics, the two lines intersect at one point, their point of intersection. If two lines are moved so that they coincide, or become one line, then they have all of their points in common.

What other arrangements are possible for two lines in a plane? One can place them so that they do not coincide (that is, one can see that they are two separate lines), and yet they do not cross, and will never cross, no matter how far they are extended. Two lines in the same plane, which have no point in common and will never meet, are called parallel lines. If one draws a grid, or coordinate system, on the plane, she can see that two parallel lines have the same slope, or steepness. Are there any parallel lines in nature, or in the human-made world? There are many models of parallel lines in the world we build: railroad tracks, the opposite sides of a picture frame, the lines at the corners of a room, fence posts. In nature, parallel lines are not quite so common, and the models are only approximate: tracks of an animal in the snow, tree trunks in a forest, rays of sunlight.

The only other possible arrangement for two lines in the plane is also modeled by a picture frame, or a piece of poster board. Two sides of a rectangle that are not parallel are **perpendicular**. Perpendicular lines meet, or intersect, at right angles, that is, the four angles formed are all equal. The first pair of lines in part (a) of the figure below meet to form four equal angles; they are perpendicular. The second pair in part (b) forms two larger angles and two smaller ones; they are not perpendicular.

plane generally considered an undefinable term, a plane is a flat surface extending in all directions without end, and that has no thickness

geometry the branch of mathematics that deals with the properties and relationships of points, lines, angles, surfaces, planes, and solids

perpendicular forming a right angle with a line or plane

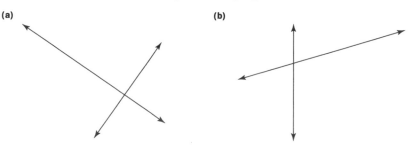

(a)   (b)

Perpendicular lines occur everywhere in buildings and in other constructions. Like parallel lines, they are less common in nature. On a coordinate system, two perpendicular lines (unless one of them is horizontal) have slopes that multiply to a product of –1; for example, if a line has a slope of 3, any line perpendicular to it will have a slope of $-\frac{1}{3}$. SEE ALSO LINES, SKEW; SLOPE.

Lucia McKay

Bibliography

Anderson, Raymond W. *Romping Through Mathematics.* New York: Alfred A. Knopf, 1961.

Juster, Norton. *The Dot and the Line: A Romance in Lower Mathematics.* New York: Random House, 1963.

Konkle, Gail S. *Shapes and Perception: An Intuitive Approach to Geometry.* Boston: Prindle, Weber and Schmidt, Inc., 1974.

Lines, Skew

For geometric figures in a plane, two straight lines must either be parallel to one another or must intersect at one point. Skew lines are non-parallel and do not intersect. Skew lines must therefore lie in separate planes from one another. Since skew lines are defined in terms of distinct planes, discussing such lines leads directly to the branch of mathematics called **solid geometry**.

Solid geometry is the branch of Euclidian geometry (named for Euclid, c. 325 B.C.E.–265 B.C.E.) that examines the relative positions, sizes, shapes, and other aspects of geometric figures that are not in a single plane. Whereas **plane geometry** is about two-dimensional space described by parameters such as length and width, solid geometry concerns itself with three-dimensional space.

One example of a three-dimensional object is a cube, which has height, length, and width. Another familiar example of a solid (three-dimensional) figure is the pyramid. Figures like these can be used to illustrate skew lines.

solid geometry the geometry of solid figures, spheres, and polyhedrons; the geometry of points, lines, surfaces and solids in three-dimensional space

plane geometry the study of geometric figures, points, lines, and angles and their relationships when confined to a single plane

Examples of Skew Lines

The edges of the pyramid above form skew lines. Each of the four faces of the pyramid (as well as its bottom) define a unique **plane**. Line segments *AB*, *AC*, and *BC*, for instance, define a unique plane, and each plane constitutes one of the four faces of the pyramid. None of the three line segments (*AB*, *AC*, *BC*) can be skew lines relative to one another because they all lie in the same plane. Recall that lines in the same plane either intersect (as do *AB*, *AC*, and *BC*) or are parallel to one another.

plane generally considered an undefinable term, a plane is a flat surface extending in all directions without end, and that has no thickness

There are, however, several pairs of line segments on the pyramid that form skew lines. Line segments *AB* and *CD* form a pair of such lines. These two segments are skew to one another because they are neither parallel nor intersecting. Even if the line segments are extended into infinite lines, they still remain skew. Though some of the line segments are hidden from view in this picture, one can envision several other pairs of skew lines formed by the edges of the pyramid.

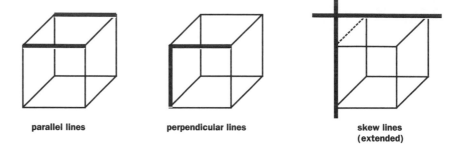

parallel lines   perpendicular lines   skew lines (extended)

A cube possesses many combinations of parallel, perpendicular, and skew line segments. The cubes above illustrate different line pairs: parallel, perpendicular, and skew. (The skew segments have been extended to indicate infinite lines.) The shortest distance between the two skew lines is the length of the dashed line segment, which is perpendicular to both of the indicated skew lines. Any other distance measured between the two skew lines will be longer than the dashed line segment.

The spatial orientation of any two skew lines can be described by two quantities: the closest or perpendicular distance between the two lines, and the angle between them. The illustration below shows these two quantities of distance and angle.

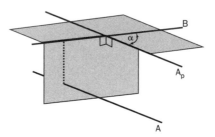

The two skew lines are *A* and *B*. Line *B* lies along the intersection of the two shaded planes. The dotted line segment joining lines *A* and *B* is perpendicular to both, and is the shortest distance between any two points on lines *A* and *B*.

To find the angle between *A* and *B*, a line, A_p, is constructed, which is parallel to *A* and which also intersects line *B*. The angle between lines A_P and *B* is designated by the Greek letter alpha (α). Because A_p and *A* are parallel lines, the angle α is also the angle between lines *A* and *B*. Therefore, by determining the distance (dotted line segment) and angle (α) between skew lines *A* and *B*, the relative position between the two is uniquely determined. SEE ALSO LINES, PARALLEL AND PERPENDICULAR.

Philip Edward Koth (with William Arthur Atkins)

Bibliography

Ringenberg, Lawrence A., and Presser, Richard S. *Geometry*. New York: Benziger, Inc. (in association with John Wiley and Sons, Inc.), 1971.

Locus

Sometimes it is useful in mathematics to describe the path that a point traces as it moves in a plane to meet certain conditions. For example, what is the path that a point on the end of the second hand of a clock traces in 60 seconds? This answer, of course, is a circle.

One way to define a circle is to say that a circle is the **locus** of all the points in a **plane** that are a given distance from a fixed point, called the center.

A locus in a plane can be thought of as all the possible locations or positions that a point can take as it moves to meet certain stated conditions. What is the locus of, or path traced by, a point in a plane that moves so that it is always three inches from point A? This locus will be a circle, with point A as the center and a radius of three inches.

What is the locus in a plane of all points that are 2 centimeters from a given line? This locus is made up of two lines, each parallel to the given line, one on each side, and at a distance of 2 centimeters from it, as illustrated in the figure below. The two dashed lines form the locus.

locus in geometry, the set of all points, lines or surfaces that satisfies a particular requirement

plane generally considered an undefinable term, a plane is a flat surface extending in all directions without end, and that has no thickness

What is the locus of all points in a plane that are the same distance from point D and from point E? To answer this, one might draw some example points that are **equidistant** from D and E, such as the points marked with a star in the left-hand illustration of the figure below.

equidistant at the same distance

These example points indicate that the locus of all the points in a plane that are the same distance from D as they are from E is a line that is the

perpendicular forming a right angle with a line or plane

parabola a conic section; the locus of all points such that the distance from a fixed point called the focus is equal to the perpendicular distance from a line

ellipse one of the conic sections, it is defined as the locus of all points such that the sum of the distances from two points called the foci is constant

hyperbola a conic section; the locus of all points such that the absolute value of the difference in distance from two points called foci is a constant

perpendicular bisector of the line segment that joins D and E, as shown in the right-hand illustration.

The idea of a locus can be used not just in a plane but also in three-dimensional space. For example, the preceding example, extended into space, becomes the locus of all points that are equidistant from points D and E. This locus will be the entire plane that is perpendicular to the plane containing DE and its perpendicular bisector and that contains the entire perpendicular bisector.

In space, the locus of all points at a given distance from a specific point is a sphere with a center at the point and a radius equal to the given distance. In space, the locus of all points at a given distance from a line segment is a cylinder with a hemisphere at each end.

The idea of locus can also be used to define the conic sections. In a plane, a circle is the locus of all points at a given distance from a specific point; a **parabola** is the locus of all points such that each point on the curve is the same distance from a specific point as its distance from a specific line; an **ellipse** is the locus of all points such that, for each point on the curve, the sum of the distances from each of two separate specific points, called the foci, remains the same; and a **hyperbola** is the locus of all points such that, for each point on the curve, the absolute value of the difference of the distances to each of two separate specific points, called the foci, remains the same. SEE ALSO Conic Sections.

Lucia McKay

Bibliography

Hogben, Lancelot. *Mathematics in the Making.* New York: Crescent Books, Inc., 1940.

Logarithms

The logarithm of a positive real number x to the base-a is the number y that satisfies the equation $a^y = x$. In symbols, the logarithm of x to the base-a is $\log_a x$, and, if $a^y = x$, then $y = \log_a x$.

Essentially, the logarithm to base-a is a function: To each positive real number x, the logarithm to base-a assigns x a number y such that $a^y = x$. For example, $10^2 = 100$; therefore, $\log_{10} 100 = 2$. The logarithm of 100 to **base-10** is 2, which is an elaborate name for the power of 10 that equals 100.

base-10 a number system in which each place represents a power of 10 larger than the place to its right

base-2 a binary number system in which each place represents a power of 2 larger than the place to its right

Any positive real number except 1 can be used as the base. However, the two most useful integer bases are 10 and 2. **Base-2**, also known as the binary system, is used in computer science because nearly all computers and calculators use base-2 for their internal calculations. Logarithms to the base-10 are called common logarithms. If the base is not specified, then base-10 is assumed, in which case the notation is simplified to $\log x$.

Some examples of logarithms follow.

$\log 1 = 0$ because $10^0 = 1$

$\log 10 = 1$ because $10^1 = 10$

$\log 100 = 2$ because $10^2 = 100$

$\log_2 8 = 3$ because $2^3 = 8$

$\log_2 2 = 1$ because $2^1 = 2$

$\log_5 25 = 2$ because $5^2 = 25$

$\log_3 \left(\frac{1}{9}\right) = -2$ because $3^{-2} = \frac{1}{9}$

The logarithm of multiples of 10 follows a simple pattern: logarithm of 1,000, 10,000, and so on to base-10 are 3, 4 and so on. Also, the logarithm of a number a to base-a is always 1; that is, $\log_a a = 1$ because $a^1 = a$.

Logarithms have some interesting and useful properties. Let x, y, and a be positive real numbers, with a not equal to 1. The following are five useful properties of logarithms.

1. $\log_a (xy) = \log_a x + \log_a y$, so $\log_{10} (15) = \log_{10} 3 + \log_{10} 5$
2. $\log_a \left(\frac{x}{y}\right) = \log_a x - \log_a y$, so $\log \left(\frac{2}{3}\right) = \log 2 - \log 3$
3. $\log_a x^r = r \log_a x$, where r is any real number, so $\log 3^5 = 5 \log 3$
4. $\log_a \left(\frac{1}{x}\right) = -\log_a x$, so $\log \left(\frac{1}{4}\right) = (-1) \log 4$ because $\frac{1}{4} = (4)^{-1}$
5. $\log_a a^r = r$, so $\log_{10} 10^3 = 3$

Logarithms are useful in simplifying tedious calculations because of these properties.

History of Logarithms

The beginning of logarithms is usually attributed to John Napier (1550–1617), a Scottish amateur mathematician. Napier's interest in astronomy required him to do tedious calculations. With the use of logarithms, he developed ideas that shortened the time to do long and complex calculations. However, his approach to logarithms was different from the form used today.

Fortunately, a London professor, Henry Briggs (1561–1630) became interested in the logarithm tables prepared by Napier. Briggs traveled to Scotland to visit Napier and discuss his approach. They worked together to make improvements such as introducing base-10 logarithms. Later, Briggs developed a table of logarithms that remained in common use until the advent of calculators and computers. Common logarithms are occasionally also called Briggsian logarithms. SEE ALSO POWERS AND EXPONENTS.

Rafiq Ladhani

Bibliography

James, Robert C., and Glenn James. *Mathematics Dictionary*, 5th ed. New York: Van Nostrand Reinhold, 1992.

Young, Robyn V., ed. *Notable Mathematicians, from Ancient Times to the Present*. Detroit: Gale Research, 1998.

Lotteries, State

State lotteries give participants the dream of winning huge jackpots while providing the state with funding for education, transportation, and other projects. State lotteries currently operate in about three-fourths of the states in the United States. These lotteries provide individuals with a relatively

inexpensive means of gambling on the possibility of winning a huge jackpot. The first legal state lottery was established in New Hampshire in 1964, culminating 10 years of legislative effort.

Probabilities of Winning

A wide range of games is offered by the numerous state lotteries across the country. The offerings of the Florida State Lottery in 2001, for example, include Florida Lotto, Mega Money, Fantasy 5, Play 4, and CASH 3, as well as numerous instant games played with scratch-off tickets. These games cater to the preferences of potential players by varying the size of the prizes awarded and the probabilities of winning.

Florida Lotto, the premier game in the Florida State Lottery, holds drawings twice a week. In this game, six balls are drawn from a container holding fifty-three balls numbered from 1 to 53. To win the jackpot, the six numbers chosen by a player must match the numbers on the six balls drawn. The order in which the numbers are selected does not matter. The Florida State Lottery claims that the odds of winning this jackpot are 1 in 22,957,480. Players can also win by matching five, four, or three numbers as well. The probability of matching five of six is 1 in 81,410, and continues to increase as the amount of matched numbers decreases.

The probability of winning the jackpot in this game can be verified by determining the amount of six-number combinations possible or by multiplying the probabilities of six consecutive successful selections. Calculating the number of combinations yields the following, which can be expressed using the notation of factorials, denoted as "!",

$$\frac{(53!)}{[(47!)(6!)]} = \frac{(53\times52\times51\times50\times49\times48)}{(6\times5\times4\times3\times2\times1)} = 22{,}957{,}480.$$

Of these combinations, only one corresponds to selecting all six numbers correctly. Alternatively, using probabilities, you could multiply the probabilities that the numbers on a ticket are selected on each of the six successive selections. The probability of the first number drawn matching one of the player's chosen numbers is 6 in 53. If this occurs, there are five favorable numbers in the remaining fifty-two, and so on. Therefore, the probability of six consecutive successful selections is $(\frac{6}{53})(\frac{5}{52})(\frac{4}{51})(\frac{3}{50})(\frac{2}{49})(\frac{1}{48})$ or 1 in 22,957,480.

Verifying the probability of correctly selecting five of the six numbers is only slightly more complex. Using the same logic as in the previous example, the probability of the first five matching numbers being selected on the first five draws is $(\frac{6}{53})(\frac{5}{52})(\frac{4}{51})(\frac{3}{50})(\frac{2}{49})$. If this occurs, there are forty-eight numbers remaining, and forty-seven are favorable to the result of correctly matching five of six numbers. Thus the probability of attaining this outcome would be $(\frac{6}{53})(\frac{5}{52})(\frac{4}{51})(\frac{3}{50})(\frac{2}{49})(\frac{47}{48})$. Though the fractions being multiplied would be different, the probability of the first number not matching and the next five matching would be $(\frac{47}{53})(\frac{6}{52})(\frac{5}{51})(\frac{4}{50})(\frac{3}{49})(\frac{2}{48})$ which is equal to the previous result. It is easily verifiable that the probability of the non-matching number occurring on any of the six selections is equal. Thus the overall probability of correctly selecting five of six is $6(\frac{6}{53})(\frac{5}{52})(\frac{4}{51})(\frac{3}{50})(\frac{2}{49})(\frac{47}{48})$ or 1 in 81,409.50355, which rounds to 1 in 81,410.

Though people do win large lottery jackpots with regularity, the odds of an individual winning the lottery are very slim.

Fantasy 5 requires the player to match five numbers selected from 26 numbers. Prizes are also awarded to those who correctly match three or four numbers. The probability calculations for this game are analogous to those of Florida Lotto. In Fantasy 5, the probabilities of matching five, four, or three numbers are 1 in 65,780, 1 in 627, and 1 in 32, respectively.

At the other end of the spectrum is Florida's CASH 3 game. This game gives the player a probability of 1 in 1,000 of winning $500 on a $1 ticket or $250 on a 50-cent ticket. In order to win, the player must match a 3-digit number, each digit of which is a number from 0 to 9. In this game, unlike Lotto, each digit is randomly selected from its own set of numbers from 0 to 9 and the order of the result is important.

The Mega Money game adds a bit of a twist. In this game the player picks four numbers from the thirty-two numbers on the top of the ticket and one number from thirty-two on the lower half of the ticket. In order to win, all four numbers on the upper portion and the number on the lower portion of the ticket must be drawn. Finding the probability of matching the first four numbers can be found in the same way as determining the jackpot probability in Lotto. In Mega Money, the probability is $(\frac{4}{32})$ $(\frac{3}{31})(\frac{2}{30})(\frac{1}{29}) = 1$ in 35,960. To determine the probability of winning the big prize in this game, you must multiply that result by the chances of correctly matching the one number on the lower part of the ticket, which is drawn from another bin of thirty-two balls. The probability of winning the big prize, which averages $200,000 in this game, is: $(\frac{1}{35,960})(\frac{1}{32}) = 1$ in 1,150,720.

Perspectives

When there are no winners in a large game, like Florida Lotto, new tickets are sold for the next drawing, increasing the value of the prize. Some feel that if the jackpot has not hit several times in a row, that it is "due to be hit." In fact, the probability of any particular combination winning does not change. However, the increase in interest and, correspondingly, in the number of tickets purchased makes it more likely that the jackpot will hit than if a smaller number of tickets were sold.

Consider a hypothetical game in which the probability of winning the jackpot is 1 in 1,000,000. If the jackpot is relatively low and only 100,000 tickets are sold, the probability of the jackpot being hit is at most 1 in 10. The probability is not necessarily equal to $\frac{1}{10}$ since almost certainly, more than one person will have selected the same combination. Now assume the jackpot has not hit for several drawings and a huge prize has accrued. If more than a million tickets have been sold covering 900,000 of the possible 1,000,000 combinations, the probability of the jackpot being hit will now be 90 percent. The chances of any individual ticket winning, however, remains 1 in 1,000,000. An interesting consequence here is that there is no guarantee that a winner will receive the entire jackpot. It is possible that two or more ticket holders will have chosen the correct combination of numbers and would then divide the jackpot equally.

Allocation of Revenue

The potential revenue generated by a lottery has provided a strong incentive for states to pass legislation to legalize them. While the exact figures vary from state to state, normally about thirty to thirty-eight percent of the intake goes toward funding state programs. A little more than half is returned in prize money and the remainder is applied to various expenses associated with operating the lottery, such as advertising and paying commissions to vendors. To put the monetary amounts from lotteries that go into state budgets into perspective, the New Hampshire state lottery provided the state department of education with over $65 million in one fiscal year, bringing the total amount of aid to education in that state to $665 million. California boasts of more than $12 billion being earmarked for its public schools since 1985, while the New York state lottery provided $1.35 billion to education in the 1999–2000 fiscal year.

Prize Payoffs

The allure of huge jackpots influences many individuals to purchase lottery tickets. Advertisements touting multi-million dollar jackpots are common. Information regarding the payoff procedures for jackpots is readily available from state lottery commissions as well as from other sources. Most lotteries allow the winner to choose between one immediate lump sum payment or yearly payments over a period of time.

A jackpot winner in the California Super Lotto Plus, for example, can opt for an immediate payment of roughly half of the jackpot amount or can take payment annually for 26 years. In the long-term plan, the first installment is 2.5 percent of the jackpot amount. Successive yearly payments increase each year, with the final payment being about twice the initial. The sum of these twenty-six payments will be equal to the originally stated jackpot amount. Thus the winner of a $6 million jackpot could take approximately $3 million immediately or could get $150,000 as a first installment with successive yearly payments increasing each year and totaling $6 million after all the payments have been made.

Of course, lottery winners must take into consideration the taxes that must be paid on their winnings. Calculating taxes at one-third, a $6 million jackpot winner choosing the one-time payment option would get approximately $4 million. An individual may find that tax savings may be realized in the long term payoff; however, the large lump sum would not be available for investing purposes. SEE ALSO PROBABILITY, EXPERIMENTAL; PROBABILITY, THEORETICAL.

Robert J. Quinn

Lovelace, Ada Byron

English Mathematician and Scientist
1815–1852

Ada Lovelace was born Augusta Ada Byron, the daughter of the poet George Gordon (Lord Byron) and the mathematician and heiress Anne Isabella Milbanke. Although Lovelace inherited poetic inclinations from her father, her mother raised her to be a mathematician, and she subsequently contributed significantly to the earliest work on mechanical computing machines.

Lovelace received her early education at home and was assisted in her advanced studies by mathematician Augustus De Morgan and scientist Mary Somerville. Presented at court in 1833, she married William, eighth Lord of King, in 1835. He subsequently became Earl of Lovelace, and she became Countess of Lovelace.

Although involved in London society, Lovelace was interested in mathematics, particularly the calculating machines proposed by Charles Babbage, professor of mathematics at Cambridge. After Lovelace met Babbage, the pair became friends and coworkers.

Babbage proposed mechanical devices—the Difference Engine in 1833 and the more complex Analytical Engine in 1838—that would be able to make numerical calculations. Lovelace translated an Italian article describing Babbage's Analytical Engine and added commentary that was three times the length of the original article. Published in 1843, this article clearly shows that she was the first person to understand fully the significance of Babbage's inventions.

In the article, Lovelace described how the calculating machine could be programmed to compute Bernoulli numbers, foreshadowing modern computer programming. She also predicted the use of mechanical mathematical devices for such purposes as music composition and the production of graphics. Although thought to be whimsical at the time, her predictions have turned out to be quite accurate. SEE ALSO BABBAGE, CHARLES; COMPUTERS, EVOLUTION OF ELECTRONIC; MATHEMATICAL DEVICES, MECHANICAL.

J. William Moncrief

Ada Byron Lovelace is credited with writing the world's first computer program when she wrote instructions for Charles Babbage's Analytical Engine.

Bibliography

Toole, Betty A., ed. *Ada, the Enchantress of Numbers: A Selection from the Letters of Lord Byron's Daughter and Her Description of the First Computer.* Mill Valley, CA: Strawberry Press, 1992.

Woolley, Benjamin. *The Bride of Science: Romance, Reason, and Byron's Daughter.* New York: McGraw Hill, 1999.

Photo and Illustration Credits

The illustrations and tables featured in Mathematics *were created by GGS Information Services. The photographs appearing in the text were reproduced by permission of the following sources:*

Volume 2

United Nations: **2**; Martha Tabor/Working Images Photographs: **4, 5, 33, 109, 140, 155**; RTKL: **7**; Photograph by Dr. Wm. M. Harlow. Photo Researchers, Inc.: **12**; The Library of Congress: **17**; © Bettmann/Corbis: **26, 36**; AP/Wide World Photos: **27, 128**; UPI/Corbis-Bettmann: **29**; Archive Photos: **32**; Photograph by Ken M. Highfill. Photo Researchers, Inc.: **37**; Art Resource: **40**; Corbis-Bettmann: **43, 56, 75, 136**; Photo Researchers, Inc.: **46, 153**; The Granger Collection, New York: **53, 103**; Wolf Foundation: **54**; © Martha Tabor/Working Images Photographs: **59, 145**; © 2001 Dr. Andrew D. Burbanks: **68**; © Jim Zuckerman/Corbis: **69**; Photograph by Eliot Glassheim: **77**; AP/Wide World Photos, Inc.: **78**; © Photograph by Martin Gardner: **81**; © Biophoto Associates/Photo Researchers, Inc.: **85**; Photograph by Tom Dunham: **87**; © AFP/Corbis: **104**; Bettmann/Corbis: **120**; © Bettmann/CORBIS: **121**; Photograph by Robert J. Huffman. Field Mark Publications: **125**; Photograph by Earl Dotter: **126**; Michael Shane Smith/Getty Images: **142**; UPI/Corbis-Bettmann: **152**; Corbis Corporation: **156**; Photo Researchers: **158**; © Reuters NewMedia Inc./Corbis: **173**; Doris Langley Moore Collection: **175**.

Glossary

abscissa: the *x*-coordinate of a point in a Cartesian coordinate plane

absolute: standing alone, without reference to arbitrary standards of measurement

absolute dating: determining the date of an artifact by measuring some physical parameter independent of context

absolute value: the non-negative value of a number regardless of sign

absolute zero: the coldest possible temperature on any temperature scale; $-273°$ Celsius

abstract: having only intrinsic form

abstract algebra: the branch of algebra dealing with groups, rings, fields, Galois sets, and number theory

acceleration: the rate of change of an object's velocity

accelerometer: a device that measures acceleration

acute: sharp, pointed; in geometry, an angle whose measure is less than 90 degrees

additive inverse: any two numbers that add to equal 1

advection: a local change in a property of a system

aerial photography: photographs of the ground taken from an airplane or balloon; used in mapping and surveying

aerodynamics: the study of what makes things fly; the engineering discipline specializing in aircraft design

aesthetic: having to do with beauty or artistry

aesthetic value: the value associated with beauty or attractiveness; distinct from monetary value

algebra: the branch of mathematics that deals with variables or unknowns representing the arithmetic numbers

algorithm: a rule or procedure used to solve a mathematical problem

algorithmic: pertaining to an algorithm

ambiguity: the quality of doubtfulness or uncertainty

analog encoding: encoding information using continuous values of some physical quantity

analogy: comparing two things similar in some respects and inferring they are also similar in other respects

analytical geometry: describes the study of geometric properties by using algebraic operations

anergy: spent energy transferred to the environment

angle of elevation: the angle formed by a line of sight above the horizontal

angle of rotation: the angle measured from an initial position a rotating object has moved through

anti-aliasing: introducing shades of gray or other intermediate shades around an image to make the edge appear to be smoother

applications: collections of general-purpose software such as word processors and database programs used on modern personal computers

arc: a continuous portion of a circle; the portion of a circle between two line segments originating at the center of the circle

areagraph: a fine-scale rectangular grid used for determining the area of irregular plots

artifact: something made by a human and left in an archaeological context

artificial intelligence: the field of research attempting the duplication of the human thought process with digital computers or similar devices; also includes expert systems research

ASCII: an acronym that stands for American Standard Code for Information Interchange; assigns a unique 8-bit binary number to every letter of the alphabet, the digits, and most keyboard symbols

assets: real, tangible property held by a business corporation including collectible debts to the corporation

asteroid: a small object or "minor planet" orbiting the Sun, usually in the space between Mars and Jupiter

astigmatism: a defect of a lens, such as within an eye, that prevents focusing on sharply defined objects

astrolabe: a device used to measure the angle between an astronomical object and the horizon

astronomical unit (AU): the average distance of Earth from the Sun; the semi-major axis of Earth's orbit

asymptote: the line that a curve approaches but never reaches

asymptotic: pertaining to an asymptote

atmosphere (unit): a unit of pressure equal to 14.7 lbs/in^2, which is the air pressure at mean sea level

atomic weight: the relative mass of an atom based on a scale in which a specific carbon atom (carbon-12) is assigned a mass value of 12

autogiro: a rotating wing aircraft with a powered propellor to provide thrust and an unpowered rotor for lift; also spelled "autogyro"

avatar: representation of user in virtual space (after the Hindu idea of an incarnation of a deity in human form)

average rate of change: how one variable changes as the other variable increases by a single unit

axiom: a statement regarded as self-evident; accepted without proof

axiomatic system: a system of logic based on certain axioms and definitions that are accepted as true without proof

axis: an imaginary line about which an object rotates

axon: fiber of a nerve cell that carries action potentials (electrochemical impulses)

azimuth: the angle, measured along the horizon, between north and the position of an object or direction of movement

azimuthal projections: a projection of a curved surface onto a flat plane

bandwidth: a range within a band of wavelengths or frequencies

base-10: a number system in which each place represents a power of 10 larger than the place to its right

base-2: a binary number system in which each place represents a power of 2 larger than the place to its right

base-20: a number system in which each place represents a power of 20 larger than the place to the right

base-60: a number system used by ancient Mesopotamian cultures for some calculations in which each place represents a power of 60 larger than the place to its right

baseline: the distance between two points used in parallax measurements or other triangulation techniques

Bernoulli's Equation: a first order, nonlinear differential equation with many applications in fluid dynamics

biased sampling: obtaining a nonrandom sample; choosing a sample to represent a particular viewpoint instead of the whole population

bidirectional frame: in compressed video, a frame between two other frames; the information is based on what changed from the previous frame as well as what will change in the next frame

bifurcation value: the numerical value near which small changes in the initial value of a variable can cause a function to take on widely different values or even completely different behaviors after several iterations

Big Bang: the singular event thought by most cosmologists to represent the beginning of our universe; at the moment of the big bang, all matter, energy, space, and time were concentrated into a single point

binary: existing in only two states, such as "off" or "on," "one" or "zero"

binary arithmetic: the arithmetic of binary numbers; base two arithmetic; internal arithmetic of electronic digital logic

binary number: a base-2 number; a number that uses only the binary digits 1 and 0

binary signal: a form of signal with only two states, such as two different values of voltage, or "on" and "off" states

binary system: a system of two stars that orbit their common center of mass; any system of two things

binomial: an expression with two terms

binomial coefficients: coefficients in the expansion of $(x + y^n$, where n is a positive integer

binomial distribution: the distribution of a binomial random variable

binomial theorem: a theorem giving the procedure by which a binomial expression may be raised to any power without using successive multiplications

bioengineering: the study of biological systems such as the human body using principles of engineering

biomechanics: the study of biological systems using engineering principles

bioturbation: disturbance of the strata in an archaeological site by biological factors such as rodent burrows, root action, or human activity

bit: a single binary digit, 1 or 0

bitmap: representing a graphic image in the memory of a computer by storing information about the color and shade of each individual picture element (or pixel)

Boolean algebra: a logic system developed by George Boole that deals with the theorems of undefined symbols and axioms concerning those symbols

Boolean operators: the set of operators used to perform operations on sets; includes the logical operators AND, OR, NOT

byte: a group of eight binary digits; represents a single character of text

cadaver: a corpse intended for medical research or training

caisson: a large cylinder or box that allows workers to perform construction tasks below the water surface, may be open at the top or sealed and pressurized

calculus: a method of dealing mathematically with variables that may be changing continuously with respect to each other

calibrate: act of systematically adjusting, checking, or standardizing the graduation of a measuring instrument

carrying capacity: in an ecosystem, the number of individuals of a species that can remain in a stable, sustainable relationship with the available resources

Cartesian coordinate system: a way of measuring the positions of points in a plane using two perpendicular lines as axes

Cartesian plane: a mathematical plane defined by the x and y axes or the ordinate and abscissa in a Cartesian coordinate system

cartographers: persons who make maps

catenary curve: the curve approximated by a free-hanging chain supported at each end; the curve generated by a point on a parabola rolling along a line

causal relations: responses to input that do not depend on values of the input at later times

celestial: relating to the stars, planets, and other heavenly bodies

celestial body: any natural object in space, defined as above Earth's atmosphere; the Moon, the Sun, the planets, asteroids, stars, galaxies, nebulae

central processor: the part of a computer that performs computations and controls and coordinates other parts of the computer

centrifugal: the outwardly directed force a spinning object exerts on its restraint; also the perceived force felt by persons in a rotating frame of reference

cesium: a chemical element, symbol Cs, atomic number 55

Chandrasekhar limit: the 1.4 solar mass limit imposed on a white dwarf by quantum mechanics; a white dwarf with greater than 1.4 solar masses will collapse to a neutron star

chaos theory: the qualitative study of unstable aperiodic behavior in deterministic nonlinear dynamical systems

chaotic attractor: a set of points such that all nearby trajectories converge to it

chert: material consisting of amorphous or cryptocrystalline silicon dioxide; fine-grained chert is indistinguishable from flint

chi-square test: a generalization of a test for significant differences between a binomial population and a multinomial population

chlorofluorocarbons: compounds similar to hydrocarbons in which one or more of the hydrogen atoms has been replaced by a chlorine or fluorine atom

chord: a straight line connecting the end points of an arc of a circle

chromakey: photographing an object shot against a known color, which can be replaced with an arbitrary background (like the weather maps on television newscasts)

chromosphere: the transparent layer of gas that resides above the photosphere in the atmosphere of the Sun

chronometer: an extremely precise timepiece

ciphered: coded; encrypyted

circumference: the distance around a circle

circumnavigation: the act of sailing completely around the globe

circumscribed: bounded, as by a circle

circumspheres: spheres that touch all the "outside" faces of a regular polyhedron

client: an individual, business, or agency for whom services are provided by another individual, business, or industry; a patron or customer

clones: computers assembled of generic components designed to use a standard operation system

codomain: for a given function f, the set of all possible values of the function; the range is a subset of the codomain

cold dark matter: hypothetical form of matter proposed to explain the 90 percent of mass in most galaxies that cannot be detected because it does not emit or reflect radiation

coma: the cloud of gas that first surrounds the nucleus of a comet as it begins to warm up

combinations: a group of elements from a set in which order is not important

combustion: chemical reaction combining fuel with oxygen accompanied by the release of light and heat

comet: a lump of frozen gas and dust that approaches the Sun in a highly elliptical orbit forming a coma and one or two tails

command: a particular instruction given to a computer, usually as part of a list of instructions comprising a program

commodities: anything having economic value, such as agricultural products or valuable metals

compendium: a summary of a larger work or collection of works

compiler: a computer program that translates symbolic instructions into machine code

complex plane: the mathematical abstraction on which complex numbers can be graphed; the x-axis is the real component and the y-axis is the imaginary component

composite number: an integer that is not prime

compression: reducing the size of a computer file by replacing long strings of identical bits with short instructions about the number of bits; the information is restored before the file is used

compression algorithm: the procedure used, such as comparing one frame in a movie to the next, to compress and reduce the size of electronic files

concave: hollowed out or curved inward

concentric: sets of circles or other geometric objects sharing the same center

conductive: having the ability to conduct or transmit

confidence interval: a range of values having a predetermined probability that the value of some measurement of a population lies within it

congruent: exactly the same everywhere; having exactly the same size and shape

conic: of or relating to a cone, that surface generated by a straight line, passing through a fixed point, and moving along the intersection with a fixed curve

conic sections: the curves generated by an imaginary plane slicing through an imaginary cone

continuous quantities: amounts composed of continuous and undistinguishable parts

converge: come together; to approach the same numerical value

convex: curved outward, bulging

coordinate geometry: the concept and use of a coordinate system with respect to the study of geometry

coordinate plane: an imaginary two-dimensional plane defined as the plane containing the x- and y-axes; all points on the plane have coordinates that can be expressed as x, y

coordinates: the set of n numbers that uniquely identifies the location of a point in n-dimensional space

corona: the upper, very rarefied atmosphere of the Sun that becomes visible around the darkened Sun during a total solar eclipse

corpus: Latin for "body"; used to describe a collection of artifacts

correlate: to establish a mutual or reciprocal relation between two things or sets of things

correlation: the process of establishing a mutual or reciprocal relation between two things or sets of things

cosine: if a unit circle is drawn with its center at the origin and a line segment is drawn from the origin at angle theta so that the line segment intersects the circle at (x, y), then x is the cosine of theta

cosmological distance: the distance a galaxy would have to have in order for its red shift to be due to Hubble expansion of the universe

cosmology: the study of the origin and evolution of the universe

cosmonaut: the term used by the Soviet Union and now used by the Russian Federation to refer to persons trained to go into space; synonomous with astronaut

cotton gin: a machine that separates the seeds, hulls, and other undesired material from cotton

cowcatcher: a plow-shaped device attached to the front of a train to quickly remove obstacles on railroad tracks

cryptography: the science of encrypting information for secure transmission

cubit: an ancient unit of length equal to the distance from the elbow to the tip of the middle finger; usually about 18 inches

culling: removing inferior plants or animals while keeping the best; also known as "thinning"

curved space: the notion suggested by Albert Einstein to explain the properties of space near a massive object, space acts as if it were curved in four dimensions

deduction: a conclusion arrived at through reasoning, especially a conclusion about some particular instance derived from general principles

deductive reasoning: a type of reasoning in which a conclusion necessarily follows from a set of axioms; reasoning from the general to the particular

degree: 1/360 of a circle or complete rotation

degree of significance: a determination, usually in advance, of the importance of measured differences in statistical variables

demographics: statistical data about people—including age, income, and gender—that are often used in marketing

dendrite: branched and short fiber of a neuron that carries information to the neuron

dependent variable: in the equation $y = f(x)$, if the function f assigns a single value of y to each value of x, then y is the output variable (or the dependent variable)

depreciate: to lessen in value

deregulation: the process of removing legal restrictions on the behavior of individuals or corporations

derivative: the derivative of a function is the limit of the ratio of the change in the function; the change is produced by a small variation in the variable as the change in the variable is allowed to approach zero; an inverse operation to calculating an integral

determinant: a square matrix with a single numerical value determined by a unique set of mathematical operations performed on the entries

determinate algebra: the study and analysis of equations that have one or a few well-defined solutions

deterministic: mathematical or other problems that have a single, well-defined solution

diameter: the chord formed by an arc of one-half of a circle

differential: a mathematical quantity representing a small change in one variable as used in a differential equation

differential calculus: the branch of mathematics primarily dealing with the solution of differential equations to find lengths, areas, and volumes of functions

differential equation: an equation that expresses the relationship between two variables that change in respect to each other, expressed in terms of the rate of change

digit: one of the symbols used in a number system to represent the multiplier of each place

digital: describes information technology that uses discrete values of a physical quantity to transmit information

digital encoding: encoding information by using discrete values of some physical quantity

digital logic: rules of logic as applied to systems that can exist in only discrete states (usually two)

dihedral: a geometric figure formed by two half-planes that are bounded by the same straight line

Diophantine equation: polynomial equations of several variables, with integer coefficients, whose solutions are to be integers

diopter: a measure of the power of a lens or a prism, equal to the reciprocal of its focal length in meters

directed distance: the distance from the pole to a point in the polar coordinate plane

discrete: composed of distinct elements

discrete quantities: amounts composed of separate and distinct parts

distributive property: property such that the result of an operation on the various parts collected into a whole is the same as the operation performed separately on the parts before collection into the whole

diverge: to go in different directions from the same starting point

dividend: the number to be divided; the numerator in a fraction

divisor: the number by which a dividend is divided; the denominator of a fraction

DNA fingerprinting: the process of isolating and amplifying segments of DNA in order to uniquely identify the source of the DNA

domain: the set of all values of a variable used in a function

double star: a binary star; two stars orbiting a common center of gravity

duodecimal: a numbering system based on 12

dynamometer: a device that measures mechanical or electrical power

eccentric: having a center of motion different from the geometric center of a circle

eclipse: occurrence when an object passes in front of another and blocks the view of the second object; most often used to refer to the phenomenon that occurs when the Moon passes in front of the Sun or when the Moon passes through Earth's shadow

ecliptic: the plane of the Earth's orbit around the Sun

eigenvalue: if there exists a vector space such that a linear transformation onto itself produces a new vector equal to a scalar times the original vector, then that scalar is called an eigenfunction

eigenvector: if there exists a vector space such that a linear transformation onto itself produces a new vector equal to a scalar times the original vector, then that vector is called an eigenvector

Einstein's General Theory of Relativity: Albert Einstein's generalization of relativity to include systems accelerated with respect to one another; a theory of gravity

electromagnetic radiation: the form of energy, including light, that transfers information through space

elements: the members of a set

ellipse: one of the conic sections, it is defined as the locus of all points such that the sum of the distances from two points called the foci is constant

elliptical: a closed geometric curve where the sum of the distances of a point on the curve to two fixed points (foci) is constant

elliptical orbit: a planet, comet, or satellite follows a curved path known as an ellipse when it is in the gravitational field of the Sun or another object; the Sun or other object is at one focus of the ellipse

empirical law: a mathematical summary of experimental results

empiricism: the view that the experience of the senses is the single source of knowledge

encoding tree: a collection of dots with edges connecting them that have no looping paths

endangered species: a species with a population too small to be viable

epicenter: the point on Earth's surface directly above the site of an earthquake

epicycle: the curved path followed by planets in Ptolemey's model of the solar system; planets moved along a circle called the epicycle, whose center moved along a circular orbit around the sun

epicylic: having the property of moving along an epicycle

equatorial bulge: the increase in diameter or circumference of an object when measured around its equator usually due to rotation, all planets and the sun have equatorial bulges

equidistant: at the same distance

equilateral: having the property that all sides are equal; a square is an equilateral rectangle

equilateral triangle: a triangle whose sides and angles are equal

equilibrium: a state of balance between opposing forces

equinox points: two points on the celestial sphere at which the ecliptic intersects the celestial equator

escape speed: the minimum speed an object must attain so that it will not fall back to the surface of a planet

Euclidean geometry: the geometry of points, lines, angles, polygons, and curves confined to a plane

exergy: the measure of the ability of a system to produce work; maximum potential work output of a system

exosphere: the outermost layer of the atmosphere extending from the ionosphere upward

exponent: the symbol written above and to the right of an expression indicating the power to which the expression is to be raised

exponential: an expression in which the variable appears as an exponent

exponential power series: the series by which e to the x power may be approximated; $e^x = 1 + x + x^{2/2!} + x^{3/3!} + \ldots$

exponents: symbols written above and to the right of expressions indicating the power to which an expression is to be raised or the number of times the expression is to be multiplied by itself

externality: a factor that is not part of a system but still affects it

extrapolate: to extend beyond the observations; to infer values of a variable outside the range of the observations

farsightedness: describes the inability to see close objects clearly

fiber-optic: a long, thin strand of glass fiber; internal reflections in the fiber assure that light entering one end is transmitted to the other end with only small losses in intensity; used widely in transmitting digital information

fibrillation: a potentially fatal malfunction of heart muscle where the muscle rapidly and ineffectually twitches instead of pulsing regularly

fidelity: in information theory a measure of how close the information received is to the information sent

finite: having definite and definable limits; countable

fire: the reaction of a neuron when excited by the reception of a neurotransmitter

fission: the splitting of the nucleus of a heavy atom, which releases kinetic energy that is carried away by the fission fragments and two or three neutrons

fixed term: for a definite length of time determined in advance

fixed-wing aircraft: an aircraft that obtains lift from the flow of air over a nonmovable wing

floating-point operations: arithmetic operations on a number with a decimal point

fluctuate: to vary irregularly

flue: a pipe designed to remove exhaust gases from a fireplace, stove, or burner

fluid dynamics: the science of fluids in motion

focal length: the distance from the focal point (the principle point of focus) to the surface of a lens or concave mirror

focus: one of the two points that define an ellipse; in a planetary orbit, the Sun is at one focus and nothing is at the other focus

formula analysis: a method of analysis of the Boolean formulas used in computer programming

Fourier series: an infinite series consisting of cosine and sine functions of integral multiples of the variable each multiplied by a constant; if the series is finite, the expression is known as a Fourier polynomial

fractal: a type of geometric figure possessing the properties of self-similarity (any part resembles a larger or smaller part at any scale) and a measure that increases without bound as the unit of measure approaches zero

fractal forgery: creating a natural landscape by using fractals to simulate trees, mountains, clouds, or other features

fractal geometry: the study of the geometric figures produced by infinite iterations

futures exchange: a type of exchange where contracts are negotiated to deliver commodites at some fixed price at some time in the future

g: a common measure of acceleration; for example 1 g is the acceleration due to gravity at the Earth's surface, roughly 32 feet per second per second

game theory: a discipline that combines elements of mathematics, logic, social and behavioral sciences, and philosophy

gametes: mature male or female sexual reproductive cells

gaming: playing games or relating to the theory of game playing

gamma ray: a high-energy photon

general relativity: generalization of Albert Einstein's theory of relativity to include accelerated frames of reference; presents gravity as a curvature of four-dimensional space-time

generalized inverse: an extension of the concept of the inverse of a matrix to include matrices that are not square

generalizing: making a broad statement that includes many different special cases

genus: the taxonomic classification one step more general than species; the first name in the binomial nomenclature of all species

geoboard: a square board with pegs and holes for pegs used to create geometric figures

geocentric: Earth-centered

geodetic: of or relating to geodesy, which is the branch of applied mathematics dealing with the size and shape of the earth, including the precise location of points on its surface

geometer: a person who uses the principles of geometry to aid in making measurements

geometric: relating to the principles of geometry, a branch of mathematics related to the properties and relationships of points, lines, angles, surfaces, planes, and solids

geometric sequence: a sequence of numbers in which each number in the sequence is larger than the previous by some constant ratio

geometric series: a series in which each number is larger than the previous by some constant ratio; the sum of a geometric sequence

geometric solid: one of the solids whose faces are regular polygons

geometry: the branch of mathematics that deals with the properties and relationships of points, lines, angles, surfaces, planes, and solids

geostationary orbit: an Earth orbit made by an artificial satellite that has a period equal to the Earth's period of rotation on its axis (about 24 hours)

geysers: springs that occasionally spew streams of steam and hot water

glide reflection: a rigid motion of the plane that consists of a reflection followed by a translation parallel to the mirror axis

grade: the amount of increase in elevation per horizontal distance, usually expressed as a percent; the slope of a road

gradient: a unit used for measuring angles, in which the circle is divided into 400 equal units, called gradients

graphical user interface: a device designed to display information graphically on a screen; a modern computer interface system

Greenwich Mean Time: the time at Greenwich, England; used as the basis for universal time throughout the world

Gross Domestic Product: a measure in the change in the market value of goods, services, and structures produced in the economy

group theory: study of the properties of groups, the mathematical systems consisting of elements of a set and operations that can be performed on that set such that the results of the operations are always members of the same set

gyroscope: a device typically consisting of a spinning wheel or disk, whose spin-axis turns between two low-friction supports; it maintains its angular orientation with respect to inertial conditions when not subjected to external forces

Hagia Sophia: Instanbul's most famous landmark, built by the emperor Justinian I in 537 C.E. and converted to a mosque in 1453 C.E.

Hamming codes: a method of error correction in digital information

headwind: a wind blowing in the opposite direction as that of the course of a vehicle

Heisenberg Uncertainty Principle: the principle in physics that asserts it is impossible to know simultaneously and with complete accuracy the values of certain pairs of physical quantities such as position and momentum

heliocentric: Sun-centered

hemoglobin: the oxygen-bearing, iron-containing conjugated protein in vertebrate red blood cells

heuristics: a procedure that serves to guide investigation but that has not been proven

hominid: a member of family Hominidae; *Homo sapiens* are the only surviving species

Huffman encoding: a method of efficiently encoding digital information

hydrocarbon: a compound of carbon and hydrogen

hydrodynamics: the study of the behavior of moving fluids

hydrograph: a tabular or graphical display of stream flow or water runoff

hydroscope: a device designed to allow a person to see below the surface of water

hydrostatics: the study of the properties of fluids not in motion

hyperbola: a conic section; the locus of all points such that the absolute value of the difference in distance from two points called foci is a constant

hyperbolic: an open geometric curve where the difference of the distances of a point on the curve to two fixed points (foci) is constant

Hypertext Markup Language: the computer markup language used to create documents on the World Wide Web

hypertext: the text that contains hyperlinks, that is, links to other places in the same document or other documents or multimedia files

hypotenuse: the long side of a right triangle; the side opposite the right angle

hypothesis: a proposition that is assumed to be true for the purpose of proving other propositions

ice age: one of the broad spans of time when great sheets of ice covered the Northern parts of North America and Europe; the most recent ice age was about 16,000 years ago

identity: a mathematical statement much stronger than equality, which asserts that two expressions are the same for all values of the variables

implode: violently collapse; fall in

inclination: a slant or angle formed by a line or plane with the horizontal axis or plane

inclined: sloping, slanting, or leaning

incomplete interpretation: a statistical flaw

independent variable: in the equation $y = f(x)$, the input variable is x (or the independent variable)

indeterminate algebra: study and analysis of solution strategies for equations that do not have fixed or unique solutions

indeterminate equation: an equation in which more than one variable is unknown

index (number): a number that allows tracking of a quantity in economics by comparing it to a standard, the consumer price index is the best known example

inductive reasoning: drawing general conclusions based on specific instances or observations; for example, a theory might be based on the outcomes of several experiments

Industrial Revolution: beginning in Great Britain around 1730, a period in the eighteenth and nineteenth centuries when nations in Europe, Asia, and the Americas moved from agrarian-based to industry-based economies

inertia: tendency of a body that is at rest to remain at rest, or the tendency of a body that is in motion to remain in motion

inferences: the act or process of deriving a conclusion from given facts or premises

inferential statistics: analysis and interpretation of data in order to make predictions

infinite: having no limit; boundless, unlimited, endless; uncountable

infinitesimals: functions with values arbitrarily close to zero

infinity: the quality of unboundedness; a quantity beyond measure; an unbounded quantity

information database: an array of information related to a specific subject or group of subjects and arranged so that any individual bit of information can be easily found and recovered

information theory: the science that deals with how to separate information from noise in a signal or how to trace the flow of information through a complex system

infrastructure: the foundation or permanent installations necessary for a structure or system to operate

initial conditions: the values of variables at the beginning of an experiment or of a set at the beginning of a simulation; chaos theory reveals that small changes in initial conditions can produce widely divergent results

input: information provided to a computer or other computation system

inspheres: spheres that touch all the "inside" faces of a regular polyhedron; also called "enspheres"

integer: a positive whole number, its negative counterpart, or zero

integral: a mathematical operation similar to summation; the area between the curve of a function, the x-axis, and two bounds such as $x = a$ and $x = b$; an inverse operation to finding the derivative

integral calculus: the branch of mathematics dealing with the rate of change of functions with respect to their variables

integral number: integer; that is, a positive whole number, its negative counterpart, or zero

integral solutions: solutions to an equation or set of equations that are all integers

integrated circuit: a circuit with the transistors, resistors, and other circuit elements etched into the surface of a single chip of silicon

integration: solving a differential equation; determining the area under a curve between two boundaries

intensity: the brightness of radiation or energy contained in a wave

intergalactic: between galaxies; the space between the galaxies

interplanetary: between planets; the space between the planets

interpolation: filling in; estimating unknown values of a function between known values

intersection: a set containing all of the elements that are members of two other sets

interstellar: between stars; the space between stars

intraframe: the compression applied to still images, interframe compression compares one image to the next and only stores the elements that have changed

intrinsic: of itself; the essential nature of a thing; originating within the thing

inverse: opposite; the mathematical function that expresses the independent variable of another function in terms of the dependent variable

inverse operations: operations that undo each other, such as addition and subtraction

inverse square law: a given physical quality varies with the distance from the source inversely as the square of the distance

inverse tangent: the value of the argument of the tangent function that produces a given value of the function; the angle that produces a particular value of the tangent

invert: to turn upside down or to turn inside out; in mathematics, to rewrite as the inverse function

inverted: upside down; turned over

ionized: an atom that has lost one or more of its electrons and has become a charged particle

ionosphere: a layer in Earth's atmosphere above 80 kilometers characterized by the existence of ions and free electrons

irrational number: a real number that cannot be written as a fraction of the form a/b, where a and b are both integers and b is not zero; when expressed in decimal form, an irrational number is infinite and nonrepeating

isometry: equality of measure

isosceles triangle: a triangle with two sides and two angles equal

isotope: one of several species of an atom that has the same number of protons and the same chemical properties, but different numbers of neutrons

iteration: repetition; a repeated mathematical operation in which the output of one cycle becomes the input for the next cycle

iterative: relating to a computational procedure to produce a desired result by replication of a series of operations

iterator: the mathematical operation producing the result used in iteration

kinetic energy: the energy an object has as a consequence of its motion

kinetic theory of gases: the idea that all gases are composed of widely separated particles (atoms and molecules) that exert only small forces on each other and that are in constant motion

knot: nautical mile per hour

Lagrange points: two positions in which the motion of a body of negligible mass is stable under the gravitational influence of two much larger bodies (where one larger body is moving)

latitude: the number of degrees on Earth's surface north or south of the equator; the equator is latitude zero

law: a principle of science that is highly reliable, has great predictive power, and represents the mathematical summary of experimental results

law of cosines: for a triangle with angles A, B, C and sides a, b, c, $a^2 = b^2 + c^2 - 2bc \cos A$

law of sines: if a triangle has sides a, b, and c and opposite angles A, B, and C, then $\sin A/a = \sin B/b = \sin C/c$

laws of probability: set of principles that govern the use of probability in determining the truth or falsehood of a hypothesis

light-year: the distance light travels within a vaccuum in one year

limit: a mathematical concept in which numerical values get closer and closer to a given value

linear algebra: the study of vector spaces and linear transformations

linear equation: an equation in which all variables are raised to the first power

linear function: a function whose graph on the x-y plane is a straight line or line segment

litmus test: a test that uses a single indicator to prompt a decision

locus (pl: loci): in geometry, the set of all points, lines, or surfaces that satisfies a particular requirement

logarithm: the power to which a certain number called the base is to be raised to produce a particular number

logarithmic coordinates: the x and y coordinates of a point on a cartesian plane using logarithmic scales on the x- and y-axes.

logarithmic scale: a scale in which the distances that numbers are positioned, from a reference point, are proportional to their logarithms

logic circuits: circuits used to perform logical operations and containing one or more logic elements: devices that maintain a state based on previous input to determine current and future output

logistic difference equation: the equation $x_{(n+1)} = r \times x_{n(1-xn)}$ is used to study variability in animal populations

longitude: one of the imaginary great circles beginning at the poles and extending around Earth; the geographic position east or west of the prime meridian

machine code: the set of instructions used to direct the internal operation of a computer or other information-processing system

machine language: electronic code the computer can utilize

magnetic trap: a magnetic field configured in such a way that an ion or other charged particle can be held in place for an extended period of time

magnetosphere: an asymmetric region surrounding the Earth in which charged particles are trapped, their behavior being dominated by Earth's magnetic field

magnitude: size; the measure or extent of a mathematical or physical quantity

mainframes: large computers used by businesses and government agencies to process massive amounts of data; generally faster and more powerful than desktops but usually requiring specialized software

malfunctioning: not functioning correctly; performing badly

malleability: the ability or capability of being shaped or formed

margin of error: the difference between the estimated maximum and minimum values a given measurement could have

mathematical probability: the mathematical computation of probabilities of outcomes based on rules of logic

matrix: a rectangular array of data in rows and columns

mean: the arithmetic average of a set of data

median: the middle of a set of data when values are sorted from smallest to largest (or largest to smallest)

megabyte: term used to refer to one million bytes of memory storage, where each byte consists of eight bits; the actual value is 1,048,576 (2^{20})

memory: a device in a computer designed to temporarily or permanently store information in the form of binomial states of certain circuit elements

meridian: a great circle passing through Earth's poles and a particular location

metallurgy: the study of the properties of metals; the chemistry of metals and alloys

meteorologist: a person who studies the atmosphere in order to understand weather and climate

methanol: an alcohol consisting of a single carbon bonded to three hydrogen atoms and an O–H group

microcomputers: an older term used to designate small computers designed to sit on a desktop and to be used by one person; replaced by the term personal computer

microgravity: the apparent weightless condition of objects in free fall

microkelvin: one-millionth of a kelvin

minicomputers: a computer midway in size between a desktop computer and a main frame computer; most modern desktops are much more powerful than the older minicomputers and they have been phased out

minimum viable population: the smallest number of individuals of a species in a particular area that can survive and maintain genetic diversity

mission specialist: an individual trained by NASA to perform a specific task or set of tasks onboard a spacecraft, whose duties do not include piloting the spacecraft

mnemonic: a device or process that aids one's memory

mode: a kind of average or measure of central tendency equal to the number that occurs most often in a set of data

monomial: an expression with one term

Morse code: a binary code designed to allow text information to be transmitted by telegraph consisting of "dots" and "dashes"

mouse: a handheld pointing device used to manipulate an indicator on a screen

moving average: a method of averaging recent trends in relation to long term averages, it uses recent data (for example, the last 10 days) to calculate an average that changes but still smooths out daily variations

multimodal input/output (I/O): multimedia control and display that uses various senses and interaction styles

multiprocessing: a computer that has two or more central processers which have common access to main storage

nanometers: billionths of a meter

nearsightedness: describes the inability to see distant objects clearly

negative exponential: an exponential function of the form $y = e^{-x}$

net force: the final, or resultant, influence on a body that causes it to accelerate

neuron: a nerve cell

neurotransmitters: the substance released by a neuron that diffuses across the synapse

neutron: an elementary particle with approximately the same mass as a proton and neutral charge

Newtonian: a person who, like Isaac Newton, thinks the universe can be understood in terms of numbers and mathematical operations

nominal scales: a method for sorting objects into categories according to some distinguishing characteristic, then attaching a label to each category

non-Euclidean geometry: a branch of geometry defined by posing an alternate to Euclid's fifth postulate

nonlinear transformation: a transformation of a function that changes the shape of a curve or geometric figure

nonlinear transformations: transformations of functions that change the shape of a curve or geometric figure

nuclear fission: a reaction in which an atomic nucleus splits into fragments

nuclear fusion: mechanism of energy formation in a star; lighter nuclei are combined into heavier nuclei, releasing energy in the process

nucleotides: the basic chemical unit in a molecule of nucleic acid

nucleus: the dense, positive core of an atom that contains protons and neutrons

null hypothesis: the theory that there is no validity to the specific claim that two variations of the same thing can be distinguished by a specific procedure

number theory: the study of the properties of the natural numbers, including prime numbers, the number theorem, and Fermat's Last Theorem

numerical differentiation: approximating the mathematical process of differentiation using a digital computer

nutrient: a food substance or mineral required for the completion of the life cycle of an organism

oblate spheroid: a spheroid that bulges at the equator; the surface created by rotating an ellipse 360 degrees around its minor axis

omnidirectional: a device that transmits or receives energy in all directions

Öort cloud: a cloud of millions of comets and other material forming a spherical shell around the solar system far beyond the orbit of Neptune

orbital period: the period required for a planet or any other orbiting object to complete one complete orbit

orbital velocity: the speed and direction necessary for a body to circle a celestial body, such as Earth, in a stable manner

ordinate: the *y*-coordinate of a point on a Cartesian plane

organic: having to do with life, growing naturally, or dealing with the chemical compounds found in or produced by living organisms

oscillating: moving back and forth

outliers: extreme values in a data set

output: information received from a computer or other computation system based on the information it has received

overdubs: adding voice tracks to an existing film or tape

oxidant: a chemical reagent that combines with oxygen

oxidizer: the chemical that combines with oxygen or is made into an oxide

pace: an ancient measure of length equal to normal stride length

parabola: a conic section; the locus of all points such that the distance from a fixed point called the focus is equal to the perpendicular distance from a line

parabolic: an open geometric curve where the distance of a point on the curve to a fixed point (focus) and a fixed line (directrix) is the same

paradigm: an example, pattern, or way of thinking

parallax: the apparent motion of a nearby object when viewed against the background of more distant objects due to a change in the observer's position

parallel operations: separating the parts of a problem and working on different parts at the same time

parallel processing: using at least two different computers or working at least two different central processing units in the same computer at the same time or "in parallel" to solve problems or to perform calculation

parallelogram: a quadrilateral with opposite sides equal and opposite angles equal

parameter: an independent variable, such as time, that can be used to rewrite an expression as two separate functions

parity bits: extra bits inserted into digital signals that can be used to determine if the signal was accurately received

partial sum: with respect to infinite series, the sum of its first *n* terms for some *n*

pattern recognition: a process used by some artificial-intelligence systems to identify a variety of patterns, including visual patterns, information patterns buried in a noisy signal, and word patterns imbedded in text

payload specialist: an individual selected by NASA, another government agency, another government, or a private business, and trained by NASA to operate a specific piece of equipment onboard a spacecraft

payloads: the passengers, crew, instruments, or equipment carried by an aircraft, spacecraft, or rocket

perceptual noise shaping: a process of improving signal-to-noise ratio by looking for the patterns made by the signal, such as speech

perimeter: the distance around an area; in fractal geometry, some figures have a finite area but infinite perimeter

peripheral vision: outer area of the visual field

permutation: any arrangement, or ordering, of items in a set

perpendicular: forming a right angle with a line or plane

perspective: the point of view; a drawing constructed in such a way that an appearance of three dimensionality is achieved

perturbations: small displacements in an orbit

phonograph: a device used to recover the information recorded in analog form as waves or wiggles in a spiral grove on a flat disc of vinyl, rubber, or some other substance

photosphere: the very bright portion of the Sun visible to the unaided eye; the portion around the Sun that marks the boundary between the dense interior gases and the more diffuse

photosynthesis: the chemical process used by plants and some other organisms to harvest light energy by converting carbon dioxide and water to carbohydrates and oxygen

pixel: a single picture element on a video screen; one of the individual dots making up a picture on a video screen or digital image

place value: in a number system, the power of the base assigned to each place; in base-10, the ones place, the tens place, the hundreds place, and so on

plane: generally considered an undefinable term, a plane is a flat surface extending in all directions without end, and that has no thickness

plane geometry: the study of geometric figures, points, lines, and angles and their relationships when confined to a single plane

planetary: having to do with one of the planets

planisphere: a projection of the celestial sphere onto a plane with adjustable circles to demonstrate celestial phenomena

plates: the crustal segments on Earth's surface, which are constantly moving and rotating with respect to each other

plumb-bob: a heavy, conical-shaped weight, supported point-down on its axis by a strong cord, used to determine verticality in construction or surveying

pneumatic drill: a drill operated by compressed air

pneumatic tire: air-filled tire, usually rubber or synthetic

polar axis: the axis from which angles are measured in a polar coordinate system

pole: the origin of a polar coordinate system

poll: a survey designed to gather information about a subject

pollen analysis: microscopic examination of pollen grains to determine the genus and species of the plant producing the pollen; also known as palynology

polyconic projections: a type of map projection of a globe onto a plane that produces a distorted image but preserves correct distances along each meridian

polygon: a geometric figure bounded by line segments

polyhedron: a solid formed with all plane faces

polynomial: an expression with more than one term

polynomial function: a functional expression written in terms of a polynomial

position tracking: sensing the location and/or orientation of an object

power: the number of times a number is to be multiplied by itself in an expression

precalculus: the set of subjects and mathematical skills generally necessary to understand calculus

predicted frame: in compressed video, the next frame in a sequence of images; the information is based on what changed from the previous frame

prime: relating to, or being, a prime number (that is, a number that has no factors other than itself and 1)

Prime Meridian: the meridian that passes through Greenwich, England

prime number: a number that has no factors other than itself and 1

privatization: the process of converting a service traditionally offered by a government or public agency into a service provided by a private corporation or other private entity

proactive: taking action based on prediction of future situations

probability: the likelihood an event will occur when compared to other possible outcomes

probability density function: a function used to estimate the likelihood of spotting an organism while walking a transect

probability theory: the branch of mathematics that deals with quantities having random distributions

processor: an electronic device used to process a signal or to process a flow of information

profit margin: the difference between the total cost of a good or service and the actual selling cost of that good or service, usually expressed as a percentage

program: a set of instructions given to a computer that allows it to perform tasks; software

programming language processor: a program designed to recognize and process other programs

proliferation: growing rapidly

proportion: the mathematical relation between one part and another part, or between a part and the whole; the equality of two ratios

proportionately: divided or distributed according to a proportion; proportional

protractor: a device used for measuring angles, usually consisting of a half circle marked in degrees

pseudorandom numbers: numbers generated by a process that does not guarantee randomness; numbers produced by a computer using some highly complex function that simulates true randomness

Ptolemaic theory: the theory that asserted Earth was a spherical object at the center of the universe surrounded by other spheres carrying the various celestial objects

Pythagorean Theorem: a mathematical statement relating the sides of right triangles; the square of the hypotenuse is equal to the sums of the squares of the other two sides

Pythagorean triples: any set of three numbers obeying the Pythogorean relation such that the square of one is equal to the sum of the squares of the other two

quadrant: one-fourth of a circle; also a device used to measure angles above the horizon

quadratic: involving at least one term raised to the second power

quadratic equation: an equation in which the variable is raised to the second power in at least one term when the equation is written in its simplest form

quadratic form: the form of a function written so that the independent variable is raised to the second power

quantitative: of, relating to, or expressible in terms of quantity

quantum: a small packet of energy (matter and energy are equivalent)

quantum mechanics: the study of the interactions of matter with radiation on an atomic or smaller scale, whereby the granularity of energy and radiation becomes apparent

quantum theory: the study of the interactions of matter with radiation on an atomic or smaller scale, whereby the granularity of energy and radiation becomes apparent

quaternion: a form of complex number consisting of a real scalar and an imaginary vector component with three dimensions

quipus: knotted cords used by the Incas and other Andean cultures to encode numeric and other information

radian: an angle measure approximately equal to 57.3 degrees, it is the angle that subtends an arc of a circle equal to one radius

radicand: the quantity under the radical sign; the argument of the square root function

radius: the line segment originating at the center of a circle or sphere and terminating on the circle or sphere; also the measure of that line segment

radius vector: a line segment with both magnitude and direction that begins at the center of a circle or sphere and runs to a point on the circle or sphere

random: without order

random walks: a mathematical process in a plane of moving a random distance in a random direction then turning through a random angle and repeating the process indefinitely

range: the set of all values of a variable in a function mapped to the values in the domain of the independent variable; also called range set

rate (interest): the portion of the principal, usually expressed as a percentage, paid on a loan or investment during each time interval

ratio of similitude: the ratio of the corresponding sides of similar figures

rational number: a number that can be written in the form a/b, where a and b are intergers and b is not equal to zero

rations: the portion of feed that is given to a particular animal

ray: half line; line segment that originates at a point and extends without bound

real number: a number that has no imaginary part; a set composed of all the rational and irrational numbers

real number set: the combined set of all rational and irrational numbers, the set of numbers representing all points on the number line

realtime: occuring immediately, allowing interaction without significant delay

reapportionment: the process of redistributing the seats of the U. S. House of Representatives, based on each state's proportion of the national population

recalibration: process of resetting a measuring instrument so as to provide more accurate measurements

reciprocal: one of a pair of numbers that multiply to equal 1; a number's reciprocal is 1 divided by the number

red shift: motion-induced change in the frequency of light emitted by a source moving away from the observer

reflected: light or soundwaves returned from a surface

reflection: a rigid motion of the plane that fixes one line (the mirror axis) and moves every other point to its mirror image on the opposite side of the line

reflexive: directed back or turning back on itself

refraction: the change in direction of a wave as it passes from one medium to another

refrigerants: fluid circulating in a refrigerator that is successively compressed, cooled, allowed to expand, and warmed in the refrigeration cycle

regular hexagon: a hexagon whose sides are all equal and whose angles are all equal

relative: defined in terms of or in relation to other quantities

relative dating: determining the date of an archaeological artifact based on its position in the archaeological context relative to other artifacts

relativity: the assertion that measurements of certain physical quantities such as mass, length, and time depend on the relative motion of the object and observer

remediate: to provide a remedy; to heal or to correct a wrong or a deficiency

retrograde: apparent motion of a planet from east to west, the reverse of normal motion; for the outer planets, due to the more rapid motion of Earth as it overtakes an outer planet

revenue: the income produced by a source such as an investment or some other activity; the income produced by taxes and other sources and collected by a governmental unit

rhomboid: a parallelogram whose sides are equal

right angle: the angle formed by perpendicular lines; it measures 90 degrees

RNA: ribonucleic acid

robot arm: a sophisticated device that is standard equipment on space shuttles and on the International Space Station; used to deploy and retrieve satellites or perform other functions

Roche limit: an imaginary surface around a star in a binary system; outside the Roche limit, the gravitational attraction of the companion will pull matter away from a star

root: a number that when multiplied by itself a certain number of times forms a product equal to a specified number

rotary-wing design: an aircraft design that uses a rotating wing to produce lift; helicopter or autogiro (also spelled autogyro)

rotation: a rigid motion of the plane that fixes one point (the center of rotation) and moves every other point around a circle centered at that point

rotational: having to do with rotation

round: also to round off, the systematic process of reducing the number of decimal places for a given number

rounding: process of giving an approximate number

sample: a randomly selected subset of a larger population used to represent the larger population in statistical analysis

sampling: selecting a subset of a group or population in such a way that valid conclusions can be made about the whole set or population

scale (map): the numerical ratio between the dimensions of an object and the dimensions of the two or three dimensional representation of that object

scale drawing: a drawing in which all of the dimensions are reduced by some constant factor so that the proportions are preserved

scaling: the process of reducing or increasing a drawing or some physical process so that proper proportions are retained between the parts

schematic diagram: a diagram that uses symbols for elements and arranges these elements in a logical pattern rather than a practical physical arrangement

schematic diagrams: wiring diagrams that use symbols for circuit elements and arranges these elements in a logical pattern rather than a practical physical arrangement

search engine: software designed to search the Internet for occurences of a word, phrase, or picture, usually provided at no cost to the user as an advertising vehicle

secant: the ratio of the side adjacent to an acute angle in a right triangle to the side opposite; given a unit circle, the ratio of the x coordinate to the y coordinate of any point on the circle

seismic: subjected to, or caused by an earthquake or earth tremor

self-similarity: the term used to describe fractals where a part of the geometric figure resembles a larger or smaller part at any scale chosen

semantic: the study of how words acquire meaning and how those meanings change over time

semi-major axis: one-half of the long axis of an ellipse; also equal to the average distance of a planet or any satellite from the object it is orbiting

semiconductor: one of the elements with characteristics intermediate between the metals and nonmetals

set: a collection of objects defined by a rule such that it is possible to determine exactly which objects are members of the set

set dancing: a form of dance in which dancers are guided through a series of moves by a caller

set theory: the branch of mathematics that deals with the well-defined collections of objects known as sets

sextant: a device for measuring altitudes of celestial objects

signal processor: a device designed to convert information from one form to another so that it can be sent or received

significant difference: to distinguish greatly between two parameters

significant digits: the digits reported in a measure that accurately reflect the precision of the measurement

silicon: element number 14, it belongs in the category of elements known as metalloids or semiconductors

similar: in mathematics, having sides or parts in constant proportion; two items that resemble each other but are not identical

sine: if a unit circle is drawn with its center at the origin and a line segment is drawn from the origin at angle theta so that the line segment intersects the circle at (x, y), then y is the sine of theta

skepticism: a tendency towards doubt

skew: to cause lack of symmetry in the shape of a frequency distribution

slope: the ratio of the vertical change to the corresponding horizontal change

software: the set of instructions given to a computer that allows it to perform tasks

solar masses: dimensionless units in which mass, radius, luminosity, and other physical properties of stars can be expressed in terms of the Sun's characteristics

solar wind: a stream of particles and radiation constantly pouring out of the Sun at high velocities; partially responsible for the formation of the tails of comets

solid geometry: the geometry of solid figures, spheres, and polyhedrons; the geometry of points, lines, surfaces, and solids in three-dimensional space

spatial sound: audio channels endowed with directional and positional attributes (like azimuth, elevation, and range) and room effects (like echoes and reverberation)

spectra: the ranges of frequencies of light emitted or absorbed by objects

spectrum: the range of frequencies of light emitted or absorbed by an object

sphere: the locus of points in three-dimensional space that are all equidistant from a single point called the center

spin: to rotate on an axis or turn around

square: a quadrilateral with four equal sides and four right angles

square root: with respect to real or complex numbers s, the number t for which $t^2 = s$

stade: an ancient Greek measurement of length, one stade is approximately 559 feet (about 170 meters)

standard deviation: a measure of the average amount by which individual items of data might be expected to vary from the arithmetic mean of all data

static: without movement; stationary

statistical analysis: a set of methods for analyzing numerical data

statistics: the branch of mathematics that analyzes and interprets sets of numerical data

stellar: having to do with stars

sterographics: presenting slightly different views to left and right eyes, so that graphic scenes acquire depth

stochastic: random, or relating to a variable at each moment

Stonehenge: a large circle of standing stones on the Salisbury plain in England, thought by some to be an astronomical or calendrical marker

storm surge: the front of a hurricane, which bulges because of strong winds; can be the most damaging part of a hurricane

stratopause: the boundary in the atmosphere between the stratosphere and the mesosphere usually around 55 kilometers in altitude

stratosphere: the layer of Earth's atmosphere from 15 kilometers to about 50 kilometers, usually unaffected by weather and lacking clouds or moisture

sublimate: change of phase from a solid to a gas

sublunary: "below the moon"; term used by Aristotle and others to describe things that were nearer to Earth than the Moon and so not necessarily heavenly in origin or composition

subtend: to extend past and mark off a chord or arc

sunspot activity: one of the powerful magnetic storms on the surface of the Sun, which causes it to appear to have dark spots; sunspot activity varies on an 11-year cycle

superconduction: the flow of electric current without resistance in certain metals and alloys while at temperatures near absolute zero

superposition: the placing of one thing on top of another

suspension bridge: a bridge held up by a system of cables or cables and rods in tension; usually having two or more tall towers with heavy cables anchored at the ends and strung between the towers and lighter vertical cables extending downward to support the roadway

symmetric: to have balanced proportions; in bilateral symmetry, opposite sides are mirror images of each other

symmetry: a correspondence or equivalence between or among constituents of a system

synapse: the narrow gap between the terminal of one neuron and the dendrites of the next

tactile: relating to the sense of touch

tailwind: a wind blowing in the same direction of that of the course of a vehicle

tangent: a line that intersects a curve at one and only one point in a local region

tectonic plates: large segments of Earth's crust that move in relation to one another

telecommuting: working from home or another offsite location

tenable: defensible, reasonable

terrestrial refraction: the apparent raising or lowering of a distant object on Earth's surface due to variations in atmospheric temperature

tessellation: a mosaic of tiles or other objects composed of identical repeated elements with no gaps

tesseract: a four-dimensional cube, formed by connecting all of the vertices of two three-dimensional cubes separated by the length of one side in four-dimensional space

theodolite: a surveying instrument designed to measure both horizontal and vertical angles

theorem: a statement in mathematics that can be demonstrated to be true given that certain assumptions and definitions (called axioms) are accepted as true

threatened species: a species whose population is viable but diminishing or has limited habitat

time dilation: the principle of general relativity which predicts that to an outside observer, clocks would appear to run more slowly in a powerful gravitational field

topology: the study of those properties of geometric figures that do not change under such nonlinear transformations as stretching or bending

topspin: spin placed on a baseball, tennis ball, bowling ball, or other object so that the axis of rotation is horizontal and perpendicular to the line of flight and the top of the object is rotating in the same direction as the motion of the object

trajectory: the path followed by a projectile; in chaotic systems, the trajectory is ordered and unpredictable

transcendental: a real number that cannot be the root of a polynomial with rational coefficients

transect: to divide by cutting transversly

transfinite: surpassing the finite

transformation: changing one mathematical expression into another by translation, mapping, or rotation according to some mathematical rule

transistor: an electronic device consisting of two different kinds of semi-conductor material, which can be used as a switch or amplifier

transit: a surveyor's instrument with a rotating telescope that is used to measure angles and elevations

transitive: having the mathematical property that if the first expression in a series is equal to the second and the second is equal to the third, then the first is equal to the third

translate: to move from one place to another without rotation

translation: a rigid motion of the plane that moves each point in the same direction and by the same distance

tree: a collection of dots with edges connecting them that have no looping paths

triangulation: the process of determining the distance to an object by measuring the length of the base and two angles of a triangle

trigonometric ratio: a ratio formed from the lengths of the sides of right triangles

trigonometry: the branch of mathematics that studies triangles and trigonometric functions

tropopause: the boundry in Earth's atmosphere between the troposphere and the stratosphere at an altitude of 14 to 15 kilometers

troposphere: the lowest layer of Earth's atmosphere extending from the surface up to about 15 kilometers; the layer where most weather phenomena occur

ultra-violet radiation: electromagnetic radiation with wavelength shorter than visible light, in the range of 1 nanometer to about 400 nanometer

unbiased sample: a random sample selected from a larger population in such a way that each member of the larger population has an equal chance of being in the sample

underspin: spin placed on a baseball, tennis ball, bowling ball, or other object so that the axis of rotation is horizontal and perpendicular to the line of flight and the top of the object is rotating in the opposite direction from the motion of the object

Unicode: a newer system than ASCII for assigning binary numbers to keyboard symbols that includes most other alphabets; uses 16-bit symbol sets

union: a set containing all of the members of two other sets

upper bound: the maximum value of a function

vaccuum: theoretically, a space in which there is no matter

variable: a symbol, such as letters, that may assume any one of a set of values known as the domain

variable star: a star whose brightness noticeably varies over time

vector: a quantity which has both magnitude and direction

velocity: distance traveled per unit of time in a specific direction

verify: confirm; establish the truth of a statement or proposition

vernal equinox: the moment when the Sun crosses the celestial equator marking the first day of spring; occurs around March 22 for the northern hemisphere and September 21 for the southern hemisphere

vertex: a point of a graph; a node; the point on a triangle or polygon where two sides come together; the point at which a conic section intersects its axis of symmetry

viable: capable of living, growing, and developing

wavelengths: the distance in a periodic wave between two points of corresponding phase in consecutive cycles

whole numbers: the positive integers and zero

World Wide Web: the part of the Internet allowing users to examine graphic "web" pages

yield (interest): the actual amount of interest earned, which may be different than the rate

zenith: the point on the celestial sphere vertically above a given position

zenith angle: from an observer's viewpoint, the angle between the line of sight to a celestial body (such as the Sun) and the line from the observer to the zenith point

zero pair: one positive integer and one negative integer

ziggurat: a tower built in ancient Babylonia with a pyramidal shape and stepped sides

Topic Outline

APPLICATIONS

Agriculture
Architecture
Athletics, Technology in
City Planning
Computer-Aided Design
Computer Animation
Cryptology
Cycling, Measurements of
Economic Indicators
Flight, Measurements of
Gaming
Grades, Highway
Heating and Air Conditioning
Interest
Maps and Mapmaking
Mass Media, Mathematics and the
Morgan, Julia
Navigation
Population Mathematics
Roebling, Emily Warren
Solid Waste, Measuring
Space, Comercialization of
Space, Growing Old in
Stock Market
Tessellations, Making

CAREERS

Accountant
Agriculture
Archaeologist
Architect
Artist
Astronaut
Astronomer
Carpenter
Cartographer
Ceramicist
City Planner
Computer Analyst
Computer Graphic Artist
Computer Programmer
Conservationist
Data Analyst

Electronics Repair Technician
Financial Planner
Insurance Agent
Interior Decorator
Landscape Architect
Marketer
Mathematics Teacher
Music Recording Technician
Nutritionist
Pharmacist
Photographer
Radio Disc Jockey
Restaurant Manager
Roller Coaster Designer
Stone Mason
Web Designer

DATA ANALYSIS

Census
Central Tendency, Measures of
Consumer Data
Cryptology
Data Collection and Interpretation
Economic Indicators
Endangered Species, Measuring
Gaming
Internet Data, Reliability of
Lotteries, State
Numbers, Tyranny of
Polls and Polling
Population Mathematics
Population of Pets
Predictions
Sports Data
Standardized Tests
Statistical Analysis
Stock Market
Television Ratings
Weather Forecasting Models

FUNCTIONS & OPERATIONS

Absolute Value
Algorithms for Arithmetic
Division by Zero

Boole, George
Calculus
Carroll, Lewis
Dürer, Albrecht
Euler, Leonhard
Fermat, Pierre de
Hypatia
Kovalevsky, Sofya
Mathematics, Very Old
Newton, Sir Isaac
Pascal, Blaise
Robinson, Julia Bowman
Somerville, Mary Fairfax
Trigonometry

TECHNOLOGY

Abacus
Analog and Digital
Babbage, Charles
Boole, George
Bush, Vannevar
Calculators
Cierva Codorniu, Juan de la
Communication Methods
Compact Disc, DVD, and MP3 Technology

Computer-Aided Design
Computer Animation
Computer Information Systems
Computer Simulations
Computers and the Binary System
Computers, Evolution of Electronic
Computers, Future of
Computers, Personal
Galileo, Galilei
Geometry Software, Dynamic
Global Positioning System
Heating and Air Conditioning
Hopper, Grace
IMAX Technology
Internet
Internet Data, Reliability of
Knuth, Donald
Lovelace, Ada Byron
Mathematical Devices, Early
Mathematical Devices, Mechanical
Millennium Bug
Photocopier
Slide Rule
Turing, Alan
Virtual Reality

Volume 2 Index